HISTORICIZING BLAKE

Historicizing Blake

Edited by

Steve Clark
University of Northampton

and

David Worrall
St Mary's College of Higher Education
Twickenham

M

St. Martin's Press

Text © The Macmillan Press Ltd 1994
Editorial matter and selection © Steve Clark and David Worrall 1994

First published in Great Britain 1994 by
THE MACMILLAN PRESS LTD
Houndmills, Basingstoke, Hampshire RG21 2XS
and London
Companies and representatives
throughout the world

A catalogue record for this book is available
from the British Library.

ISBN 0–333–56819–2

Printed in Great Britain by
Antony Rowe Ltd
Chippenham, Wiltshire

First published in the United States of America 1994 by
Scholarly and Reference Division,
ST. MARTIN'S PRESS, INC.,
175 Fifth Avenue,
New York, N.Y. 10010

ISBN 0–312–10393–X

Library of Congress Cataloging-in-Publication Data
Historicizing Blake / edited by Steve Clark and David Worrall.
p. cm.
Includes bibliographical references and index.
ISBN 0–312–10393–X
1. Blake, William, 1757–1827—Knowledge—History. 2. Blake,
William, 1757–1827—Criticism and interpretation.   3. Literature and
history—England—History—18th century.   I. Clark, S. H. (Steven
H.), 1957– . II. Worrall, David.
PR4148.H5H57   1994
821'.7—dc20

93–43706
CIP

Contents

v

Contents

List of Plates

Notes on the Contributors

John Beer is the author of *Blake's Humanism* and *Blake's Visionary Universe*; he has also published books on Wordsworth, Coleridge and E.M. Forster, edited Coleridge's *Aids to Reflection* for the *Collected Coleridge* and written articles on a variety of authors and topics. His new book *Romantic Influences* is also published by Macmillan.

Helen Bruder teaches English at Oxford Brookes University. She has recently completed a PhD thesis entitled 'Historicizing Blake in "A Land of Men and Women Too"' and has written reviews for several academic journals, including *Blake/An Illustrated Quarterly.*

Steve Clark teaches at Osaka University and the University of Northampton. He is the author of *Paul Ricoeur* (1990) and *Sordid Images: The Poetry of Masculine Desire* (1994), has published on Blake and eighteenth-century philosophy, and has edited a selection from Akenside, Macpherson and Young.

Philip Cox is a Lecturer in the School of Cultural Studies at Sheffield Hallam University. He is the author of articles on Blake and Emily Brontë and is currently working on two book-length projects: *William Blake and the Politics of Pastoral* and *The Gendered Discourse of Romantic Pastoral.*

D. W. Dörrbecker teaches art history at the University of Trier, Germany. For many years he was bibliographer for *Blake/An Illustrated Quarterly*, and he rediscovered five copies of Blake's illuminated books in Cologne, Munich and Vienna. His most recent publication on Blake's art is *Konvention und Innovation* (1992). He is currently co-editing Volume IV in the William Blake Trust series of reproductions of 'Blake's Illuminated Books'.

Mary Lynn Johnson, formerly on the faculty of the University of Illinois and Georgia State University, has been assistant to the president of the University of Iowa since 1983. She is co-author of *Blake's*

'Four Zoas': The Design of a Dream (1978), co-editor of the Norton Critical Edition, *Blake's Poetry and Designs* (1979), compiler of the Blake chapter in *The English Romantic Poets: A Review of Research and Criticism* (1985), and author of several articles on Blake and on other Romantic poets.

Edward Larrissy is Senior Lecturer in English, Warwick University. He is the author of *William Blake* (1985), *Reading Twentieth-Century Poetry* (1990), and *Yeats The Poet: The Measures of Difference* (forthcoming). He is currently preparing the Oxford Authors *Yeats*.

Andrew Lincoln teaches in the English Department of Queen Mary and Westfield College, University of London. His edition of Blake's *Songs of Innocence and of Experience* was published by the William Blake Trust in conjunction with the Tate Gallery in 1991.

Jon Mee is a Lecturer in the English Department of the Australian National University. His *Dangerous Enthusiasm: William Blake and the Culture of Radicalism in the 1790s* was published in 1992.

Iain McCalman is Associate Director of the Humanities Research Centre, Australian National University. He has written *Radical Underworld: Prophets, Revolutionaries and Pornographers in London, 1795–1840* (1988) and is the editor of *Horrors of Slavery: The Life and Writings of Robert Wedderburn* (1992).

David Worrall teaches English at St Mary's College, Strawberry Hill. He is Associate Editor of *Blake/An Illustrated Quarterly* and the author of *Radical Culture: Discourse, Resistance and Surveillance, 1790–1820* (1992). He is co-editing Volume IV of the William Blake Trust facsimiles.

Preface

The essays collected here were given, in earlier forms, at the conference 'Historicizing Blake' held at St Mary's College, Strawberry Hill, Twickenham, on 5–7 September 1990. Not all the papers delivered at the conference were available to the editors but we have tried to indicate the range of issues discussed in the notes supplementary to the Introduction. The British Academy helped support the conference and we are grateful to them. We also wish to thank Professor Stephen Prickett of the University of Glasgow for his support at a crucial stage of this project.

Our thanks are also due to Margaret Cannon and Charmian Hearne of Macmillan for their patience and to St Mary's College for providing the congenial conditions for the original conference as well as for subsequent facilities. All the errors contained within are the responsibility of the editors.

Steve Clark and David Worrall

Abbreviations and
References

References to Blake's works are from *The Complete Poetry and Prose of William Blake*, edited by D.V. Erdman (New York: Anchor Books, 1982), abbreviated to E.

The following abbreviations for Blake's titles are used:

Ann. Lav.	Annotations to Lavater
Ann. Sw. Div. Love	Annotations to Swedenborg's *Divine Love and Divine Wisdom*
Ann. Thorn.	Annotations to Thornton's *The Lord's Prayer*
Ann. Wat.	Annotations to *An Apology for the Bible* by R. Watson
BofA	*The Book of Ahania*
BofU	*The [First] Book of Urizen*
DC	*A Descriptive Catalogue*
FZ	*The Four Zoas*
IB	Erdman (1974)
J	*Jerusalem*
MHH	*The Marriage of Heaven and Hell*
Songs	*Songs of Innocence and of Experience*
Thel	*The Book of Thel*
VLJ	*A Vision of The Last Judgment*

1

Introduction

STEVE CLARK AND DAVID WORRALL

While Blake studies in the 1980s witnessed an impressive burgeoning of post-structuralist methodologies, contextual methods appeared to lie somewhat abjectly dormant, as if neutralized by the publication in 1954 of David Erdman's *Blake: Prophet Against Empire* and the wider, more detailed perspective offered a decade later by E.P. Thompson's *The Making of the English Working Class*. The introduction to a recent anthology, *Critical Paths: Blake and the Argument of Method*, has no compunction in stating that 'in one book, Erdman fully establishes the historical dimensions of Blake's art and the political commentary pervading it', and then proceeding to denigrate its supposed tendency 'to resolve poetry into history' (Miller, Bracher and Ault, 1987: 6); and another book of essays, *Unnam'd Forms*, emanating from a similar geographic and demographic formation of North Americans and a single Briton, similarly bypasses the supposedly reductive historicist consensus by concentrating its efforts on Blake's relationship with 'the whole institution of print' (Hilton and Vogler, 1986: 4). The past decade, from Nelson Hilton's pioneering and highly influential study of Blake's polysemy, *Literal Imagination: Blake's Vision of Words* (1983), to Robert N. Essick's *William Blake and the Language of Adam* (1989) seems to have been awash with studies preoccupied with semiotic practices and assorted methodologies of reading.

The original impulse for the conference on which this anthology is based was a reluctance to acquiesce in the apparently cursory dismissal of historicist approaches to Blake, combined with a curiosity as to why the development of 'New Historicism' in Renaissance studies had had comparatively little impact on Romantic period scholarship. Our introduction therefore is divided into four sections: the first examines the recent debate about the historical materiality of Blake's text; the second is concerned with the influence of E.P. Thompson on Blake studies in Britain; the third considers the

1

treatment of Blake in recent historicism, as represented by the work of Jerome J. McGann; and the fourth seeks to situate the essays which appear in this volume, and offer some collective rationale for the project as a whole.

I

It is worth noting how supportive, even cosseting, of Blake recent work in the post-structuralist idiom has been: a deconstructive criticism that prizes the instability of the material signifier above all else is left with little to do but applaud Blake's refusal of the stable text and pre-emptive self-demystification. For all their preoccupation with writing (or if one prefers, *écriture*), such studies have largely ignored the cultural history and context of books, print and writing.[1] The only history of reading offered has been that of the self-conscious preoccupations of late twentieth-century academic practices.[2] This is evident in the heated debate occasioned by the publication of a new standard edition of Blake's text in the early 1980s. New (and hard-won) ground in post-structuralist theory produced dissatisfaction with editorial compromise because of perceived inauthenticity with regard to Blake's mode of literary production. In this one respect, the case was strenuously argued for a restitution of the original historical moment insofar as it concerned textual production.

The normative Blake text for *Historicizing Blake*, as a matter of international convenience, is this new standard edition, the revised *The Complete Poetry and Prose of William Blake* (1982) edited by David V. Erdman. In the early 1980s its publication posed a challenge to an emergent, post-structuralist Blake scholarship. Here was the first book explicitly sanctioned by the Modern Language Association Committee of Scholarly Editions and carrying its 'emblem of approval' with the double-bordered cartouche of that powerful institution stamped on the back cover (E vi). Erdman's editorial solutions to the problems of rendering into conventional typography the inconsistencies and indeterminacies of Blake's text provoked a fierce reaction from the post-structuralist tendency of the American academy. This was an indicative contest when viewed from the vantage of the early 1990s, an illuminating synecdoche of critical possibilities. On the one hand, Erdman had been prepared to compromise the intractable complexities of Blake's text, on the other hand, the 'Santa Cruz Blake Study Group' were committed to an overtly philosophical probing of their semiotic possibilities.[3] This 'unnam'd' professional collectivity (to this day the SCBSG form as anonymous an élite institution-within-an-institution as one could find) challenged the deficiencies of Erdman's deviation from the precise historicity of Blake's text with its unconforming punctuation and design. The points raised are, indeed, not easily dismissable. For example, does close inspection of plate 3 of *The Book of Ahania* reveal that Urizen had 'fixed / The sinew in its rest: ' or 'fixed / The sinerv in its rest: ' (*BofA* 3: 31–2 E86)? The SCBSG were asking, with fastidious empirical scholarship, what might be lost in an editorial assimilation which restores linguistic orthodoxy.

The insistence of the Santa Cruz Group on the 'materiality of the printed sign-vehicle' in Blake's text did not extend to a consideration of the materiality of the historical culture. And yet works like *Songs of Innocence* (1789) and *For Children / The Gates of Paradise* (1793) address a young audience already placed within a virulently counter-revolutionary context. One 'EM', a 'friend to Church & State', wrote in December 1792 to the Secretary of the anti-progressive pressure group, the 'Association for the Preservation of Liberty and Property from Republicans and Levellers', telling him that the sight of two poor children in Oxford Street had caused 'the following Rhime, to Jingle in My Mind' and that he 'should Not be displeased to hear [it] Re-echoed by Every little Boy in the Streets during the Christ**[*sic*] Holidays':

Long May Old England, Possess Good Cheer and Jollity
Liberty and Property, and No Equality –[4]

Putting such sentiments 'by twenties into the hands of Ballad Singers, who might Sing them for the sake of selling them' was exactly an attempt to capture the 'child' figured in Blake's 'Introduction' to *Songs of Innocence*, one who might indeed ask the piper to 'pipe that song again' (*Songs* 4: 2, 7, E7). Hearing a song could be a political act in the London of the early 1790s but the Santa Cruz Group's insistence on the 'important functional component of the auditory experience' seems content to restrict itself to questions of late twentieth-century reception. Blake's *Songs* were politicized in their originating historical moment because their visual innovation was an attempt to capture the attention, and the allegiance, of a crucial section of the population.

'EM's plans of December 1792 (the month Tom Paine was outlawed in his absence for *The Rights of Man* Part II) came hard on that May's Royal Proclamation against seditious writings. If Blake's text and design were the subject of material physical constraints, as Robert N. Essick has meticulously argued, so too were the political conditions under which Blake's utterances circulated.[5] Recent theoretical rigour has not solved, or even adequately addressed, the problem of defining Blake's contemporary discursive conditions. Much influential recent criticism has ignored the question of the interventions (or accommodations) of Blake's medium, message and method in their precise historical moment. In principle there is no reason why deconstructive strategies should preclude historical understanding, but in practice they have rarely strayed beyond the formal boundaries of Blake's text and then usually only to reproduce, somewhat credulously, his supposed critiques of mainstream European cultural history.

II

American post-structuralist readings of Blake, it should be stressed, have flourished within, rather than broken from, the idealist tradition established in 1947 by *Fearful Symmetry,* Frye's magisterial, and in many respects still unsurpassed, devotional homage. There is an easy enough transition from myth to textuality with a few detours via influence theory, reader-response and psychoanalysis. The contrast with the text occupying a similarly dominant role in recent British studies – E.P. Thompson's *The Making of the English Working Class* (1963) – could hardly be more pronounced. (One might somewhat facetiously summarise the divergence as 'they have the theory but we have the facts'). To present Blake's work as an articulation of an emergent working-class consciousness was not in itself novel. The broadly symbolist assimilation which had dominated his reception in the Modernist period took on a more politically engaged inflection in 1930s Marxism. That curious mixture of personality and principle comprises Thompson's ideological roots and lies behind the presentation of Blake as a radical which was to become a formative influence on subsequent generations of social and literary historians.[6] *The Making of the English Working Class,* although not dedicated to literary issues, was the product of Thompson's place in a British Left movement which had a tradition of particularly prizing the English Romantic poets.[7]

The distinctive force of Thompson's account lies in Blake's dramatic function within his own historical text. 'In London a Jacobin engraver went to the "Garden of Love" and "found a Chapel . . . built in the midst,/Where I used to play on the green"' (1963: 41). Leaving aside questions of if and when Blake was a wholly committed 'Jacobin', and the determinative status granted 'engraver', it is striking that Thompson finds no discontinuity between the stylized lyric emblems and his own rhetoric. This incorporation occurs not only in detail such as the transformation of London artisans into 'myriads of eternity' (1963: 446) or the strictures on generalisation, and praise for Mayhew's grasp of 'awkward particularities' (1963: 250), but also in the authorial voice, whose 'veritable fury of compassion' at the 'exploitation of little children' (1963: 349) replicates the response of the poet: 'It was the pall of moral equivocation which settled upon Britain in these years which stung Blake to fury' (1963: 57).

Blake serves as a cross between a presiding deity and a diffused rhetorical presence. The opening epigraph of *The Making of the English Working Class* ('The Beast and the Whore rule without control' [1963: 15]) accords him a metatextual status rather than seeking to locate him as a participant. His work is invoked as a stable point of comparison and illumination not itself subject to historical interpretation. Paine, for example, is indicted for 'a glibness and a lack of resource which remind one of Blake's strictures on the "single vision"'(1963: 98). Citation of Blake allows a convenient reinforcement of some sparsely-documented links with seventeenth-century radicalism ('many, like Blake', we are told, must have 'remembered that their own forbears once executed a king' [1963: 52]) while, elsewhere in the book, some specific claims are, at the very least, questionable. 'Like Blake', in Thompson's approving citation of W.H. Reid, the London artisans 'yielded to the stronger impulse of the French Revolution and became "politicians"' (1963: 52)' Thompson's *Witness Against the Beast: William Blake and the Moral Law* (1993) undoubtedly supplements this account, and reminds us of the folly of seeking to disentangle political from religious discourses during the period. Nevertheless this attribution of representative status ('it is Blake, himself a craftsmen by training, who gives us the experience' [1963: 446]) glides over the fundamental problem (for Blake scholars) of the absence of any documentary record of overt political engagement. The Blake mentioned in the London Corresponding Society lists is Arthur Blake (Erdman, 1977: 160).

In this context, the significance for Blake studies becomes apparent of Iain McCalman's *Radical Underworld: Prophets, Revolutionaries and Pornographers in London, 1795–1840*. McCalman opens up a previously occluded world of artisan textuality and orality in the 'one pair of stairs' back rooms and upper storeys of London, the very places where the Blakes lived. In particular, *Radical Underworld* proposes that we address history not from the standpoint of wondering whether literature affects culture but rather of demonstrating that literature is far from being radicalism's primary signifying practice. McCalman offers us a perspective from which Blake might be seen as the product of an extremely complicated, sometimes apparently contradictory, set of cultural forces. His meticulous reconstruction of the shifting human alliances within the milieu of radical London brings to light the centrality of Thomas Spence, the Holborn and Oxford Street writer, publisher and organizer whose ability to produce and sell his own pamphlets and periodicals is analogous, in a separate sphere, to Blake's self-contained productions in art. The parallels between them may be extended further: both were marginal figures in their fields and considered eccentric by their contemporaries; both expounded a complexly eclectic 'system'; both were subjected to political arrest for sedition; and both were sufficiently charismatic to gather around them groups of dedicated followers in later life. Another illuminating point of reference is provided by the discussion of artisan poets, such as Allen Davenport and Edward James Blandford, or the sometime-print-colourer and author Thomas Evans, whose careers were stretched and pressured by changing circumstances of employment and general economic exigencies in the same way that Blake was forced to invent, protest and accommodate in the craft of engraving (see Eaves, 1977).

For Thompson, 'moral sobriety was a demonstrable product of the old Radical and rationalist agitation itself' (1963: 740). There is nothing anarchic or carnivalesque about his marginal subcultures: they are populated with selfless, purposeful, devoted figures, with little or no trace of the seediness, opportunism, and picaresque resilience revealed by McCalman's fuller tracing of their biographies. It was this aspect of Thompson's historical sense that enabled him to interpret a culture which displayed such a propensity to hoax, lie and repress its representation of itself. Thompson's indictment of the 1816 Spa Fields rising informer John Castle might extend to the whole milieu; 'each word must be critically fumigated before it may be admitted to historical intercourse' (1963: 493).

However, it is no disparagement to acknowledge that Thompson's major work gives us an eloquently idealising narrative and that its valedictory thanks 'for these years of heroic culture' (1963: 832) is less a belated tribute than a generic decision. His own rhetoric shows an obvious debt to Romanticism: the experience of class, for example, is defined as 'a fluency which evades analysis if we attempt to stop it dead at any given moment and anatomise its structure' (1963: 9). Renata Rosaldo goes so far as to ascribe the 'sentimental heroics of victimisation' to the 'melodramatic imagination', but a fairer categorisation, particularly given the influence of Morris, would be romance.[8] In this context, the sharp repudiation of theatricality, of the 'histrionic' element in Thelwall, or the 'romantic derivative postures' of the Cato Street conspirators (1963: 616) becomes a pre-emptive denial of the highly effective rhetoricity of his own text.

Thompson gives us a dual and, one would have thought, self-contradictory narrative of origins. He repeatedly emphasises that 'making' of the working-classes is 'an active process which owes as much to agency as to conditioning', yet the radicalism that emerges between 1780 and 1832 is also prefigured, bequeathed. ('To read the controversies . . . in the 1790s is to see the Putney debates come to life once again . . . it is the old debate continued' [1963: 23–4]). It is proclaimed rather than argued that 'the wilder sectaries of the English revolution were never wholly extinguished', and a 'continuous thread of communitarian ideas' were handed down in an almost somative collective memory: 'Bunyan in their bones' (1963: 47, 52). The insistence on indigenous roots at times approaches parochial nationalism. Whereas the French engaged in 'extermination', this was 'an English agitation, of impressive dimensions, for an English democracy' drawing upon 'the Dissenting and libertarian traditions' that 'reach far back into English history' (1963: 102).

The problems with the thesis lie not merely in establishing connections back to the Civil War period, but also internally between 1795 and 1816: 'the claims made in the 1790s by Mary Wollstonecraft, William Blake and Thomas Spence were never wholly abandoned; they recur' (1963: 415).[9] It is surely anything but 'natural to assume a direct causal relationship' between the two outbreaks of radicalism (1963: 192); and Thompson himself is obliged to resort to such 'constructive speculation' as positing that the very absence of testimony 'lends weight' to the thesis of the 'secret history' of an effective Luddite underground (1963: 497).

Casual invocations of Blake's exemplary radicalism are therefore at the very least double-edged.[10] One may choose to emphasise his work's coincidence with the general political effervescence of the 1790s, what Thompson calls the 'reflected glow from the storming of the Bastille' (1963: 102). Nevertheless the single most significant fact about the English French Revolution is that it never happened. (The nearest equivalent, the Irish risings in 1798, and the appalling subsequent retribution, are seldom discussed).[11] 'It is wrong to see this as the end, for it was also a beginning: in the 1790s something like an English Revolution took place, of profound importance' (1963: 177). Thompson's disingenuous phraseology disguises the degree to which his own narrative provides the requisite satisfaction of a fictive event as its first two hundred pages present the London Corresponding Society as heroic protagonist (narratology has taught us that not only persons but also logically second-order entities can serve as agents or pseudo-characters).[12] The initial ascription of significance – 'it is extraordinary that so brief an agitation should have diffused its ideas into many corners of Britain' (1963: 183) – proves chimerical: it transpires that what we had been led to believe was a mass movement was only a 'handful of Jacobin sheets' ekeing out a 'precarious existence in a score of towns' (1963: 191). Yet the narrative's animistic sense of the general will ('less a movement of an organised minority than the response of the whole community' [1963: 605–6]) remains undeterred and undiminished despite the acknowledgement that 'every detail of the story illustrates the weakness of the revolutionary organisation, and the lack of an experienced leadership' (1963: 669). Even Thompson's central thesis depends on a dialectical reversal that would make an Althusserian blush: the 'working class presence' became 'the most significant factor in British political life' despite the ruling class having 'gained in cohesion' through its ruthlessly effective suppression (1963: 11–12).

The absence of revolutionary turmoil is by no means a disadvantage from certain perspectives: it allows Romantic literature to serve as a beguiling simulacrum of political activism untarnished by cruelty, compromise or corruption. (One of the recent '1789' commemorative anthologies opens: 'with the bicentenary of the French Revolution a focus was provided for re-examining the rhetoricity of texts that have traditionally been seen as politically determined and determinative'.[13]) This move to 'rhetoricity' is not confined to literary criticism: Thompson himself is far from unwilling to locate political contestation in a rhetorical sphere (Burke and Paine, for example, become 'publicists of genius' [1963: 90]). Much attention has been expended on the politics of language during the period; but in some ways, such studies have simply been re-inventing wheels already in use by social historians like Gareth Stedman Jones in his work on Chartism.[14]

What one might have expected to be the strength of the British tradition of Blake studies – a commitment to restore historical density to literary interpretation – in this case simply has not happened. Thompson's work quickly provoked other waves of historical re-examination of radicalism during the period from less committed viewpoints.[15]

Yet while the historical pickings have been unusually rich recently, remarkably little of this work has impinged on literary perceptions of the period. John Lucas's blithe dismissal of Blake's later work as a 'mistaken tactic' is by no means unrepresentative:

> But the Prophetic Books quite lack an answerable style . . . You could not perhaps expect Blake to realise it was too late in history for the kind of epic at which he laboured . . . But Blake's problem goes deeper . . . The passage from 1789 to 1794 is a tragic one, but in *Songs of Experience*, Blake takes the weight of this tragedy. Having done that he is left convinced of his isolation. Hence, the increased private 'system', of alternative history in an alternate style, of the Prophetic Books. (Lucas, 1990: 85–6)

The claimed lack of an 'answerable style' due to a loss of community may be refuted simply by invoking the subsequent history of reception: the prophecies have been read and read well, by whatever minimal pragmatic criteria one might choose to adopt. Blake's supposed 'isolation', therefore, becomes a kind of self-fulfilling prophecy, a vacuum permitting the uncontested interpolation of large-scale cultural narratives. The assumption that it is 'too late in history' for this 'kind of epic' (regardless of poems such as the *Cantos* of Ezra Pound or David Jones's *Anathemata*) is part of a broader complacency as to what history does and does not permit. 'Blake's dilemma is familiar in English radical experience', and 'his vision is necessarily utopian in the sense that he cannot imagine the transition from present to future', a view which seems to have consolidated itself into a critical orthodoxy (Lucas, 1990: 86).[16] The viewpoint is condescendingly diagnostic: Blake has a 'problem' rather than an achievement. Yet the supposedly public history so confidently expounded in opposition to the private 'system' is highly questionable, both for its dependence on an increasingly unconvincing Marxist meta-narrative, and more immediately for its arbitrary assumption that historical study has no relevance to Blake after the mid-1790s.

Thompson's own citations (for example 1963: 57, 119) suggest a fundamental unity to Blake's work, but his explicit argument holds to the thesis of fracture. 'As the Jacobin current went into more hidden underground channels, so his own prophecies became more mysterious and private' (1963: 175). Homology assumes a causal status: because of Blake's representative status political failure must lead to private withdrawal. Thus contradicting the earlier argument that the millenialist idiom, far from being 'mysterious and private' was both intelligible and politically resonant; and also, by its emphasis on internal exile, the final assertion that 'after William Blake no mind was at home in both cultures (artisan and romantic), nor had the genius to interpret the two traditions to each other' (1963: 832).

Whatever reservations one might hold about certain aspects of American criticism, one cannot but admire its ready engagement with Blake's later prophecies: as Frye puts it 'they are what a great poet chose to spend most of his time on' (1947: 5), and the most influential critics (Adams, Bloom, Mitchell, Hilton) have tended simply to assume their primacy. The comparative stultification of British criticism can be seen in its myopic preoccupation with early Blake, specifically the lyrics; an alliance of radical politics and conservative aesthetics which may be traced as least as far back as Bronowski's 'we must learn to read Blake's prophetic manner, not as poetry, but as rhetoric' (1944: 21). The pedagogic inconvenience of dealing with long texts requiring a high degree of initial application has been routinely elevated to a judgement of value: the question posed is not how to read the prophecies but if they should be read at all. A particularly fatuous tautology results: Blake's later work is unreadable because of his withdrawal from history, and because of his withdrawal from history, need not be read.

It must be conceded that one immediate obstacle to the historical study of Blake, at least in comparison to the other major Romantic writers, is the disproportion between the meagre finitude of documentary resources for his life and the infinitely complex status of his verbal and visual texts. Yet despite the comparatively scant record of direct peer intersection, an impressive breadth of cultural affiliations can be demonstrated. Professionally, Blake was to remain well connected and highly regarded in artistic and engraving circles throughout his career. Culturally, his apparent retreat from vivid politically radical statements is matched by the fluctuations of others who considered themselves to be politically active but who were tossed and tried by the after-shock of a thirty-year period of systematized Government surveillance and discursive repression.

The extreme internalization of Blake's mythology in its exclusive, elusive and recondite forms in *Milton* and *Jerusalem* can be illuminated by knowledge of the topical conditions of his time: in a culture of surveillance and the prosecution of sedition, where every printing press in the land had to be licensed (Worrall, 1992). An exploration of the ultra-radical environment, the political and revolutionary fringe clearly beyond Blake's own position, remains a useful point of departure for future studies. It is nonetheless startling that nearly 30 years after the publication of Thompson's magnificent narrative, so little work of substance has been accomplished in his wake; one is tempted to conclude that in the sphere of literary studies his work has served as a substitute for rather than a spur to historical understanding.

III

David V. Erdman's *Blake: Prophet Against Empire* remains the most highly regarded historically contextualised study of the poet and his times. One might have expected his achievement to have inaugurated a tradition of American Romantic historicist scholarship but this has proved not to be the case. Instead, explicating historical allusion has tended to be regarded as yet another dimension of the text, an interpretative option coexisting with other methods. As Jerome J. McGann puts it, post-war American Blake studies have been a series of 'experimental alliances' between 'three distinct interpretative schedules' (1989: 18): the starting-points of Blake as symbolist poet, painter and engraver, and political activist have been treated as virtually mutually exclusive planes.

American historicism has tended towards a tolerantly eclectic empiricism within a comparatively unassertive liberal perspective. Erdman's book undoubtedly lacks Thompson's impassioned moralizing, though the courage of its determinedly pacifist stance, in the context of its publication, at the height of the Cold War in 1954 should not be underestimated. Nevertheless there is resulting equivocation over Blake's political position. On the one hand, he is lauded as a hero who, unlike other writers of his generation, never reneges on a fundamental revolutionary commitment; on the other his isolation subsequent to the mid-1790s is insisted upon, despite Erdman's own copious documentation to the contrary. In striking contrast to the tendency of British criticism to regard Blake's apparent cultural marginalization as debilitating, this has presented little difficulty for the majority of American criticism. Instead this dislocation becomes a kind of principled self-ostracism that makes his work infinitely available to successive waves of idealist appropriation.

This tendency to accept the 'isolation of the literary work from its social and historical contexts' (1985: 3) in both the American New Criticism and its post-structuralist successors has been forcefully challenged in a series of recent books by Jerome J. McGann. These may be considered the nearest equivalent to Renaissance 'New Historicism' in Romantic studies; and for the purposes of our discussion will be regarded as a composite argument.[17] McGann himself regards *The Romantic Ideology* (1983), *The Beauty of Inflections* (1985), *A Critique of Modern Textual Criticism* (1983), *Social Values and Poetic Acts* (1988), and *Towards a Literature of Knowledge* (1989) as a continuous project (1988: vii). *The Textual Condition* (1991) amplifies but does not significantly deviate from the cumulative rationale.

McGann offers a salutary reminder of the 'worldliness' of Romanticism (1989: 96): its eager and prosperous integration into the high culture of its own time prefiguring the academic incorporation of its major tenets a century later. In the US context, its move inwards away from the public sphere behind what Thompson calls the 'ramparts of disenchantment' (1963: 832) has tended to be all too readily equated with archetypal wisdom.[18] McGann seeks to shift the major axis of the period away from the poignancy of recantation in Wordsworth and Coleridge to the satiric and prophetic modes of Byron and Blake. This refusal to accept the Romantic epiphany at its own exalted valuation, through simple demonstration of continued habitation of a social world, is designed to provoked 'a critical awakening would strip away such modes of deception (and self-deception)' (1988: 223).

McGann's protest against the continued enshrinement of a highly restricted canon and predominance of holistic accounts of Romanticism have been deservedly influential. The positive side of

his agenda – 'to reintegrate the entire range of socio-historical philological methods with an aesthetic and ideological criticism of individual works' (1985; 3) – is markedly more problematic.

Renaissance 'New Historicism', as articulated in the work of
Stephen Greenblatt, deploys a model of culture as text stemming
from the anthropology of Geertz and the genealogy of Foucault.
One can read a society; the process of decoding the underlying dis-
placements, rhetorical mobility (*energeia*), within a given symbolic
system is comparable to understanding a network of ironic tensions or undermining of apparently stable hierarchies within a
written text.

McGann, in contrast, urges us 'to reconceive the literary "text" as
the "literary work"' (1985: 10) which may be comprehended in
terms of the immanence represented by the process of publication
and reception. Its trajectory as an object, commodity, allows a factual and archival documentation of its transmission. The work does
not exist solely as a network of semantic meanings but as a material
trace. McGann puts a distinctive emphasis on collaborative interchange, whether with editor, amanuensis, revision or through audience response. One discovers relative stability of meaning not so
much a originary mental event as an inaugural dialogue: socialisa-
tion rather than personal creativity becomes the normative, even
optimum, condition of literary production.

'Romantic poetry incorporates Romantic Ideology as a drama of
the contradictions which are inherent in that ideology' (1983: 2): the
critic may expose its pretensions to transcendence by revealing 'the
human limits which history imposes even on these famous words'
(1985: 65). This may be distinguished from a Macherayan position
by its downgrading of the aesthetic, which ceases to be the medium
that reveals cultural contradictions, but is itself exposed as displaced and concealed ideology. The critic laying claim to understand the objective conditions of the text does not dispel but
perpetuates the mystificatory pretensions of the art-object to produce disinterested insight. The literary work is not merely a '*vehicle
for ideology*' but is itself an 'ideological form *per se*' (1983: 159). Its
'meanings' must be removed from an illusory sphere of aesthetic
autonomy and instead 'grasped as parts of the histories which
poems reflect and reproduce' (1985: 10).

Several immediate lines of objection may be raised. Firstly, as the
phrasing ('reflect and reproduce') indicates, McGann acknowledges
neither the possibility of the creative transformation of ideology, nor

of semantic innovation as such. And though the 'histories', which precede and determine linguistic meaning, may appear undogmatically plural, their intelligibility is only achieved through an impoverishing and arguably tautologous curtailment of focus.

Secondly, McGann's usage of ideology remains, at best, composite. It appears to function as both a necessary cultural bonding in Mannheim's sense, and a form of false consciousness as in classic Marxist analysis. The 'differential' nature of the past is said to allow us to 'gain a measure by which our own present interests may be critically observed'; the literary works which provide this point of displaced vantage are themselves 'constantly being reformulated into new forms of finishedness' (1985: 12). Yet this mutual interpenetration offers no extrinsic standard of truth, equivalent to Althusser's epistemological break or Habermas's ideal speech-context, against which ideology may be measured: by default it becomes inevitable, therefore necessary.

Thirdly, the self-consciousness envisaged is, in its way, as recessive and disabling as the familiar deconstructive paradoxes. We are in history therefore our actions are culturally determined; our freedom lies in our proclamation of the impossibility of autonomous choice. Where Thompson insists on the recovery of a common heritage to orientate future struggle, McGann insists that 'the precise specification of historical details' makes us newly aware of 'the deeply felt distance between us and our pasts' (1985: 64). So the study of history prevents facile or premature appropriation of the past. But this awareness remains disconnected from subsequent intervention or application, to use Gadamer's term, of the act of interpretation. All we learn from the past is that we have nothing to learn from it. Hence despite the insistence that 'art' works 'like a set of actions carried out in the world' (1988: 4), it is difficult to see how historical understanding, on McGann's terms, can result in anything other than ethical passivity.

Fourthly, more technically, no attempt is made to modify a speech-act terminology based upon the premise of spoken dialogue when it is transposed into a context of textual interpretation; one of several points where the absence of an adequately theorised moment of distanciation seriously undermines the entire argument. (In the preceding quotation, for example, the phrase 'deeply felt distance' confuses ontological and psychological levels of response, and the way in which recognition of apartness in one domain leads to denial of empathy in the other.)

In particular, McGann may be criticised for assuming the relative continuity of the process of publishing, circulation, and review. This is perhaps the nearest one can find to the 'collective intentions' embodied in the Renaissance theatre, but comprehending its own internal rationale apparently involves no comparable effort of estrangement. The context of material production which may itself be understood as a cultural text remains unanalysed. Its intelligibility is taken as self-evident, an unargued assumption that explains the retrojected Victorianism that colours McGann's account of the period.

The normative status granted to a historically determined mode of producing literature has a paradoxical effect on McGann's attitude to Blake. He is described, somewhat banally, as 'probably the most private and individualistic artist ever to emerge from England' (1985: 119). His marginal status is not merely uncontested, but enthusiatically accentuated: 'in his own day Blake insisted upon having his artistic freedom, and the proper measure of success on this aim – ironic though it seems – lies in his contemporary artistic anonymity' (1985: 120). This is inferred on the basis of his 'deliberate defiance of his period's avenues of publication' (1983: 44): the empirical difficulty of the élitist nature of Blake's work in terms of simple cost preventing access to their envisaged audience becomes his chief insight, itself an ontological statement. His 'prophecy against empire' resides in an utter refusal of complicity equivalent to Adorno's 'negative or reactive movement' of the art-work 'by which it casts an anathema upon the social dysfunctions of actuality' (1989: 2). Its radicalism lies in the way it 'consistently foregrounds the material, social and institutional bases of its own productive modes' (1989: 96). Far from transmitting a common radical heritage, Blake's achievement lies in his very denial of communication. The texts do not properly exist as such until the pre-Raphaelite coterie 'initiated the process of full social integration which his work has since achieved' (1985: 120).

It should be acknowledged that McGann highlights a genuine problem for Blake scholarship – his apparent isolation and entire lack of an audience. His reading, though consistent on its own terms, may, however, be questioned on several levels.

Firstly it assumes a stance of proprietorial solipsism: 'Blake strove so resolutely, even so obsessively, to produce work that was wholly his own' (1985: 120). It is tempting simply to quote in response the famous reply to Dr Trusler: 'And tho I call them Mine I know that they are not Mine' (16 August 1799 E701). The problem, however, disappears with a simple methodological adjustment. If we see the illuminated books ('each of his engraved works was a unique publication by itself' [1985: 119]) as merely one part of an output quantitatively dominated by engravings (which may in this context be regarded as texts), it becomes immediately possible to construct a series of contexts of response (though there undeniably remains a conjectural element). Far from mechanical reproduction of his work representing, as McGann claims, 'a final splendid insult to the equally splendid principles of a genius' (1983: 47), it is crucial, on his own terms to any attempt to reconstruct a history of reception.

Secondly, the broad antithesis of Blake's 'activist and contestatory poetics' (1988: 43) opposed to a Kantian ideal of disinterested art is empirically questionable. (If nothing else, Kantianism is decontextualised into a continuous intellectual tradition rather than understood on McGann's own terms as specificable manifestations of a physical entity.) Blakean imagination transposes the Shaftesbury-Akenside premise of the intuitive capacity for aesthetic response onto all perceptual judgements and so can be seen as a parallel rather than contrasting development to Kant; the doctrine of 'Eternal Forms' may be primarily Platonic in origin, but nevertheless remains analogous to the Kantian categories; and both thinkers display a substantial common debt to Burkean aesthetics.

Thirdly, and most importantly, the priority accorded to understanding the originary moment (albeit defined in social terms) remains irredeemably monocausal. Historical understanding of Blake results in the recognition of its own impossibility due to the artist's own gesture of severance. 'Blake's ideas', we are told, 'carry a certain historical importance' from 'his philosophical significance' which 'is to be sought, and defined, in his graphic and poetical work, and not in his ideas as such' (1989: 16, 32–3). In so elevating the 'philosophical' to a supra-historical dimension (and one apparently devoid of 'ideas'), McGann remains eminently compatible with the idealist tradition which he ostensibly condemns.

There is a pleasant irony that a historicist project originally justified in terms of the restitution of philological rigour should produce a conclusion diametrically opposed to that of Thompson: 'although Blake is often associated with radical London circles of the 1790s, his poems did not interact within that circle in any important or observable way' (1991: 43).

It will now be helpful to situate the contributions to this volume, and see whether they manage to escape this impasse of rival historicisms.

IV

Iain McCalman's essay in this collection, 'The Infidel as Prophet: William Reid and Blakean Radicalism', charts the progress, reversals and general political vicissitudes in the life of the London Corresponding Society member, informer, reactionary polemicist and (consecutively) re-born radical William Hamilton Reid who was Blake's demographic contemporary. The series of analogies established allows Blake's class position, as a self-employed and self-educated engraver, to be differentiated in a more nuanced fashion from the bulk of the urban artisan class. As a result, his work can no longer be simply assumed to be synonymous with an emergent radical consciousness: a more accurate delineation is required.

On the basis of Thompson's declaration – 'Against the background of London Dissent, with its fringe of deists and earnest mystics, William Blake seems no longer the cranky untutored genius that he must seem to those who know only the genteel culture of the time' (1963: 52) – a wide variety of exotic Protestant sects have all too often been loosely invoked as a kind of cover-all explanatory context. Thompson's own undeniably attractive emphasis on Blake's 'almost antinomian affirmation' against the 'all-enveloping Thou shalt not which permeated all religious persuasions' itself involves a highly selective reading; the claim that he 'drew his bow against the teaching of humility and submission' (1963: 374) ignores, for example, the ethic of self-annihilation central to the later work. Jon Mee's essay, 'Is there an Antinomian in the house? William Blake and the After-Life of a Heresy', focuses on the minute particularities of contemporary dissent in order to substantiate this claim. His exemplary empirical investigation raises the question of whether the cultural context documented in such detail can bear the burden of significance placed upon it. At the very least, more detailed investigation into the milieu and practices of these engaging communities is likely to emphasize the degree of their unlikeness at least as much as of their similarity with Blake.[19]

The historicizing of Blake needs to advance on all fronts, not merely to see him within the 'traditional' radical context, but also by avoiding unnecessary polarizations with mainstream eighteenth-century culture. Blake's protestations of 'Contempt & Abhorrence' (E660) have been taken at face value far too readily. The dinner-party in the *Marriage of Heaven and Hell* with 'the Prophets Isaiah and Ezekiel' (*MHH* 12, E38) is adapted from Voltaire's *Dictionnaire Philosophique*; the tirades in *Jerusalem*, 'O Woman-born/ And Woman-nourishd & Woman-educated & Woman-scornd!' (*Jerusalem* 64: 16–17 E213) from Rousseau's *Emile*; and the 'visionary' spaces to be found within a 'red Globule of Mans Blood' in *Milton* (29 [31]:19–23 E127) from Locke's comments on the 'wonders' in the 'Figure and Motion of the minute Particles in the Blood'.[20] The assumption of a purely oppositional relation to a monolithic and oppressive Enlightenment has precluded fuller understanding of Blake's diverse, unpredictable, and by no means unproductive responses to the culture of his time.

From Yeats and Ellis through to Kathleen Raine, Blake's relation to Neoplatonism has tended to be regarded in absolutist terms. Critics have tended either to commit themselves to the primacy of a relatively unchanging perennial philosophy, or seek to deny its presence altogether. Edward Larrissy's essay, '"Self-Imposition": Alchemy, and the Fate of the "Bound" in later Blake', seeks to move away from the presupposition of a self-contained and essentially static occult tradition, and instead to stress its precise impingement on and reciprocal interchange with radical thought. Instead of Blake's interest in alchemy implying a removal from public history, it must be understood as part of a continuous renegotiation in which any clear-cut distinction between the political and the esoteric ceases to be operative. Furthermore, a more precise understanding of such contexts need not work solely on the level of direct explication: as Larrissy goes on to argue, it can serve to illuminate the concerns of recent post-structuralist criticism through historically situating their problematic.

Blake's aesthetic, at least in its more overtly neo-Platonic formulations, appears to endorse unequivocally the realm of vision and eternity at the expense of time and the 'Outward Creation' that 'is as the Dirt upon my feet No part of Me' (*VLJ* E565). The famous denunciation in the *Descriptive Catalogue* of the 'reasoning historian, turner and twister of causes and consequences' (E543) might appear to demonstrate beyond doubt Blake's antipathy to the possibility of historical understanding *per se*. Andrew Lincoln's essay, 'Blake and the "Reasoning Historian"' refuses any such dichotomy. Instead he brings out the striking degree of continuity between Blake's mythological mode and Enlightenment philosophical history, particularly in their interrelation of economic, social and religious spheres and their interest in the genealogy of culture. The significance of this recognition lies in three areas. Firstly, it makes available to us alternative sources for a Blakean historiography than a theological schema of creation, fall and redemption, whether or not mediated through radical millenialism. Secondly, closer analysis of the relation between Blake and the dominant culture of his time reveals a complexity of interchange that contradicts his more intemperately idealist pronouncements. Thirdly, it transpires that the prophecies, far from representing solipsistic withdrawal, are in certain respects the most self-consciously historical of Blake's work.

Blake criticism has customarily engaged in a leap-frogging over the poetry of his more immediate contemporaries in its haste to return to more respectable antecedents in Milton and Spenser. In '"Among the flocks of Tharmas": *The Four Zoas* and the Pastoral of Commerce', Philip Cox challenges this foreshortening by insisting on the generic continuity of Blake's prophecies with mid-century poems such as Dyer's *The Fleece* and Young's *Ocean*. What becomes clear is that the ideological freighting of these texts is precisely what is at stake in Blake's reworkings, and provides a further context in which the charge of an absence of 'answerable style' may be refuted.

Blake's relation to Newton may seem to have been definitively treated in Donald Ault's impressive *Blake's Visionary Physics* (1974) which analyses the poetic appropriation and inversion of the underlying metaphoric paradigm of Newtonian physics. But as Mary Lynn Johnson's essay, 'Blake, Democritus and the "Fluxions of the Atom"', reminds us, eighteenth-century natural philosophy must be regarded not as a unitary phenomenon but as a diverse and even internally contradictory formation. As James Thomson observed, in *A Poem Sacred to the Memory of Sir Isaac Newton* 'but a few/ Of the deep-studying Race can stretch their minds/ To what he knew' (11. 133–5); the *Principia* does not exist as a series of self-contained theorems but through a variety of mediations to which one cannot assume Blake was simply hostile. A more nuanced response needs to be adopted to the bold if often reductive clarity of his polemics if we are to understand their relation to the complex textual dissemination of Newton and the other major proponents of Enlightenment rationalism.

D.W. Dörrbecker's 'Innovative Reproduction: Painters and Engravers at the Royal Academy of Arts' is concerned with the material conditions of visual production in Blake's time, in particular the constitution of the subordinate position of the artist-engraver in the eighteenth-century art market. Such a reconstruction serves two major purposes for Blake criticism. Firstly it provides a context in which his apparently irascible and dogmatic hostility to Reynolds may be reassessed; it is not a personalized resentment, another regrettable side-effect of his isolation, but an accurate diagnosis of the process of exclusion which the craft of engraving was undergoing during his lifetime. Secondly, the marginalization of and condenscension towards Blake's own artistic oeuvre can, as Dörrbecker points out, be regarded as determined by and continuous with the institutional hegemony established during the period. The recent powerful contextualization of Blake's theoretical statements provided by John Barrell's *The Political Theory of Painting from Reynolds to Hazlitt: 'The Body of the Public'* (1986) may need modification in the light of Dörrbecker's argument. Barrell sees the disagreements between Blake and Reynolds as superficial in comparison to the underlying continuity of an idiom of civic humanism. This position may be challenged for a residual idealism in its decoupling of a self-sufficient textual sphere from the exercise of institutional power.[21]

Helen Bruder's essay, 'The Sins of the Fathers: Patriarchal Criticism and *The Book of Thel'*, offers the poem as a striking instance of how a radical poet may attract reactionary readings, indeed how his presumed radicalism in one area may be taken as licensing repressive attitudes in another. Her discussion of the tradition of commentary serves as a salutary warning that the situation of male critics passing judgement on female sexuality remains deeply problematic. But Bruder also goes on to suggest that many of the accomplished, indeed now classic, feminist readings of Blake (Fox, Ostriker, Mellor among others) are themselves limited by their tendency to discuss the issue of gender in broadly ahistorical terms: male power, female passivity. Her own interpretation offers a simple and elegant re-formulation of the poem's narrative: the sudden descent to an underworld in the sixth plate should not be regarded as subsequent to the pastoral realm of the preceding five, but rather as the simultaneous manifestation of an equivalent condition. The prescriptive implications of a sentimentalist idiom in terms of female conduct – maternity, domesticity, self-sacrifice – are made apparent through juxtaposition with a harshly surreal representation of essentially the same ideological structure.

John Beer's essay, 'Blake's Changing View of History: The Impact of the Book of Enoch', reminds us that it may be premature to attempt to establish direct relations between Blake's work and the events of his time. Instead his interventions may occur in more localized spheres, in this case the undermining of a tradition of biblical exegesis directed towards the triumph of law. The rediscovery of the Book of Enoch presented an occasion for Blake to contest this authoritarian version of sacred history, and instead to insist upon the availability of this new scriptural text for a utopian reappropriation. At this point we may appear to be rejoining a deconstructive emphasis upon competing interpretations within a purely textual continuum, but Beer insists on the necessity of attention to the specifics of material composition in order to comprehend the precise force of such interventions. The date altering alters all.

The rubric of the conference perhaps dictated the absence of the types of theoretical interests dominant in recent American criticism.[22] This does not, however, imply intransigence or hostility to these modes of inquiry: *Historicizing Blake* attempts both to reassess and continue the historicist tradition, so as to be able to resume a more productive dialogue with its counterpart.

It would be folly to anticipate the future directions which Blake scholarship in all its unwieldy diversity might take, but insofar as this collection may claim to be representative, it reflects a current move towards a more historically engaged assessment of the Romantic period.

Notes

1. A suggestive article is Roger Chartier, 'Texts, Printings, Readings', in *The New Cultural History*, ed. Lynn Hunt (Berkeley and Los Angeles: University of California Press, 1989) pp. 154–75.

2. For contributions to a critical awareness of current institutional and reading practices, see Marjorie Levinson, 'The New Historicism: Back to the Future' and Jerome McGann, 'The Third World of Criticism', in *Rethinking Historicism: Critical Readings in Romantic History*, ed. Marjorie Levinson (Oxford: Basil Blackwell, 1989) pp. 18–63; 85–107.

3. SCBSG (1982). See also Jerome J. McGann, 'What is Critical Editing?', *The Textual Condition* (Princeton: Princeton University Press, 1991) esp. pp. 52–8.

4. Association Papers, BM Add. Ms. 16922. fol. 45.

5. See Essick (1985).

6. For Modernism see Symons (1907), for an early development of Blake criticism out of a Left disposition, see Bronowski (1972) first published in 1944 as *William Blake: A Man Without Mask*. On Thompson

see Harvey J. Kaye, *The English Marxist Historians* (Cambridge: Polity Press, 1984) chap. 6.

7. The British Left's post-war reception of English Romanticism was the subject of a paper by Phillip Gorski, 'Blake, Romanticism and English Marxism'.

8. Renata Rosaldo, 'Celebrating Thompson's Heroes: Social Analysis in History and Anthropology', in *E.P. Thompson: Critical Perspectives*, ed. Harvey J. Kaye and Keith McClelland (Oxford: Polity Press 1991) pp. 103–24, see especially pp. 117–19.

9. The survival of the 'Ranter' nomenclature, if not the tradition, is confirmed by the identifier of an open air meeting of Nottinghamshire 'Ranters' in a letter to the Home Office the same year as Peterloo. Public Records Office, Home Office 42/168.9, 3 June 1819. See also E.P. Thompson, 'Eighteenth Century Ranters: did they exist?', in *Reviving the English Revolution*, eds Geoffrey Eley and William Hunt (London: Verso, 1988).

10. Terry Eagleton, *Against the Grain: Essays 1975–1985* (London: Verso, 1986) p. 185; Susan Matthews, 1992, p. 79.

11. For a vivid account, see Thomas Pakenham, *The Year of Liberty: The Story of the Great Irish Rebellion of 1798* (London: Hodder & Stoughton, 1969).

12. Paul Ricoeur, 'The First-Order Entities of History', *Time and Narrative*, trans. K. McLaughlin and D. Pellauer, (Chicago: University of Chicago Press, 1984) 3 vols, vol. 1, pp. 193–206.

13. Keith Hanley and Raman Selden, eds, *Revolution and English Romanticism: politics and rhetoric* (Hemel Hempstead: Harvester Wheatsheaf, 1990). See also Swearingen (1992).

14. Gareth Stedman Jones, *Language and Class: Studies in English Working Class History, 1832–1982* (Cambridge: Cambridge University Press, 1983).

15. Radicalism on both sides of the Channel can be pieced together by combining Albert Goodwin's *The Friends of Liberty: The English Democratic Movement in the Age of the French Revolution* (London: Hutchinson, 1979), part synthesis, part first-hand research in the 1790s, with Gwyn Williams's vivid *Artisans and Sans-Culottes: Popular Movements in France and Britain during the French Revolution* (London: Libris, 1968; 2nd edn 1989). For the London context, in addition to McCalman (1988), the last decade or so has been especially productive: Iowerth J. Prothero's *Artisans and Politics in Early Nineteenth-Century London: John Gast and his Times* (Folkestone: Dawson, 1979) emphasises the persistence of ultra-radical pro-revolutionary organization, with richly-sourced documentation of its personalities and its setbacks, and J. Ann Hone's *For the Cause of Truth: Radicalism in London 1796–1821* (Oxford: Clarendon Press, 1982) is especially illuminating on middle-class participation and the role played by the radical press.

16. Compare Graham Pechey, '1789 and After: Mutation of "Romantic" Discourse', in *1789: Reading, Writing, Revolution: Proceedings of the Essex Conference on the Sociology Literature, July 1981*, Francis Barker et al. eds, (Colchester: University of Essex, 1982) p. 60, and Aers (1987).

17. For McGann's influential role, see the comment that *The Romantic Ideology* produced the 'buzz phrase' of 1980s Romanticism, Stephen Copley and John Whale, 'Introduction', in *Beyond Romanticism: New Approaches to Text and Context. 1780–1832*, eds. S. Copley and J. Whale (London: Routledge, 1992) p. 4.

18. See M.H. Abrams, 'English Romanticism and the Spirit of the Age', in *Romanticism Reconsidered*, ed. Northrop Frye (Columbia, NY: English Institute Papers, 1963); Jon Klancher, 'English Romanticism and Cultural Production', in *The New Historicism*, ed. H. Aram Veeser (London: Routledge, 1989) pp. 77–88.

19. The mid eighteenth-century hinterland to Mee's study was also discussed in a paper by Désirée Hirst, 'Undercurrents of Thought in the late Eighteenth Century'.

20. Voltaire, *Dictionnaire philosophique* (1764), *Oeuvres Complètes*, ed. L. Moland (Paris, 1877-85) 52 vols, vol. 19, p. 58; Jean Jacques Rousseau, *Emile ou de l'éducation* (Genève: 1764) 4 vols, bk v, pp. 29–30; John Locke, *An Essay Concerning Human Understanding* (1690), ed. P.H. Nidditch (Oxford: Clarendon Press, 1975) 2:23:13.

21. Alexander Gourlay's paper on '"Idolatry on Politics": Blake's Chaucer and the Powers of 1809' argued that Blake's explicit claim to present Chaucer's pilgrims as eternal 'characters' is undermined by his actual practice of using them to denote precise, topical, individuals. The political context of *A Descriptive Catalogue* was also discussed in the paper 'Blake and the Theology of the Aesthetic' by Suzanne Matheson.

22. Papers on Blake's relationship to contemporary figures were given by Peter Kitson, 'Blake, Richard Brothers and Popular Millenialism', and Bruce Woodcock, 'Reason and Energy: Paine, Blake and the Dialectic of Revolution'. Papers on the *Songs* were given by Michael Phillips on 'The First Issue of *Songs of Experience*' and by John E. Grant in 'Historicizing Blake Historifying: From Joseph of Arimathea to "London"'. *Milton* and *Jerusalem* were considered in papers by Marilyn Butler, Susan Matthews and Young Ok-an.

2

The Infidel as Prophet: William Reid and Blakean Radicalism

IAIN McCALMAN

William Hamilton Reid occupied the margins of his world – as a deist, prophet, Jacobin and writer – now he appears occasionally in the footnotes of scholarly studies of English popular radicalism. If he is remembered, it is for having published in 1800 *The Rise and Dissolution of the Infidel Societies in this Metropolis*. Yet even this remains a fringe source. Despite its claim to have exposed 'the most secret operations' of a revolutionary, freethinking and millenarian underworld, much of the 117-page contents remains unknown or unused. Modern historians tend to reproduce the same few passages to enliven accounts of metropolitan Jacobin clubs in the 1790s. True, there is good reason to be wary of Reid's *Infidel Societies*. He does not establish Jacobin credentials and he writes in the style of an extreme loyalist. Not unreasonably, a *Gentleman's Magazine* reviewer of 1800 described him as 'a converted penitent' a view shared by modern authorities on both anti-Jacobinism and radical free-thought.[1]

I wish to argue, however, that the *Infidel Societies* can, if read sensitively, offer unique insights into the origins and character of London's revolutionary political culture during the French wars, especially when used in conjunction with Reid's other writings. Notwithstanding its hostile tone, the underlying attitudes of *Infidel Societies* are ambivalent. Reid's divided outlook reflects peculiar personal circumstances, but is symptomatic also of the wider tensions and struggles of marginal romantic-radical literati during the Napoleonic Wars. That some popular radicals were swept up in the patriotic revulsion against the French Revolution and France is undeniable, but the permanency of the swing to conservatism has been too readily presumed. Reid did modify some of his ideas in the late 1790s, but he was never a true penitent. He and others like him swiftly realigned themselves with oppositionist causes during the second half of the Napoleonic War years. Their radical commitment ultimately survived the seismic shocks of counter-revolution at home and abroad because it had been built on foundations laid well before the French Revolution.

I hope by analysing Reid to contribute also towards the elusive task of historicizing the culture and milieu of William Blake. The two men probably never met and their talents cannot be compared. Reid's were as minor as Blake's were major. Yet as artisan seekers and intellectuals both men spoke a common language of prophecy, art and revolution: they helped shape, and were shaped by, essentially the same late eighteenth-century *Weltanschauung*. They both struggled to make their living as romantic-radical artists and literati during the painful Napoleonic War years, and they responded similarly to the crucible of this experience.

I

William Hamilton Reid's *Infidel Societies* conforms in many ways to a fashionable sub-genre of loyalist writing inspired by the infidel conspiracy thesis of Abbé Barruel, whose seminal *Memoirs of Jacobinism* appeared in English translation in 1797. Barruel traced the excesses of French revolutionary Jacobinism to a long-germinating European conspiracy of infidel and anti-monarchical *philosophes* led in France by Voltaire and supported in Germany by occult lodges of 'Illuminati'. The passion, documentation and timing of Barruel's book ensured an explosive impact in English intellectual circles already primed by Burke's prophecies.[2] The Abbé's thesis was adapted by scores of loyalist pamphleteers, pressmen, theologians and preachers, all claiming on minimal evidence the existence of parallel or related conspiracies in England and Ireland. Reid promised to authenticate the London conspiracy from personal experience as a former infidel and Jacobin.

The result reads like the work of someone straining to ingratiate himself with the Establishment. It quotes the anti-infidel sermons of loyalist clerics, praises the Government for timely suppression of the popular radical movement and ostentatiously parades Reid's credentials as a translator and man of letters.[3] Reid was evidently touting for patronage. He sent a copy to the famed editor of the *Anti-Jacobin* weekly, George Canning, who evidently encouraged him to publish two short summaries in the *Anti-Jacobin Review* of July–August 1800.[4] The Bishops of Durham and London probably received similar overtures in the mail, for both sent encouraging letters. Bishop Porteus enclosed an offer of ordination, and probably helped secure Reid a brief editorship of a Church of England periodical.[5]

But if worldly advancement and commercial opportunism played a part in the decision to publish the *Infidel Societies*, Reid also had another more pressing motive. The tract describes a police raid of February 1798 on an infidel debating club at the Angel tavern, St Martins Court, which aimed to catch the United movement revolutionary John Binns.[6] Reid fails to mention that he himself was amongst those netted, and that Guildhall magistrates singled him out as a man of letters amongst a group of artisans. His further claim that the club had been innocent of politics was also disingenuous. He had been a member of the London Corresponding Society since 1793 at least, probably belonging to section five which met from 1795 at the Angel.[7] By February 1798 many of these sections had become covert cells of the United Movement revolutionary underground, operating under the guise of alehouse debating and singing clubs. Another similar club which he also attended and described, the Green Dragon in Cripplegate, hosted republican plotting from 1797 until the smashing of the Despard conspiracy in 1803. John Binns frequented both places before his capture in 1798 on the point of embarking for France with messages from the United Movement in London and Ireland.[8]

All this would seem to confirm a contemporary opinion that Reid was 'a zealous advocate of the republican doctrines with no small tinge of infidelity'.[9] At the very least he had been keeping dangerous company. He had also chosen a bad time to be compromised. As Blake well knew, the year 1798 brought the most draconian anti-radical crackdown of the entire Pittite 'Terror'; few figures of significance amongst London's surviving democrats escaped interrogation, harassment and, in some cases, lengthy prison sentences without trial. Reid wrote his anti-Jacobin exposé primarily to save his skin through public recantation. This also explains his zeal in 1800–1 to give anti-Jacobin information to the Secretary of State. He might have been somewhat discomforted, however, to know that Canning forwarded a copy of his pamphlet to Privy Council Under-Secretary John King with an ambiguously worded note saying that the author was 'little better than one of the wicked'.[10]

II

Reid's wickedness, like Blake's, went back a long way. The trajectory of their careers suggests a similar birth date, though Reid's
origins were, if anything, humbler. Born to domestic servants of the
Duke of Hamilton, he managed some early education at St James's
parochial school before the death of both parents left him dependent
on the parish. His apprenticeship with a Soho silver buckle maker
was completed in 1779, the same year as Blake's, and he worked
throughout the 1780s as a journeyman in Smithfield. Here he
presumably learned the late-eighteenth century London craftsman's
characteristic pride in skill and status, and truculent commitment to
social and economic independence. But on top of such endemic
artisan hazards as wartime inflation, trade fluctuations and sweated
competition, Reid had to contend with the vagaries of fashion
influenced in part by the French Revolution itself. The demand for
silver buckles suddenly declined at the turn of the century with a
shift in taste towards simpler clothing styles.

In a sense Reid was saved by the vitality of his culture. From the
age of sixteen he had – like Blake – plunged himself into the world
of artisan autodidact letters, devoting every spare penny and
moment to the study of divinity, history, poetry, antiquities and
foreign languages. Successive mastery of French, Italian, Spanish
and German, and later Hebrew, Greek and Portuguese, gave him a
marketable alternative skill. He weathered the collapse of his trade
by translating foreign language newspapers until that job too disappeared when the Post Office suddenly claimed a monopoly over
newspaper translations. Fortunately he had also begun in 1781 to
publish occasional periodical articles. For the remainder of his life
he struggled to keep a large family by working as a hack writer
and journalist among London's swelling ranks of Grub Street
Dunces.[11]

Through this autodidact artisan milieu surged some of the
earliest currents of romanticism. From boyhood Reid showed a
passionate interest in antiquarian culture and folklore. Around the
same time that the young apprentice engraver William Blake was
fascinatedly sketching tombstones in melancholy graveyards, Reid
was spending hours exploring old churches. Both were drawn to
works of Gothic sensibility such as Hervey's *Meditations Among the
Tombs* and both seem to have felt themselves part of a national
cultural renaissance.[12] Reid discovered his poetic talent 'by a kind

of electrical contact', when a fellow silversmith produced a poem
'On Masonry' in 1785. According to an early admirer, Reid became
a 'rapt enthusiast' who dashed off poems full of 'passion', 'pathos',
'bold imagery' and love of 'the sublime and beautiful', reflecting
'eccentric abilities, unequalled by any of the modern untutored
bards, except Robert Burns'.[13] A projected book of poetry was never
published, and the few poems that did make it into print show that
he was no Blake. A major influence seems to have been the proto-
romantic Hugh Blair.[14] This stanza from a sonnet 'To Absence,
written in 1800', conveys the flavour:

> Rudely awake the fev'rish burning flame
> That Reason long had labour'd to controul
> Now, like a Mariner, I hear those sounds
> As distant winds which threatening do away;
> So, from the beach the dashing surge rebounds
> Or wastes its fury in the whitening spray.[15]

But it was probably as an antiquarian that he attracted the notice
of Scott's close friend, George Ellis, another proto-romantic, who
compiled important collections of early English poems and metrical
romances. Perhaps this antiquarianism had a radical tincture, as
Erdman suggests, for it was almost certainly Ellis who introduced
Reid to the Esto Perpetua club, a circle of bohemian anti-tories who
met in the mid-1780s to honour Fox and dishonour Pitt.[16] No doubt
Reid was already predisposed to artisan oppositional causes: retrospective writings sympathize with the libertarian struggles of the
American colonists and with rakish John Wilkes.[17] Ellis and cronies
enrolled him to help write a scurrilous mock epic celebrating the
mythical ancestor of a bovine parliamentary Pittite called John
Rolle. The *Rolliad* sold widely and is now regarded as a seminal
work in the history of English political satire. Blake's own satire,
historical drama and prophetic painting of this time echoes some of
its themes, including the 'cold and leprous' tyranny of Pitt and the
corrupt warmongering of the American War years. The *Rolliad* and
Blake both criticize the latter by linking the visitation of the Great
Plague of 1348 to British military aggression, an idea which might
have come from Reid who was fascinated by the plague.[18] We do
know that he composed the celebrated sixth number of the *Rolliad*
which lambasted Pitt and Dundas in the language of mock prophecy, described as 'unintelligible, perhaps, to those to whom it is

addressed, but perfectly clear, full and forcible to those who live in the time of the accomplishment.'[19]

Though willing to use prophecy as a vehicle for satire, Reid generally treated it with the utmost seriousness. Sensibilities like his were drawn naturally to the powerful currents of Illuminism which still circulated among London's artisan seekers. He immersed himself in the works of William Law, the Anglican divine who popularized Boehme, and also in the writings of an early eighteenth-century English mystic, Francis Lee, himself a disciple and publicist of millenarian prophetess Jane Lead. The young silversmith became – like his engraver counterpart – 'long bewildered in the labyrinths of mystical divinity.'[20] He first learned the mystical nostrum that God existed wholly in the human mind from reading 'Cobbler' How's Ranter work, *The Sufficiency of the Spirit's Teaching*, reprinted, as Jon Mee tells us elsewhere in this volume, during the early 1790s.[21] The explosive eschatology of early Methodists offered another important, often overlooked, source of prophetical inspiration. Reid claimed to have been transported as a young man by the preaching of Calvinist Methodists Martin Madan and William Romaine, both of whom came under an official cloud in the 1780s – the one for a work advocating polygamy, the other for creating antinomians by his preaching.[22] Madan's work has been claimed as the inspiration for the *Book of Thel* and *Visions of the Daughters of Albion* (Murray, 1981).

From here it was a short step to involvement with congregations of Muggletonians and Swedenborgians who met, preached and published in the central and eastern districts of late eighteenth-century London. Reid, like Blake, knew the books, doctrines and meeting places of both these mystical sects whom he saw as important precursors of the prophetic and revolutionary infidels of the 1790s. Muggletonian field disputants around Moorfields had been the first 'after the protectorship of Oliver', he claimed, to propagate the idea that 'the whole Godhead is circumscribed in the person of Jesus Christ, still retaining the human form in heaven'. Swedenborgians had also disputed the atonement, the epistles, and the day of resurrection which they thought 'more a figure than a fact'.[23]

However much Swedenborgians influenced Reid in the 1780s, he had by 1800 arrived at a remarkably Blakean view of their defects, summarized as, 'too much of the metaphysics for the head, and too little energy for the heart'. He had also sought the proper linking of head and heart within the vibrant milieu of metropolitan liberal Dissent. True, he again sounds Blakean when castigating Socinianism in

1800 as a 'frozen zone of religion' afflicted with the 'heart deadening' and mechanistic doctrines of Priestley.[24] Yet the universalism, intelligence and scientific character of Unitarianism engaged his deeper sympathies to the extent that he decided around 1806–7 to join Thomas Belsham's celebrated Hackney congregation, earlier led by both Price and Priestley. He had earlier rejected the temptingly lucrative offer of ordination from the Bishop of London because it would compromise his independence by subscription to the Anglican articles of faith.[25]

A careful reading of the *Infidel Societies* discloses notable inconsistencies in his ostensibly hostile portrayal of rationalist Dissent. He includes, for example, a sympathetic description of a rationalist preacher known as 'The Priest of Nature' – actually Dr David Williams – who delivered deistic sermons in 1775–6 at a chapel in Margaret Street.[26] And if a simultaneous immersion in Boehmist mysticism and Dissenting rationalism seems inconsistent with modern categories of thought, eighteenth-century artisans like Reid and Blake were never bound by our antinomies. Priestley had been as famed for thunderous anti-establishment prophecies as for his materialism.[27] Elsewhere in the *Infidel Societies* Reid describes fervent Jacobin debaters of the mid-1790s who believed that 'they were the very persons designated by Dr Priestley, but a few years before, for the important and momentous task of setting fire to the train so long accumulating under the Established Church'.[28] Blake encountered such rationalist visionaries amongst the Unitarian coteries which gathered at Johnson's premises, and though he later chose to satirize Priestley as a gaseous scientist, he did at least grant him the property of inflammability.

Still more volatile compounds of materialist scepticism, biblical prophecy and libertarian politics could be traced back to the mechanic preachers who had turned the world upside down in the 1640s. Reid's intimacy with this tradition caused him to diverge sharply from conventional accounts of the origins of Jacobin infidelity. The 'true parent' of English revolutionary infidelity, he insisted, had been the sectaries of the seventeenth century rather than Voltairean *philosophes*. This linkage between the Puritan and French revolutions was eventually to become something of a commonplace in the fiction of Scott and other romantics, but Reid backed his claim with an impressive knowledge of the eighteenth-century 'Commonwealthmen' like Tindal, Chubb, Collins and Annet who had helped connect the two epochs. He also showed detailed knowledge of schoolmaster Peter Annet's Robin Hood debating club whose proceedings, ideology and membership had, he believed, anticipated the forms of 1790s radical freethought.[29]

To see the Robin Hood Club as a Jacobin precursor was not particularly original given its Grub Street notoriety, but Reid also stressed the importance of a tantalizingly obscure late eighteenth-century coterie. The whole welter of subversive and sceptical ideas circulating amongst metropolitan artisans on the eve of the French Revolution had converged, he claimed, in a circle of Hoxton 'seekers' known as the Ancient Deists. Noting that it had contained some 'above the common rank' in ability – his way of signalling his own presence – he described the group as 'a kind of vortex, attracting the restless and dissatisfied of every sect. Here, human learning was declaimed against, as one of the greatest enemies to human happiness or the improvement of the intellect, and dreams, visions, and immediate revelations were recommended as a substitute'. Some members had exercised 'the faculty of foretelling future events', some 'the discernment of spirits by physiognomy'; others had believed in 'the possibility of conversing with departed souls', in 'the hearing of supernatural voices' and in 'the daily ministrations of angels'.[30] Blake would surely have felt at home here. This 'assemblage . . . of Alchymists, Astrologers, Mystics, Magnetiziers, Prophets and Projectors' parallels the febrile mesmerist milieu which Robert Darnton has seen as an immediate precursor of French romanticism and revolution.[31] Reid made a similar claim for the Hoxton circle which 'almost immediately yielded to the stronger impulse of the French Revolution, and terminated in the general conversion of the members into *politicians* and *inquirers after news*'.[32]

III

If Reid's account of the origins of popular infidelity contains as much disguised autobiography as loyalist polemic, what of his analysis of the more immediately controversial period of the 1790s? Here again, a vigorous mouthing of anti-Jacobin orthodoxies fails to conceal persisting fascination and complicity. Reading between the lines of the *Infidel Societies*, we sense why marginal literati were attracted to this social borderland of the respectable and the rough, the profane and the pious, the plotter and the *philosophe*. Poised

between the communality of the London artisan and the individualism of the 'uneasy' lesser professional, they could perhaps find a
measure of cultural reconciliation and fulfilment within the carnivalesque milieu of Jacobin debating clubs. Here, Reid admitted,
talented Jacobins were 'encouraged to cite their own productions',
and sometimes earned money for the privilege. He gives the interesting example of an unnamed engraver who was voted half a
guinea at the Whitecross Street 'Temple of Reason' in 1796 for an
emblematic work 'exhibiting Truth with a speculum in her hand
concentrating her rays upon the figure of Error recumbent on the
ground'.[33] And though he did not say so, Reid himself benefited
from this type of Jacobin patronage when the London Corresponding Society (LCS) voted to distribute printed copies of a rollicking
song he had composed in 1793.[34] No doubt it joined the orther 1d.
and 2d. 'swivels against established opinions' which he saw strewn
on the tables of low alehouses. Possibly he translated some of the
popular editions of Voltaire, Volney and Holbach, which the *Infidel
Societies* describes with such accuracy. To men of his kind alehouse
fraternities not only served as plebeian counterparts of Voltaire's
salons – London's real republic of letters – but also offered cathartic
and convivial pleasures. '[S]arcastic or facetious conversation
across the tables', 'noisy approbation' of entertainments, 'extem-
poraneous effusions', bloodthirsty, comical and inspirational toasts,
mutualist rituals, theatrical gestures debunking the mystique of
church and state: all are vividly, almost lovingly, evoked.

Denunciations of infidelity's stark rationalist spirit are undercut
by passages describing the feverish millenarian excitement which
gripped London's revolutionary freethinkers during the mid-
1790s. Debaters hurried from East to West End late at night in the
hope of catching several meetings, or walked to Moorfields every
Sunday afternoon to debate with Methodist field preachers. Dis-
ciples of Priestley anticipated an apocalyptic explosion in 1796 that
would purge Christendom of slavery and superstition. These were
hardly the sort of infidels to read the *philosophes* with 'single
vision'. Reid trumpets his knowledge of the 'more learned and
elaborate' writings of Holbach and Volney, cites Mesurier's *Le Bon
Sens* in the original French, and admits the exhilaration of first
encountering 'the luminious scrutinizing genius of Montesquieu,
the splendid levity of Voltaire, the impassioned and fascinating
eloquence of Rousseau, the precision and depth of d'Alembert, the
bold and active investigations of Boulanger, the daring paradoxical

spirit of Helvetius, the profound astronomic researches of Baille, the captivating elegance of Marmontel and the impressive condensed thoughts of Diderot'.[35] This was the same spirit that led Blake to exult in 1791 that 'the fiery cloud of Voltaire' has smashed Europe's mental manacles (*FR*: 276, E298). Around the same time that Blake made his angry annotations of Watson's An *Apology for the Bible* (E611–20) another Jacobin-Spencean debater George Cullen was scribbling in the margins of Boulanger's *Christianity Unveiled*: 'They say the Devil was chained up in Hell once, how came they let him loose again? and to get among the women', and 'What do you think of the justice of God who first permitted the French Revolution and then destroyed millions of lives to prevent its effects, ask yourself that Mr Christian'.[36]

Reid's criticisms of 1790s infidelity carry real conviction only when he skirts this visionary side of the movement to attack its abstract and mechanistic philosophies. Like Blake he disliked the bloodless materialism of thinkers such as Hume and Holbach who failed, he said, to 'seize the imagination or interest the passions'. Without such reservoirs of feeling and imagination, artistic creativity and true social morality must atrophy. Excitement at reason's destructive powers gives way to ennui: 'our hearts sicken at the sameness of the scene. Here the heavens above are as brass, and the earth as iron beneath our feet. Our ears are torn by the screaming of the bittern, or alarmed by the howling of the beasts of prey. The voice of the turtle is not heard in this land, and the time for singing birds never comes'.[37] Such sentiments are commonly associated with the anti-jacobin recoil of Wordsworth, Coleridge and Southey, but they belong equally within a popular romantic tradition that remained broadly sympathetic to the spirit of the French Revolution. It includes Blake and Shelley, as well as the culture of popular deists, infidel preachers, Zetetics, Owenites, Anglo-Carbornarians and St Simonians which sprang up in London during the 1820s and 30s.

Romantic infidels like Reid were characteristically impressed by Volney's *Ruins of Empires*, with its Gothic imagery, orientalist mythology, sacramental language and dream-fairytale plot structure. They were also drawn to neoclassical forms; Reid praised 'the pagan systems of the ancients' which 'propagated an infinity of ideas and motives for consideration'. Less common was his admiration of German romantic-rationalist poets and philosophers such as Johan Fichte and Christoph Wieland. All this helps to explain Reid's preoccupation with the closure of the Parisian Society

of Theophilanthropists in 1799.[38] The collapse of a popular movement which had tried to marry Rousseauist nature worship, Catholic
sacramental ritual and theistic rationalism seemed to offer 'convincing proof' of infidelity's failure to develop a viable popular alternative to Christianity (p. 60).

Given this type of mystical and romantic sensibility, Reid's hostility to the enthusiasts, visionaries and millenarian prophets
whom he claimed as 'auxiliaries' of 1790s freethought might seem
puzzling. His sensational claims of prophetic and infidel interac-
tion and collusion probably derived from personal experience – of
the apocalyptic prophecies of Richard Brothers, of the rich amalgam of revolutionary and prophetic discourses expounded by the
Spencean-Jacobin tavern underground, and of the covert financing
of prophetic, deists and revolutionary causes by the banker, black-
mailer Jonathan 'Jew' King. Blake was touched by this same culture.[39] In May 1800 Reid's personal investigations at his old haunt
the Green Dragon even helped to link a recent assassination
attempt on George III by a deranged ex-soldier, James Hadfield,
with the machinations of a chiliastic Methodist fieldpreacher and
LCS revolutionary named Bannister Truelock.[40]

No doubt attacks on such enthusiasts pandered to the kind of
government paranoia that prompted the incarceration of Brothers in
Bedlam in 1795 and Spence in Newgate in 1801. Blake scarcely exaggerated the risks of professing oneself a radical Christian in the year
1798. At the same time Reid's earlier and later writings also reveal
that Methodist proselytizing and bigotry affronted an ingrained
belief in religious toleration, something that Blake again would
surely have endorsed.

Certainly Reid's diatribes against Methodist enthusiasts did not
signify a rejection of prophetic modes of exegesis; like many of his
contemporaries he assumed that prophecy functioned both as predictor and agent of social change. The *Infidel Societies* borrowed
freely from a rich corpus of a recent millenialist scholarship, particularly from *History, the interpreter of Prophecy* by an Oxford divine
named Henry Kett.[41] *Infidel Societies* also carried a faint imprint of
Reid's mystical past. His impatience with Paine's blinkered literal-
ism seems to owe something to the popular doctine of correspond-
ences – the belief, in John Harrison's words, 'that all things have an
outward and inward form, and the former is a reflection or parable
of the latter'.[42] Paine's inability to see such underlying allegories or
metaphors, Reid argued, had blinded him to the fact that the 19th

Psalm was 'almost a complete allegory' and led him to dismiss *Revelations* as a 'book of enigmas'. Seventeenth-century mystics had long anticipated Paine's deistic belief in the individual's inner and personal apprehension of divinity. Reid held to the Blakean-sounding ideal that 'Christianity is . . . more a principle than a profession'; many pagans and Mahometans were, he believed, 'in the best sense, true Christians'.[43]

IV

Overall, the *Infidel Societies* is a palimpsest that partially conceals traces of earlier texts and discourses; no clear or coherent ideology prevails throughout. It captures Reid in a moment of irresolution between his commitment to a revolutionary past and the temptations of a retreat to the safety of loyalism. Despite sharing some of the celebrated romantic disenchantment of this period, he chose ultimately not to snap his squeaking baby trumpet of sedition. Rather, like Blake during the Felpham period, he regathered something of his Christian prophetic and libertarian radicalism of the 1770s and 80s. By relinquishing the editorship of a Church of England periodical to join the Unitarians in 1806, he sentenced himself to conservative disapproval and future penury, only exacerbated by rejecting Unitarianism in turn because of its excessive formality.[44]

He could console himself that he was not alone in opting to return to the radical fold. Though the anti-Jacobin revulsion of the early nineteenth century is sometimes exaggerated, the revival of popular radical politics during the same period is underestimated equally. In 1808–9, for example, a group of ultra-radical journalists broke the news that the mistress of the royal Commander-in Chief had been using her considerable influence to run a promotions racket within the armed services. Oppositionist politicians led by Colonel Gwillam Lloyd Wardle capitalized on the government's embarrassment to force the resignation of the Duke of York and the appointment of a parliamentary inquiry. The Mary Anne Clarke affair, as it was called, roused populist passions, gathered diverse radical supporters and helped reverse the wartime equation between monarchy and patriotism. From this point 'Old Corruption' displaced 'Popery' within the demonology of the political prints.[45] Blake fiercely called on Colonel Wardle 'to give those rascals a dose of cawdle' (*Epigrams*, E514) and Reid published a chronicle of the affair which urged that the associated popular radical agitation be given 'the approbation of all ranks'.[46]

Historians have also overlooked the Irish contribution to such political scandals and anti-war agitations during the Napoleonic wars. The unwavering anti-government animosity of former United Irishmen such as Peter Finnerty, Patrick Duffin and Roger O'Connor fortified embattled London radicals, especially within Westminster electoral circles and the oppositionist press. Finnerty, a parliamentary reporter for the *Morning Chronicle* and one of Cobbett's closest friends, proved an implacable anti-government propagandist. A year after instigating the Mary Anne Clarke exposé, he faced trial for repeatedly publicizing government complicity in torturing Irish peasantry after the Rebellion. His imprisonment in 1810–11 made him a *cause célèbre* and gave heart to those opposing the war and supporting Catholic Emancipation. Blake, who may have had tenuous links to this metropolitan Irish-radical coterie through Barry, chose this moment to introduce into *Jerusalem* the visionary figure of Erin (*J* 9: 34, E152), a symbol of renewed radical hope in England as much as Ireland.

At the same time Reid was developing his own symbol of radical continuity, integrity and redemption in a commemorative biography of Horne Tooke which traced the veteran radical's libertarian political activities through the American Wars, the Wilkite agitation, the French Revolution, up to his death. At a time of festering popular dissatisfaction with the war and government, Reid recast his interpretation of the history of the 1790s into an attack on Pitt's bellicose, corrupting and famine-creating policies.[47] And in a final work published shortly after his own death in 1826, he completed this process of radical retrospect and reaffirmation by presenting the French Revolution as a fount of liberty, perpetuated by none other than Napoleon Bonaparte.[48]

For those imbued with Reid's cast of mind, no mention of Bonaparte could be innocent of prophetic implication. Blake was not alone during these years in linking history and prophecy. Conservative exegetes like Kett, Faber and Burnett pondered particularly how the enigmatic and menacing figure of Bonaparte should be fitted into the providential scheme and what form the predicted restoration and conversion of the Jews would take.[49] News of the convergence of these concerns in 1807 sent shock-waves through English millenialist circles: Napoleon had summoned the Sanhedrin of European Jewry to Paris to build a new Jerusalem based on civil and religious liberty. A more literal restoration also seemed possible because of Napoleon's advances on Palestine, especially at a time when European Jewry were supposedly hailing him as the new Messiah. In London the Society for the Conversion of Jews, and other evangelical prosyletizers, redoubled their efforts to convert local Jewry, whom they also berated for lax worship practices and for infidel and Napoleonic sympathies.[50] In spite of Erdman's disclaimers, it is this issue, surely, which provides the context for a late passage in *The Four Zoas* when Blake links the 'Synagogue of Satan in dire Sanhedrim' with a new revival of deism and natural religion (Erdman 1969, pp. 418–19; *FZ* 105: 5, E378).

Blake's overall attitude to Bonaparte seems, however, to have been ambivalent: if there was any substance in the charges levelled against him by the soldier Scholefield in 1803, he continued to feel a residual sympathy for Napoleon also shown by many other London radicals right up to 1815 (Bronowski, 1972). Reid responded to Napoleon's action of 1807 by writing a substantial book, *The New Sanhedrin: Causes and Consequences of the French Emperor's Conduct Towards the Jews* (1807), under the significant pseudonym of 'An Advocate of the House of Israel'. Here and in supporting articles published in the *Gentleman's Magazine* over the next five years, he and several other radical pamphleteers developed a sustained prophetic-historical defence of Bonaparte's liberation of European Jewry, urging the English to extend the same toleration to their Jewish countrymen.[51] Rejecting the literalist and conservative interpretations of the restoration circulated by scholars like Faber and Mede, he and other 'seekers' intellectuals like the bookseller-mystic Henry Lemoine worked to revive the powerful seventeenth-century Dissenting tradition of restorationism which had represented the scriptural restoration of the Jews as both an inspirational symbol of Puritan fortitude and the prelude to the advent of a literal or allegorical millennium of peace and enlightenment.

Reid predicted that world Jewry would be restored figuratively 'from captivity, from oppression, and from the condition of aliens in every country where they have been settled'.[52] Bonaparte's actions, when coupled with the abolition of the slave trade in 1808, filled him with expectation that a New Jerusalem, an age of universal freedom and toleration was beginning to dawn. What he called 'those beneficial changes' of the French Revolution had set in train a providential process which Napoleon now continued. It would bring about the end of the corrupt Babylon of 'old ecclesiastical and political establishments' characterized by 'narrow minded politics' and 'persecuting priests', and it would 'subvert the old [Empire], the parent of false policy, persecution and strife'. Though a spiritual city whose 'splendour' would shine like 'crystal', the New Jerusalem belonged emphatically 'to this life and not another beyond the grave'. Above all, it would be 'a city of peace, because its conquests are to make war to cease upon the earth' and its gates would be thrown open permanently, signifying a new universal catholicity, the end of 'exclusive confessions' and 'contradictory creeds'.[53] Needless to say, Blake, too, felt this breath of hope that freedom of blacks and Jews prophesied in his *Song of Liberty* might at last be coming to pass, and it is against this background that his last great visionary poem *Jerusalem* should be interpreted. Reid, Lemoine and a variety of Jewish pamphleteers gave Providence a push by demanding in print that Englishmen put a stop to the 'lash of persecution'. Reid testified from personal experience to the dignity of worship at the Duke Street synagogue and to the generosity, integrity and industriousness of metropolitan Jewry.[54]

Reid's sympathies for Jewish emancipation hearked back consciously to the restorationist writings of seventeenth-century Dissent, including Frenchman Isaac Lapeyree's, *Recal of the Jews* (1643), Thomas Beverley's *Charter for the Interpretation of Prophecy* (1694) and, above all, the works of eighteenth-century mystic Francis Lee. The latter had invoked the apocryphal text of Esdras, much favoured by 1790s enthusiasts, to predict that France would generate a princely Messiah – similar, Reid thought, to Napoleon.[55]

Some of the ideas in *The New Sanhedrin* had also been anticipated in Priestley's prophetic *Letters to the Jews* of 1794. To the evangelical London Conversion Society Reid was simply 'a modern infidel, an advocate for Bonaparte, a Jacobin . . .', as well as 'a famished Devotee' who had hired himself out to Jewish interests.[56] This last claim hit home. Marginal literati like Reid, Lemoine and Blake had been forced to struggle more desperately than usual to make a living during the middle years of the Napoleonic wars, partly because of the atmosphere of heresy sniffing that prevailed in their literary and artistic circles. Reid was twice saved from ruin during these years by handouts from the Literary Foundation. He admitted, too, to having been helped by 'a few enlightened Jews in this Metropolis' when gravely embarrassed by the costs of publishing *The New Sanhedrin*.[57]

The mysterious banker and revolutionary Jonathan 'Jew' King was probably one of these benefactors.[58] Their political trajectories had converged in Foxite opposition circles of 1783–4, in Jacobin and United movement debating clubs, and in the coteries of radical literati whom King had financed during the Mary Anne Clarke affair. However shady his reputation, King was always notoriously willing 'to bleed' for ultra-radicals and to offer loans or patronage to those involved in philo-Semitic and millenarian causes of all kinds. Around 1807 King began a militant reassertion of his Jewish origins and faith – his father had been a poor Sephardi street hawker named Moses Rey. He took up cudgels against the London Society for Converting the Jews and later republished a prophetic work of the 1790s written by the Jewish hatter, David Levi, which Reid had thought virtually 'unanswerable'. King's bitter introduction to the 1817 edition of Levi's *Dissertations and Prophecies of the Old Testament* proclaimed the superiority of Judaism over Christianity and inverted orthodox Anglican prophecy by extolling Unitarians and infidels for serving as providential anti-Christian corrosives in the 'approaching period of God's judging the earth and redeeming his faithful people'.[59]

'Jew' King, a former shoe-black and long-time patron of radical art and letters, clearly had 'seekers' like William Hamilton Reid in mind. Autodidact revolutionaries like Reid and Blake displayed a political tenacity during the French wars that is rarely appreciated. Born in humble circumstances in mid eighteenth-century London, they fashioned their revolutionary cosmologies during the ferment of the American and French revolutions, survived the Pittite 'Terror' to witness a rebirth of popular radicalism between 1810–20, and died within a few years of each other in the mid twenties still committed to a prophetic vision of an age revolution. 'After so much desolation, so much distress of nations, only to behold the dawn of the day of restitution is no mean privilege . . . in the feast of life', wrote Reid in 1807. The coming millennium would see, he promised, '. . . *no more death* on account of what has erroneously been called religion, *nor sorrow, nor crying, nor any more pain*, because the *former* state of *things* shall *pass* away, and all political and ecclesiastical things become new'.[60]

Notes

1. *Gentleman's Magazine* (hereafter *GM*) 70 (1800) pp. 970–1; see also Edward Royle, *Victorian Infidels* (Manchester and New Jersey: Manchester University Press, 1974) p. 13; and Emily Lorraine de Montluzin, *The Anti-Jacobins 1798–1800; The Early Contributions to the 'Anti-Jacobin Review'* (London: Macmillan, 1988) pp. 139–40.

2. I.D. McCalman, *Radical Underworld: Prophets, Revolutionaries, and Pornographers in London 1795–1840* (Cambridge: Cambridge University Press, 1988) pp. 2, 238; Robert Hole, *Pulpits Politics and Public Order in England 1760–1832* (Cambridge: Cambridge University Press, 1989) pp. 153–6.

3. Reid (1800) pp. 20, 80, 93–7

4. Privy Council Papers PC1/2490, correspondence between George Canning, W.H. Reid, John King and Sir Richard Ford, May 1800; *Anti-Jacobin Review* vi (July, 1800) pp. 354–6; vi (Aug., 1800) pp. 468–72.

5. See *Annual Register* 68 (1826) p. 254. The obituary is by Reid's wife.

6. Reid (1800) p. 13.

7. British Library, Francis Place Papers, Add, MS 27812, 'Journal/Minute Book of the London Corresponding Society', 30 May 1793; Add, MS 27818, 'General Committee', 20 Aug, 1795, fo. 111 and 3 Sept. 1795, fo. 122.

8. On this milieu in general, see McCalman (1988) pp. 11–16. On Binns and debating clubs, see PC1/43/A152, confiscated 'School of Eloquence' ticket; John Binns, *Recollections* (1854), vol. 1, pp. 41, 56; Mary Thale, 'London Debating Societies in the 1790s', *The Historical Journal* 32 (1989), pp. 58–9, 70, 86.

9. De Montluzin, *The Anti-Jacobins* (1988) pp. 140–1.

10. PC1/3490 20 May 1800.

11. *Annual Register* 68 (1826) pp. 253–4; *GM* 96 (1826), pp. 184–6. For further discussion of Reid as an early radical journalist and common labourer poet, see Robert Haig, *The Gazetteer, 1735–97: A Study in the Eighteenth-Century Newspaper* (Carbondale: University of Illinois, 1960) pp. 204–9, 224–5, 252–3.

12. For an excellent discussion of Blake and this antiquarian milieu, see Erdman (1977), pp. 35–55, 111–12; and Bindman (1973).

13. *GM* 58 (1788) pp. 593–5.

14. From whose work Reid produced an anthology; see *Sentimental Beauties from the Writings of Dr. H. Blair . . .* (1809).

15. *GM* 81 (1811) p. 264.

16. For further details, see *The Cambridge History of English Literature*, vol. IX, eds A.W. Ward and A.R. Waller (Cambridge: Cambridge University Press, 1914) pp. 33–8.

17. W.H. Reid, *Memoirs of the Public Life of John Horne Tooke . . . with his most celebrated Speeches . . . letters, etc.* (1812) pp. iii–xxv, 9.

18. *GM* 95 (1825) pp. 311–16; see also Erdman (1977) pp. 56–63.

19. *The Rolliad: Criticisms on the Rolliad* (1784), 8th edn, part one, no. 6 (1790) pp. 67–8. The identification of Reid's contributions is made in *Notes and Queries* 1st series, ii (20 July 1850) p. 114.

20. *GM* 81 (1811) pp. 631–2; *Annual Register* 68 (1826), p. 254.

21. Reid (1800) p. 69.
22. *GM* 81 (1811) p. 231; *DNB* vol. 12, pp. 732–4, 175–7.
23. Reid (1800) pp. 19, 52–5.
24. Reid (1800) pp. 54, 89.
25. *GM* 81 (1811) p. 232; *Annual Register* 68 (1826) p. 254.
26. Reid (1800) p. 90.
27. On this aspect of Priestley, see Clarke Garrett, *Respectable Folly: Millenarians and the French Revolution in France and England* (Baltimore and London: Johns Hopkins University Press, 1975) pp. 133–43; and W.H. Oliver, *Prophets and Millenialists, The uses of Biblical Prophecy in England from the 1790s to the 1840s* (Auckland: University of Auckland Press, 1978) pp. 42–6.
28. Reid (1800) pp. 23–4.
29. Reid (1800) pp. 83–7.
30. Reid (1800) p. 91.
31. Robert Darnton, *Mesmerism and the End of the Enlightenment in France* (Cambridge, Mass.: Harvard University Press, 1968), passim.
32. Reid (1800) p. 92.
33. Reid (1800) pp. 13, 23
34. *Hum! Hum! a new song* [1793]; BL, Place Papers, Add. MS. 27812, 'Journal/Minute Book of the London Corresponding Society', 30 May 1793.
35. See Reid (1800) for these translations, pp. 6–7, 25–7 and alehouse fraternities, pp. 8–15. See also McCalman (1988) pp. 21–3, 113–27.
36. Reid (1800) pp. 12–14, 17, 24, 27. Cf. Boulanger [Baron Holbach], *Christianity Unveiled* (1795), BL shelf mark, 900. h. 24(7), signed MS notes by George Cullen, pp. 108–9, 232, Cullen also parallels Blake's famous comment that Tom Paine was 'a better Christian than the Bishop' (E620). In Cullen's annotations of *A Letter from the author to a friend* (bound with T. Spence, *The Important Trial of Thomas Spence* (1803) BL), he writes 'The Great Thomas Paine says, all religious duties consists in doing Justice, loveing mercy, and endevouring to make our fellow creatures happy and that all others are only human inventions set up *to monopolise, power and profit and to enslave mankind*' (p. 22).
37. Reid (1800) pp. 60, 65, 76–7; 38; 28.
38. Reid (1800) pp. 37, 105–7, 26, 60, 82; 60.
39. McCalman (1988) pp. 50–72. On the links between Brothers and popular millenarianism, see J.F.C. Harrison, *The Second Coming: Popular Millenarianism. 1780–1850* (Cambridge: Cambridge University Press, 1979) pp. 64–85; James K. Hopkins, *A Woman to Deliver Her People: Joanna Southcott and English Millenarianism in an Era of Revolution* (Austin: University of Texas, 1982) esp. pp. 149–69. On Blake's relation to enthusiastic culture, see Thompson (1963) pp. 50–2; Paley (1973) and Mee (1992).
40. PC1/3490, correspondence May–June 1800; Treasury Solicitor's TS 11/223/973.
41. Henry Kett, *History the interpreter of Prophecy: or, a View of Scriptural Prophecies and their Accomplishments in the past and present Occurrences of the world: with conjectures respecting their future Completion* (1799) 3 vols. The last volume seems to have influenced Reid most.

42.   Harrison (1979) p. 42. See also Thompson (1978), esp. pp. 25–6.
43.   Reid (1800) pp. 70–1.
44.   *GM* 81 (1811) p. 232.
45.   Iain McCalman, '"Erin go Bragh": the Irish in British Popular Radical-ism c. 1790–1840', *Irish Australian Studies: Papers delivered at the Fifth Irish–Australian Conference,* ed. Oliver MacDonagh and W.F. Mandle, (Canberra: Australian National University Press, 1989), esp. pp. 174–6.
46.   W.H. Reid, *Memoirs of the life of Colonel Wardle, including thoughts on the state of the nation . . .* (London, 1809) p. iv.
47.   Reid (1812) pp. iii–xv, 57.
48.   W.H. Reid, *Memoirs of the Public and Private Life of Napoleon Bonaparte: with copious historical illustrations and original anecdotes. Translated from the French of M.V. Arnault, C.L.F. Panckoucke and Count Segur. Preceded by a sketch of the French Revolution.* [Compiled by William Hamilton Reid] (London, 1826), see esp. 'Sketch of the French Revolution', pp. 2–3; 'Introduction' to *Memoirs,* p. vii; 'Supplement', pp. 959–61.
49.   W.H. Oliver (1978) pp. 45–56.
50.   Todd M. Endelman, *The Jews of Georgian England, 1714–1830, Tradition and Change in a Liberal Society,* (Philadelphia: Jewish Publication Society of America, 1979) pp. 65–78.
51.   [W.H. Reid] *The New Sanhedrin and Causes and Consequences of the French Emperor's Conduct Towards the Jews: Including Official Documents, and the Final Decisions of their Dispersion: Their Recent Improvements in the Sciences and Polite Literature upon the Continent: and the Sentiments of their Principal Rabbis, fairly stated and compared with some Eminent Christian Writers. Upon the Restoration, the Rebuilding of the Temple, the Millenium, With Consideration of the Question, 'Whether there is anything in the Prophetic Records that seems to point particularly to England?' By an Advocate for the State of Israel* (1807). See also W.H. Reid, 'On the State of the Jews in England', *GM* 80 (1810) pp. 12–14; 'On the Present State of the Jews', pp. 108–9; 'On Proselytising Societies', *GM* 81 (1811), pp. 627–32, See also Simon Schwarzfuchs, *Napoleon, the Jews and the Sanhedrin* (London: Routledge & Kegan Paul, 1979) esp. pp. 24–7, 64–5.
52.   *GM 81* (1811) pp. 627–32.
53.   Reid (1807) pp. 421–2, 430–1, 472.
54.   *GM* 80 (1810) pp. 12–14, 108–9.
55.   Reid (1807) pp. 120, 153, 177; *GM* 81 (1811) p. 631.
56.   *GM* 81 (1811) pp. 529–35.
57.   *Annual Register* 68 (1826) pp. 253–4; *GM* 81 (1811) p. 232.
58.   On King, see McCalman (1988) pp. 35–9, 66–7; Todd M. Endelman, 'The Chequered Career of 'Jew' King: A Study in Anglo-Jewish Social History', *Association for Jewish Studies Review,* 78 (1982–3) pp. 69–100 (esp. pp. 95–7).
59.   Reid (1807) p. 123; Jonathan King, *Dissertations on the Prophecies of the Old Testament, containing all such prophecies as are applicable to the Coming of the Messiah, the Restoration of the Jews and the Resurrection of the Dead . . .* ed. David Levi, 2 vols (1817), esp. vol. 1, pp. lxxiii–lxxvi,
60.   Reid (1807) p. 131.

3

Is there an Antinomian in the House? William Blake and the After-Life of a Heresy

JON MEE

There has been an abiding interest in the relationship between Blake and popular traditions of religious heterodoxy. A historical context for Blake's millenarianism has been provided in the prophetic radicalism of his contemporaries Richard Brothers and Joanna Southcott, but critics seeking a context for his antinomianism have gone back to seventeenth-century sources. A.L. Morton, for example, traced Blake's antinomianism to the Ranters and Seekers on the radical fringe of Puritan dissent. He concluded that Blake was 'the greatest English Antinomian, but also the last' (Morton, 1958 p. 36)[1]. I shall be offering evidence of manifestations of antinomianism in the London of Blake's time which show that he was far from being the last antinomian. At the same time I shall suggest that critics who have discussed the similarities between Blake's ideas and seventeenth-century antinomianism were correct to the extent that there seems to have been a conscious revival of ranting ideas from the previous century in the 1790s.

Before discussing the historical evidence for these claims, I want briefly to turn to the thorny task of definition. A contemporary of Blake's described antinomianism as 'the doctrine of imputed righteousness' carried to lengths which could destroy 'the very obligation to moral obedience'.[2] This notion of free grace has its biblical origins in texts such as I John 3. 9: 'Whosoever is born of God doth not commit sin; for his seed remaineth in him: and he cannot sin because he is born of God'. There are a range of responses to such texts which could be called antinomian. The claim that the

Mosaic dispensation is not binding upon the faithful can be merely theoretical and maintain an actual obedience to the law. Practical antinomianism, on the other hand, involves a conviction of an already achieved state of salvation for the believer which makes the need to guard against sin redundant. The celebration of transgression in Blake's *The Marriage of Heaven and Hell* often comes close to this kind of antinomian extremism. A more passive version of the heresy promises unconditional forgiveness for what it still recognizes as sin. Perhaps the often noted stress on forgiveness in Blake's later prophecies ought to be seen as a similar change in the tenor of his antinomianism, though it should be noted that both were found equally alarming by the authorities in the late eighteenth century.

Fundamental to antinomianism is an emphasis on the quickening of the spirit over the letter of the law which involves an anticlerical antipathy to the ceremonial and institutional aspects of religion. Such values play an important part in Blake's writing and designs. Their antinomian basis is perhaps clearest in his annotations to Watson's *Apology for the Bible*:

> The laws of the Jews were (both ceremonial & real) the basest & most oppressive of human codes. & being like all other codes given under pretence of divine command were what Christ pronouncd them The Abomination that maketh desolate. i.e. State Religion which is the Source of all Cruelty. (*Ann. Wat.* E618)

Blake's hostility to 'State Religion' illustrates the way that radical antinomianism can run over into a broader antipathy for the hegemonic institutions of civil and religious authority. The work of Marxist historians like Christopher Hill and A.L. Morton has provided fascinating examples of this phenomenon from the period of the Civil War in Britain. In what follows I shall show that other late eighteenth-century antinomians besides Blake gave their theology a similarly radical political dimensions.[3]

A final point to be made in outlining the nature of antinomian heterodoxy is that it can produce widely different accounts of who is to receive the gift of free grace. Some eighteenth-century commentators identified the heresy with a universalist conception of redemption that 'supposes the church of Christ to consist of all mankind, and that at the day of judgement, the whole human race will comprise the sheep at the right hand of the Judge, and that the goats on the left hand will be their sins'. *The Analytical Review* claimed such universalism was being promoted among the populace in the 1790s by the 'publication of pretended visions' and books like Elhanan Winchester's *The Universal Restoration Exhibited* (1788).[4] Yet antinomianism could also produce a much more exclusive view of salvation. William Huntington's *Advocates for the Devil Refuted* (1794) argued that Winchester offered a dangerously open version of salvation. Hyper-Calvinists such as Huntington believed only the Elect were free from the curse of the Decalogue.

The paragraphs above should make it clear that I am not considering antinomianism as a sect but as a tendency. It is a mistake to limit the heresy to any one of its variants. Often antinomianism is to be found fused with other currents, such as millenarianism, and operative within very different sectarian guises. James Relly, for instance, offers an example of someone led into antinomianism by Methodism. Relly, originally an apprentice cow-farrier, was a convert of Whitefield's. He soon outran his teacher in enthusiasm and set up for himself as a preacher in London. His followers are mentioned in Maria de Fleury's *Antinomianism Unmasked* which characterizes them as believing 'sin is for ever pardoned and done away with' (p. 37). Relly's later theology does indeed fit her version of antinomianism. He attacked the ceremonial law and the Decalogue as 'that yoke which galled the neck of the nations and made them sigh for deliverance' and subscribed to a universalism which sounds very Blakean: 'Christ is considered as compounded of the people, as the one body is of its various parts and members'. Walter Wilson agreed with de Fleury that Relly had preached a 'finished salvation'. He also thought Relly a dangerous universalist who believed 'all shall be restored to holiness and happiness'.[5]

Relly is an example of the type of mechanic preacher that so alarmed polite opinion throughout the eighteenth century. It was always assumed that such characters had an investment in traducing the established clergy and some commentators feared that they promoted beliefs subversive of both civil and religious authority. This fear became much more pronounced in the 1790s when popular preachers were suspected of being in league with Painite reformers and revolutionaries. W.H. Reid's *Rise and Dissolution of the Infidel Societies in this Metropolis* (1800) is only one example of a number of texts which represented popular enthusiasm as an auxiliary of Jacobinism. Notwithstanding that Reid had an investment in exaggeration, there is plenty of evidence that connections between popular enthusiasm and political radicalism did exist in the 1790s.

Contacts between Richard Brothers and the London Corresponding
Society, for instance, are known to have existed. The history of
William Huntington's Providence Chapel shows that antinomian-
ism could also lead into Painite politics.[6]

Huntington seemed the very epitome of the combustible, popular
field-preacher to most commentators at the time. He came from a
humble background and had turned his hand to a variety of labour-
ing jobs (which earned him the nickname of 'the Coal-Heaver')
before 'a special providence' led him to itinerant preaching. The
events of his unrespectable past and the multiple interventions of
his special providence were detailed in his massively popular *God
the Guardian of the Poor and the Bank of Faith* (1784) which had run
into ten editions by 1813. A sturdy populism runs through all of
Huntington's publications. *The Utility of the Books*, for instance,
announces that eternal punishment awaits 'the rich overgrown
farmer' and those who 'grind the faces of the poor of this nation',
but even more typical is a fierce anticlericalism which has a distinc-
tively antinomian emphasis on the misguided attachment of the
clergy to the letter over the spirit: 'Satan has furnished the world
with ministers who revile the Gospel and cry up the law'.[7]

Huntington was consistently accused of antinomianism from the
beginning of his preaching career in the 1780s to his death in 1813.
The charge was justified to the extent that his sermons do have a
hyper-Calvinist stress on the freedom of the Elect from the bondage
of the law: 'they who go to the Law for justification, in any sense, or
even to be made perfect, Christ shall perfect them nothing'.[8] The
strength of his conviction that 'the letter killeth but the spirit giveth
life' (II Cor. 3.6) prompted many attacks upon his sermons. His
critics believed that Huntington foolishly discarded 'the moral law
as the rule of a Christian's life' so that 'all the fences of restriction,
and the penalties of disobedience, are completely taken away'. The
colloquial vigour of his language and often indelicate use of the
Bible 'swept away the boundaries of Christian liberty, and over-
spread the minds of many with the polluted waters of licentious-
ness'. The last charge led easily on to the accusation, standard
against proponents of free grace, of sexual misconduct. Huntington's theology was seen as a licence to promiscuity and subjected to
ridicule both in print and in salacious engravings like those published in *The Satirist*.[9]

Huntington represented his mission as the ministry of 'the everlasting gospel', a phrase which had often been used by seventeenth-

century champions of free grace to describe their beliefs. The notion of an 'everlasting gospel' was current among other eighteenth-century antinomians besides Huntington. Winchester, for instance, was converted to his belief in universal redemption by a German tract he translated as *The Everlasting Gospel* in 1792. Though Huntington and Winchester differed in their theology, both agreed that the everlasting gospel swept away the legalistic language of transgression and damnation. Blake interpreted the phrase in a similar way, making it the title of a late poem which promotes 'the Indwelling of the Holy Ghost' (E519) over the letter of the law.

The antinomians of the 1790s were far from being unaware of their predecessors in the seventeenth century. Huntington provided a preface for a reprint of a text from the 1640s, the 1792 edition of John Saltmarsh's *Free Grace*. Modern historians know Saltmarsh as a supporter of the Levellers and rank him among the most radical sectarians of his time. Huntington's contemporaries were equally aware of the originating context of Saltmarsh theology. A list of the 'fanatics' who sprang up after the execution of Charles I, drawn up by Joseph Moser in 1795, included Saltmarsh along with the fifth monarchy men and other radical sectarians such as Abiezer Coppe, William Erbery, and James Nayler. Huntington's preface to *Free Grace* reveals that he too was aware that Saltmarsh's reputation had 'enrolled his name in the black register of antinomians'.[10]

Nevertheless Huntington decided that the slur of antinomianism could be taken over as a badge of honour: 'many have changed their names to enjoy an inheritance by choice; and if we are compelled thereto, let us pocket the affront'. He was sponsoring a book which was itself unapologetically antinomian:

> The Spirit of Christ sets a believer as free from hell, the law, and bondage, here on earth, as if he were in heaven; nor wants he anything to make him happy in enjoyment of it, but a revelation of it to him.[11]

It is worth noting that, although seemingly unaware of the existence of a new edition of *Free Grace* in the 1790s, Michael Ferber quotes exactly this passage from Saltmarsh's tract as evidence of similarities between the Ranter doctrines of the seventeenth century and Blake's theology (Ferber, 1985: 124). W.H. Reid, Joseph Moser, and other commentators believed that the 'fanaticism' of the seventeenth century was resurfacing in the London of the 1790s. I shall offer evidence below that Saltmarsh's *Free Grace* was certainly not the only such tract to be republished in the later period. This context suggests that Blake's antinomianism was part of a more general revival going on around him in the popular culture of London.[12]

Despite his willingness to 'pocket' the title in 1792, Huntington was often more equivocal about identifying himself with antinomianism. He became increasingly cautious as the 1790s went on. By 1794 he was retreating from Saltmarsh's unabashed confidence in the permanence of free grace and putting forward instead the idea that those who 'stood not fast in their liberty' could be 'entangled again within the yoke of bondage'. Apparently not all of Huntington's congregation were happy with this compromise. One of them, Thomas Hacker, went into print to condemn his preacher for backsliding.[13] As with Wesley earlier in the eighteenth century, Huntington could not always curb the radical implications of the doctrines that he preached. Thomas Hacker's pamphlet is one indication that, whatever Huntington's ambivalence, 'in his own Chapel, there was an inconsistent practice which gave some ground for this charge [of antinomianism] in the minds of many'.[14]

The shift in Huntington's position may have been fuelled by political developments in the 1790s. Once Burke had painted the English partisans of the French Revolution as crazed enthusiasts out of the same mould as the regicides of the 1640s and 50s, it became increasingly common for loyalists to identify religious heterodoxy with political radicalism. For all his populist anticlericalism, Huntington was a vociferous monarchist and a staunch defender of civil authority. Nowhere is Huntington's concern that religious enthusiasm should not become a platform for republicanism clearer than in his response to the millenarian prophet Richard Brothers. Huntington vilified Brothers as a dangerous subversive in a pamphlet entitled *The Lying Prophet Examined* (1795). Where Brothers celebrated the French Revolution as the onset of the Millennium, Huntington stressed that the Apocalypse would neither happen in the near future nor, when it did come, involve the destruction of civil authority.

No doubt the ferocity of Huntington's attack on Brothers was given edge by the fact members of Providence Chapel were attracted to radical politics. Several of Huntington's pamphlets discuss the problems he had in controlling his congregation. He was forced to caution those who 'let fly the anguish of their souls in open rebellion against the higher powers'.[15] His warnings were hissed by one section of his audience: 'a knot of young wise men among us, who were great readers and admirers of Tom [Paine]'. The dis-affection in Providence Chapel seems to have come to a head in 1796 while Huntington was away preaching in Plymouth Dock. During his absence the dissident element in the congregation began openly to promote 'the sentiments and rebellion of Tom Paine'. Huntington was forced to hurry back from Plymouth and could only purge the spread of radicalism by cancelling 127 seatholder's tickets.[16]

Huntington discovered that some 'who lay near to my heart' were involved in spreading Paine's principles.[17] A prime candidate for inclusion in this group is Garnet Terry to whom I want to devote the second half of this essay. The details of Terry's biography are not easy to establish, but it is clear that he was an engraver rescued by Huntington from the unsuccessful practice of his trade some time in the 1780s. Huntington set Terry up as his bookseller. Terry's name can be found on the title-page of most of Huntington's publications from the late 1780s till 1795. After 1795 Terry is no longer listed, it seems likely that he was one of the those who left Providence Chapel in 1796.[18]

Evidence suggests that Terry was much more of a radical than Huntington even while still favoured by the preacher as a book-seller. Terry produced several publications on his own during this time which reveal millenarian tendencies. The earliest of these, *A Description accompanying an Hieroglyphical Print of Daniel's Great Image*, published in 1793, already records a move towards the sort of exposition of the biblical prophecies associated with Richard Brothers. Terry's tract indicts civil and religious authority with creating a society in which 'righteousness falls in the street and equity cannot enter'.

He believed the golden image of Nebuchadnezzar's dream to be the ante-type of London in the 1790s, its destruction prophesied the downfall of its rulers; 'Woe to them that turn aside the needy from judgement, and take away the right of the poor of my people'.[19] The same reading of Daniel was precisely the interpretation that Huntington was to denounce when he attacked Brothers in 1795.

If we can trace similarities between Terry and Brothers, analo-gies have already been drawn between the engraving Terry pub-lished in *A Description* and the religious imagery of Blake's designs (Bindman, 1986). I'd like to discuss a different parallel between the two men which illuminates their artisan origins. Terry described Babylon as a great centre of trade where morality has become a matter of commerce, 'to make merchandize of men, and to sell them by kingdoms, bishopricks, parishes, or parcels'.[20] Brothers similarly based his identification of London with Babylon on the fact that both were great trading powers which dealt in human slavery. The same complex of ideas and images recurs in Blake's prophecies, typified by the claim in *America* that 'pity is become a trade' (*America* 11:10, E55). Both Blake and Terry objected to the ascendancy of the market over the moral economy, a shared perspective that can be related to their socio-economic experience as reproductive engravers. Both found difficulty commanding the rewards they felt their skills deserved. Terry's description of the belly and thighs of Daniel's image as 'the merchandize, arts, crafts' of Babylon which the powerful 'often affect to despise . . . but not withstanding, they cannot do without their ARTS and CRAFTS' perhaps reflects the bitterness of the unsuccessful engraver of the 1780s.[21] Blake's own chequered career as an engraver and his inability to establish himself as a writer-painter may equally lie behind the demand:

> Who commanded this? what God? what angel!
> To keep the gen'rous from experience till the ungenerous
> Are unrestraind performers of the energies of nature;
> (*America* 11: 7–9, E55).

Terry had also had his own ambitions to make the transition from artisan to artist thwarted. For both men an antinomian insistence on the universality of free grace seems to have been related to the personal experience of exclusion.

Terry's other millenarian publications, a series of pamphlets published under the title *Prophetical Extracts* (1794–5), move even closer to the radical millenarianism of Brothers and Blake. The series is only one among several collections of visions and prophecies published during the Brothers controversy of 1793–5. Much the same material is to be found both in *Prophetical Extracts* and the collections put out by Brothers's publisher George Riebau. Most of these millenarian anthologies reprinted old material, often drawing on seventeenth-century texts. The rest of the texts were drawn mainly from contemporary visionaries such as Brothers himself. Blake has been described as much more democratic in his conception of prophetic inspiration than Brothers (Paley, 1973: 273), but this contrast overlooks the insistence in the various collections put out by

Riebau and Brothers on the continuing and general availability of prophetic inspiration. Although he styled himself the 'Nephew of the Almighty', Brothers and his publisher were prepared to sponsor pamphlets which reiterated that prophecy was not 'confined either to the Jews or any other particular rank, age, sex , or condition of men'.[22] Such an attitude comes close to Blake's view that 'Every honest man is a Prophet' (*Ann. Wat.*, E617). Terry's *Prophetical Extracts* shares this democratic conception of the prophetic role. The frontispiece to the fourth number celebrates the plenitude of its prophetic contents by quoting Acts 2.17:

> And it shall come to pass in the last days, saith God. I will pour out of my spirit upon all flesh, and your sons and your daughters shall prophesy.

The fifth number, in particular, is very keen to emphasize the continuing reality of prophetic inspiration. Introductory comments castigate the complacency of those who believe God no longer 'speaks to any by prophetic spirit' concluding 'the spirit of prophecy has not wholly left the world, even in this age'.[23]

Prophetical Extracts also reiterates the central polemical point of Richard Brothers's publications, his perception that the French Revolution was a fulfilment of biblical prophecy. The contents of Terry's series consistently identify the French monarchy with the Beast of Revelation. Returning to the subject matter of Terry's 1793 print, the first number of *Prophetical Extracts* notes the similarity between prophecies of the destruction of the French monarchy and Nebuchadnezzar's dream 'which foretold the destruction of himself, his family, and monarchy'.[24] The fourth and fifth numbers of *Prophetical Extracts* are entirely given over to prophecies 'Relative to the Revolution in France, and the Decline of the Papal Power'. Few readers in the 1790s would have failed to see the congruence between this kind of rhetoric and the radical millenarianism which was Richard Brothers's distinctive contribution to the Revolution controversy.

During a later dispute between the two men, which took place in 1806, Huntington was explicitly to accuse Terry of having disseminated the idea that biblical prophecies were fulfilling in the French Republic. The cue for the dispute was Terry's publication, under the pseudonym of Onesimus, of *Letters on Godly and Religious Subjects* (1806). Huntington believed that Terry's book contained veiled attacks on him. He was provoked to publish two typically vitriolic replies which reveal details of Terry's activities while a member of Huntington's Providence Chapel in the 1790s.[25] Among other things Huntington claimed that Terry had absented himself from the Chapel on official fast days for the French War and that Terry had also recommended Paine's *Rights of Man* on the congregation. Huntington concluded that Terry's *Letters* showed him to remain 'the same in religion as he is in politics – a leveller and for all things common'.[26] Nor was Huntington alone in making such charges against Terry. The minister Vigors M'Culla published an attack which claimed Terry was preaching 'avowed rebellion against Christ, Church, King, and State' in order to 'level all posts and offices'.[27] Terry was evidently nervous about these charges, perhaps because he now had a respectable post as the Engraver to the Bank of England. He threatened Huntington with a libel action and made moderating changes to the second edition.[28]

Although I have only been able to locate the modified second edition of Terry's book, even this version makes the radical orientation of his theology clear. *Letters on Godly and Religious Subjects* maintains the commitment to the democratic conception of prophecy found in Terry's publications of the 1790s. Letter VI, possibly the veiled attack which upset Huntington, is addressed to Utychus, a man who had formerly been content to prophesy in 'a common tradesman's dress' but who was now seeking to take on the more respectable role of a licensed clergyman. Utychus is an apostate as far as Terry is concerned, bowing down before 'the world's power or authority' where once he had 'not only refuted, but openly rebuked it as contemptible'.[29] Terry's condemnation of Utychus typifies a hostility to 'hirelings' which runs through *Letters*. It is a hostility predicated on the belief that anyone has a right to prophesy if the spirit moves them. To set oneself up as a licensed preacher, from this perspective, is to reify the letter of the law over the universal promise of free grace.

Central to Terry's antagonism to priestcraft is his conviction that the Bible does not need the mediation of commentaries or sermons:

> The scriptures are plain and easy – as is Christ's example clear and obvious to view: he is no hard master, nor are the scriptures a sealed book to you, but a plain clear guide, and easy to be understood, written to suit the meanest capacities, independent of the glosses of mercenaries who would make us believe to the contrary.

Blake shared Terry's antagonism for the view that the Bible could not 'be understood at all by the unlearned'. He believed 'the Beauty of the Bible' was that 'Ignorant & Simple Minds Understand it Best' (*Ann. Thorn*: E667). Terry went so far as to claim that a congregation did not need a preacher nor any regular form of worship bar 'a private and domestic ordinance'. Again this attitude is echoed in Blake's outlook; 'henceforth every man may converse with God & be a King & Priest in his own house' (*Ann. Wat.* E615). Terry's anti-clericalism was not a quietist version of inner-light theology but an actively and overtly oppositional enthusiasm. From his point of view, where once civil authority 'sets aside God's ordinances' it is 'to be resisted for the Lord's sake'. Such opinions make it easy to see how enthusiasts like Blake and Terry could believe Paine to be 'a better Christian' (*Ann. Wat.* E620) than a member of the episcopate. Terry had come to believe that 'the poorest soul in Zion' was 'just as forward toward perfection as his glorified saint in heaven'.

It was a move towards the universalism of Winchester which Huntington despised. Certainly Huntington suspected Terry of promoting a dangerously open salvation: 'There is not one line drawn; there is no distinction made between the elect and the reprobate'.[31] No doubt Huntington also construed this inclusiveness as dangerously democratic and evidence of Terry's political radicalism. Michael Ferber has argued that similar universalist tendencies underpin Blake's various representations of redemption (Ferber, 1985: 190–1). Huntington believed that Terry had been attracted to such ideas through contact with seventeenth-century radical heresy:

> Nor should we have been favoured with these discoveries, cautions, and warnings, if the book of an old ranter, long extant, had not fallen into his hands. His whole mystical fabric is, I have no doubt, built upon that man's wild rant, which pulls down everything, but builds up nothing.[32]

There are two possible candidates for the text referred to by Huntington. The first is the edition of Saltmarsh's *Free Grace*, discussed above, which was published by Terry in collaboration with Huntington. Despite his participation, Huntington was soon to retreat from the extreme antinomian positions espoused in the tract. It seems reasonably safe to assume that Terry shared the disgust of Thomas Hacker at this apostasy.

The other 'book of an old ranter' republished by Terry was Samuel (Cobbler) How's *The Sufficiency of the Spirit's Teaching*. On this volume Terry worked in collaboration with J.S. Jordan, an early member of the London Corresponding Society and the first publisher of Paine's *Rights of Man*. That Terry should have published in partnership with Jordan lends more substance to Huntington's claims that Terry became involved with Painite radicalism in the 1790s.[33] What makes the publication even more interesting is that, as Iain McCalman has pointed out elsewhere in this volume, W.H. Reid specifically named How's pamphlet as a source of the Painite doctrine that 'every man's mind is his own church'.[34] It is possible that Reid had Terry's edition in mind. What Reid's argument should alert us to is that enthusiasm and infidelity were often not far apart in the artisan culture of the 1790s. The longstanding assumption that Blake's enthusiasm meant he could only find limited interest in Paine's iconoclasm needs to be re-examined in this context.

How's tract has as its basic thesis that spiritual inspiration is more important than scholarship to preaching. More pointedly How argued that the poor and unlearned were more likely to be open to such illumination than the powerful and educated, charging the learned with the importation of heathen corruptions into the original simplicity of the Christian faith. How's populist antagonism to 'Plato and Artistotle, and a multitude more of heathen philosophers', calls to mind Blake's anti-classicism. Indeed much of the structure of feeling of How's pamphlet is recurrent in the work of both Blake and Terry. How's belief that the mysteries of the scriptures were open to 'mean and simple things as we are' reappears in their conviction that the poor understood the Bible best. How also contends that the Bible sanctioned any loose gathering of Christians as a church blessed with Christ's presence. The idea that a building of lime and brick is the temple of Christ or even that the performance of prayers is necessary is another priestly corruption.[35] Blake shared these prejudices. There is no evidence that he ever attended church and he ceased his involvement with the Swedenborgians close after their decision to constitute themselves as the Church of the New Jerusalem. Blake believed that 'the Whole of the New Church is in the Active Life & not in Ceremonies at all'. (*Ann.Sw.Div.Love*, E605). Reid claimed Paine's notion that 'every man's mind is his own church' had its origins in How's pamphlet. Did Blake's conviction that 'every man may converse with God & be a King & Priest in his own house', written in annotations defending Paine against a modern Pharisee, have similar origins?

The attraction of How's claim that the unlearned were better able to understand and preach the gospel than the 'wise, rich, noble, and learned' for those, like Blake and Terry, without formal education or access to the universities is fairly obvious. Such a claim offered a sense of autonomy and self-esteem to people normally cast in roles of economic and cultural dependency; 'to see with his own eyes, knowing that the just is to live by his faith'. Terry's edition of How is militant in its antagonism to received cultural authority. It promotes How's sermon as 'an attempt to draw the veil of ignorance, from the minds of the deluded multitude, . . . high treason against the rulers, principalities, and powers of darkness'.[36] The celebration of high treason in 1792, the year of the Royal proclamation against seditious writings, suggests how religious enthusiasm could lend itself to radical politics. It was a vision of the world which often already suspected the powers-that-be of anti-Christian allegiances.

The complicated and fugitive history of Providence Chapel indicates that the fears held by alarmists like W.H. Reid about the subversive potential of popular enthusiasm were sometimes justified. More specifically it serves to illustrate the vigorous survival of the antinomian heresy in Blake's London. My discussion of William Huntington and Garnet Terry is not intended to construct them as direct influences on Blake. Rather the continuities between their rhetoric and Blake's indicate that attempts to place him in an antinomian context do not have to leap back into the seventeenth century, though the evidence is that eighteenth-century enthusiasts had a greater awareness of their predecessors than is often allowed. The point is that antinomianism and millenarianism of varying degrees of extremism remained available in the popular culture of the eighteenth century. If this is accepted Blake seems less the mystic who reproduced beliefs that had generally disappeared than someone whose radicalism was the product of a dialogue with the complex nexus of popular enthusiasm.

Notes

1. The seventeenth-century context discussed by Morton has been given a new treatment in Ferber (1985). The most informative study of the millenarian context in the 1790s remains Paley (1973).

2. See John Evans's *A Sketch of the Denominations of the Christian World*, eighth edition (1803) pp. 80–1.

3. See Christopher Hill, *The World Turned Upside Down: Radical Ideas during the English Revolution* (1972); Harmondsworth: Penguin, 1975), and A.L. Morton, *The World of the Ranters: Religious Radicalism in the English Revolution* (London: Lawrence & Wishart, 1970).

4. See Maria de Fleury, *Antinomianism Unmasked and Refuted and the Moral Law Proved from the Scriptures of the Old and New Testament to be Still in Full Force as the Rule of Christian Conduct* (1791) p. 37; and *The Analytical Review* 20 (1794) pp. 39–41.

5. See James Relly, *Christian Liberty: or, The Liberty wherewith Christ hath made us Free* (1775) pp. 6–7; and Walter Wilson, *The History and Antiquities of Dissenting Churches and Meeting Houses in London. Westminster, and Southwark*, 4 vols (1808–14) vol.1, pp. 358–60.

6. For details of the relationships between the London Corresponding Society and Brothers and his following, see J.F.C. Harrison, *The Second Coming: Popular Millenarianism 1780–1850* (Cambridge: Cambridge University Press, 1979) pp. 223–4. Iain McCalman's *Radical Underworld: Prophets, Revolutionaries and Pornographers in London, 1795–1840* (Cambridge: Cambridge University Press, 1988) consistently demonstrates the connections between currents of political radicalism and religious enthusiasm in the period.

7. See Huntington, *The Utility of the Books and the Excellency of the Parchments* 2nd edn (1796) p. 30, and *Living Testimonies: or, Spiritual Letters on Divine Subjects* (1795) p. xxvii.

8. See Huntington, *The Moral Law not Injured by the Everlasting Gospel* (1792) p. 81.

9. For the attacks on Huntington, see the anonymous pamphlet *The Barber's Mirror: or, A Portrait of the Rev. William Huntington* (1791) pp. 20, 6, 19. The engravings mocking Huntington, *The Bank of Faith* and *the New Light and Love Feast*, are to be found in *The Satirist* (1808) vol. 2 p. 337 and (1808), vol. 3, p. 225.

10. See the 'Preface' to Saltmarsh's *Free Grace: or The Flowing of Christ's Blood Freely to Sinners*, 11th edn (1792), For Moser's views, see his *Anecdotes of Richard Brothers, in the Years 1791 and 1792, with some Thoughts on Credulity* (1795) pp. 8–9.

11. Saltmarsh, *Free Grace*, preface and p. 154.

12. Apart from the How tract discussed below, other texts republished included the prophecies of William Lilly and Anna Trapnel which are to be found in several of the millenarian anthologies published during the Brothers controversy.

13. See Huntington, *The Child of Liberty in Legal Bondage: or, the Son and Heir in the Servant's Yoke* (1794) p. 76. Thomas Hacker's reply was

made in the pamphlet entitled *The Believer's Entanglement by the Moral Law Proved Inconsistent with the Abolition of the Law* (1794).

14. Ebenezer Hooper, *The Celebrated Coalheaver: or, Reminiscences of the Reverend William Huntington, S.S.* (1871) p. 89.
15. Huntington, *The Utility of the Books* (1796) pp. 33–4.
16. See Huntington's *A Watchword and Warning from the Wall's of Zion* (1798) p. 82, and *God the Guardian of the Poor and the Bank of Faith*, 10th edn (1813) p. 43. Details of the purge conducted by Huntington on his return to Providence Chapel are given in Thomas Wright's *The Life of William Huntington, S.S.* (London: Farcombe 1909) p. 127.
17. Huntington, *A Watchword* (1798) p. 83.
18. Terry, like Blake, had tried to make the transition from artisan to artist, M. Bryan's *A Biographical Dictionary of Engravers* 2 vols (1889), 2: 560, describes Terry as an engraver in mezzotint who flourished between 1770 and 1780, chiefly employed in engraving portraits. Huntington was amongst those whose portraits he engraved. Thomas Dodd's manuscript history of British engravers gives a brief mention of Terry, snootily describing him as an engraver of shop bills and card plates who 'took it upon himself' to engrave the portraits of various non-conformist ministers. BM Add. Mss, Dodd 33, 406.
19. I am extremely grateful to Robert Essick for providing me with photo-copies and photographs of Terry's tract from his personal collection. Both references are to Terry, *A Description* (1793) p. 6.
20. Terry (1793) p. 10.
21. Terry (1793) p. 12.
22. Richard Brothers, *Wonderful Prophecies, being a Dissertation on the Existence, Nature, and Extent of the Prophetic Powers in the Human Mind*, 4th edn (1795) p. 5.
23. Garnet Terry, *Prophetical Extracts,* (1794–5), pamphlet 5 p. 4.
24. Terry (1794–5), pamphlet 1 p. 31.
25. See Onesimus [that is, Garnet Terry], *Letters on Godly and Religious Subjects*, 2 vols, 2nd edn (1808) and Huntington's *Onesimus in the Balance, or the Eternity of Hope Considered* (1806 [a]) and *Onesimus in the Balance and Obedience to the Civil Powers Proved* (1806 [b]).
26. Huntington (1806 [b]) pp. 13, 59.
27. Vigors M'Culla, *The Bank Note: or, The Engraver Carved in Answer to Onesimus, the Ecclesiastical State Thinker* (1806) pp. 44, 49.
28. Wright (1909), pp. 142–3, J.A. Jones *Bunhill Memorials* (1849), p. 275, offers more information about Terry's later career. It seems Terry had built a 'Meeting' (significantly not a chapel) in Shoreditch where he preached without receiving payment (again a significant detail). At his death in 1817, aged 73, he left a large sum to be divided equally between the congregation – presumably the proceeds of his profitable later years at the Bank. His gravestone bore the inscription: 'inasmuch as ye did it to the least of these my brethren, ye did it to me'.
29. Onesimus (1808) vol. 1, pp. 28–9.
30. Onesimus (1808) vol. 1, pp. iii; 5–6; vol. 2, p. 71.
31. Huntington (1806 [a]) pp. 49, 60.

32. Huntington (1806 [b]) p. 27.
33. Samuel How, *The Sufficiency of the Spirit's Teaching without Human Learning*, 8th edn (1792), first published 1651. Note, however, that Huntington collaborated with Terry and Jordan on the publication of one of his sermons, *A Feeble Dispute with a Wise and Learned Man* (1793).
34. William Hamilton Reid, *The Rise and Dissolution of the Infidel Societies in this Metropolis* (1800) p. 69.
35. How, *The Sufficiency of the Spirit's Teaching without Human Learning* (1792) pp. 47, 54, 64.
36. How, *The Sufficiency of the Spirit's Teaching without Human Learning* 8th edn (1792), pp. 41, 52.

4

'Self-Imposition', Alchemy, and the Fate of the 'Bound' in Later Blake

EDWARD LARRISSY

Figures derived from the concepts of outline and 'the bounded' are to be discovered in every period of Blake's work. I have suggested elsewhere how important is a certain ambiguity about this, especially in the period before about 1800 (Larrissy, 1985). On the one hand, 'The bounded is loathed by its possessor' (*There is No Natural Religion* [b], E2), on the other, 'Truth has bounds. Error none' (*Book of Los*, 4: 30, E92). One thing that can be inferred from this is that Blake feels an ambivalence about his own activity as an artist. He is committed to definiteness and firm outline, and to the idea – for which he finds some Neoplatonic support – that the Infinite can be apprehended through definite form. At the same time he rejects the more essentially Neoplatonic idea that the Infinite is, in the last analysis, incompatible with boundedness. But he is concerned lest he become a priestly Druid rather than a Bard; lest his influence should set bounds to the Infinite for himself and his readers, becoming the cause of 'imposition' – an idea about which he was more concerned than *The Marriage of Heaven and Hell* passages (plates 12 and 20) might suggest.

This is not a matter merely of Blake's 'ambiguity'. As a poet of strong convictions Blake is unambiguous about a multitude of things. Correspondingly, when he is ambiguous, or ironic, he is still profoundly serious and conscientious. And those who would defend him from such imputations do him an equally profound disservice. He is concerned not to limit the horizons of his readers, and at the same time not to deceive them about the clarity and passion of his own conceptions. It is precisely because of this concern that his works are marked by a degree of indeterminacy, and by the dialogic.

In what follows I hope to suggest that Blake's use of alchemical imagery provides an important thread in the symbolism of the later work by means of which one can demonstrate that the 'bound' in its malign sense of 'limit' is removed from the outside, or boundary, or 'circumference' of the symbolic figures intended to convey it, and comes to rest in their centre. It is internal division, 'doubt', 'self-contradiction', 'cloven fiction', 'self-imposition', which became the leading negative ideas. The self-divided consciousness is afflicted by an internal line or bound, on one side of which is an abstracted and corrupt form of imagination, and on the other an imaginary material world. Or, conceived in different terms, on one side a repressive Law, on the other diseased passion. This, of course, is a transmutation of the earlier sense of external compulsion, which had always been uneasy. It is, however, a weighty change, and one which shifts the responsibility for redemption far more towards the individual.

Yet I take it as axiomatic not only that internal division is, in myriad guises, the story of the fallen world in *Milton*, *Jerusalem* and *Illustrations of the Book of Job*, but that these works for the most part tell only the story of that fallen world, though with significant and decisive indicators of the ways in which unity can be recovered from division. These premises can yield some illuminating conclusions about Blake's subject-matter and techniques. But the proper place for these is at the end of the essay.

But why alchemy? One should never attempt to reduce Blake's myth to one determinant. Possibly there are other ways of reaching the conclusions I advance. Certainly, alchemy is only one of the range of Blake's symbolic vocabularies, and one which, as usual, he makes his own: I shall, at least, be able to adduce an important, related non-alchemical emblem, from the iconography of Moses. But of the importance of 'Paracelsus & Behmen' (Letter to Flaxman, 12 September 1800, E707), not just in his statements, but also in his symbolism, there can be no doubt. I would agree with those, such as Jon Mee, who see the persistence of radical Protestant interest in hermeticism in the eighteenth century. And I would add that this is not merely a matter of reprints of seventeenth-century works. The hermetic tradition was still alive in the late eighteenth century, in the sense that it was the subject of new theories, and even new practice.

In particular, interest in alchemy in general, both speculative and practical, was still current in the eighteenth century, and in Blake's own time. Thus the anti-Newtonian philosopher Robert Greene (one of the main opponents of Newton who might be called scientific) believed that the transmutation of base metals into gold was possible.[1] The other main school of pseudo-scientific anti-Newtonians were the Hutchinsonians (Larrissy, 1986). Of these, William Jones of Nayland believed not only in the doctrine of the four elements, but also in the alchemical idea that two of these were active and two passive.[2] Berkeley's *Siris*, which Blake annotated, shows an alchemical conception of matter (so to speak); and indeed, it has been suggested that he thought of his tar-water as the elixir.[3] We should not like to adjudicate in this. However, Kathleen Raine believes that the Hermetic philosophy was 'among the more important sources of Berkeley's philosophic answers to Newton and Locke' (Raine, 1969, vol. 1: 272). In Blake's own time there is the curious case of James Price, MD, FRS (1752–83) who claimed to have performed the great work of making gold.[4] Price committed suicide in front of a team of inspectors from the Royal Society. But this was not before the Fellows had become concerned at the need to dissuade others from following his example in alchemy.[5]

Why concern ourselves with the survivals of practical alchemy? First, I think, because of what J.H.S. Green says of the Royal Society's concern to combat Price's ideas: 'That this was necessary at so late a date shows how small an impact 18th-century science had made outside a narrow circle'.[6] This must be of interest to any Blake scholar. And the second reason is related to the first: it is too easy to assume that Blake's imaginative interpretation of various scientific and antiquarian data can be automatically prescinded from the data themselves. But though Blake's critique of the eighteenth-century world-view is hardly rigorous in a scientific sense, nevertheless it seems to be true that he was interested in scientific controversies. And his description of the universe in *Milton* (29 [31]: 5–20, E127) is strikingly reminiscent of that offered as scientific by a Muggletonian who wrote against the Newtonian system as late as 1846.[7] We may at least suspect that the primacy Blake accorded to vision did not entail his completely ignoring questions that we should think of as being about 'fact'.

Of course there is no evidence whatsoever that Blake had any interest in the transmutation of metals. We may disagree with Milton O. Percival when he says that 'By the end of the eighteenth century alchemy had run its course'. But he is right to say that Blake's interest in it was 'purely speculative' (Percival, 1938: 197).

Percival does, however, show how strong that 'speculative' interest was, though on different grounds from those advanced here.

We may therefore turn for enlightenment to those eighteenth-century writers who were interested in 'philosophical alchemy'. But one soon learns that the separation of 'philosophical' from 'practical' alchemy, even at this late date, is, though useful, somewhat artificial. Thus, as Robert E. Schofield points out, the Behmenist John Byrom was interested in Robert Greene's philosophy.[8] He was also, we should add, interested in Hutchinson, though he did not like his system; and he corresponded with the Hutchinsonian Jones of Nayland. Byrom reports that William Law told him that Newton's 'attraction and the three first laws of motion were from Behmen'.[9]

Richard Clark is another Behmenist whose work Blake very probably knew, according to Désirée Hirst. And he too was interested in alchemy (Hirst, 1964: 254–5).

It is now clear that radical Protestantism and Hermetism were closely allied, and that the alliance lasted at least until the end of the eighteenth century.[10] The most pertinent example of this connection has been discovered by S. Foster Damon: De Brahm, an American alchemist, was also the author of the antinomian *Voice of the Everlasting Gospel* (Philadelphia, 1792); read Boehme and George Fox; and inveighed against 'Reasoning' and its 'Harlot Church'.[11]

'Reasoning' is decried both in the tradition of Paracelsus and Boehme and in the tradition of antinomian Protestantism: correspondingly, both traditions stress the spirit, rather than the letter, of Holy Scripture. The insistent derogation of 'outward reason' in the Paracelsus-Behmenist tradition contributes to Blake's conception of Reason and Urizen. We shall show that an understanding of the alchemical symbolism associated with the *tria prima* and the great work is essential to the description of the iconography and meaning of Urizen and his relations with Orc/Luvah and Satan. But what are the alchemical teachings? First, a warning:

> one must not imagine for a moment that the alchemists always understood one another. They themselves complain about the obscurity of the texts, and occasionally betray their inability to understand even their own symbols and symbolic figures.

Jung records his opinion that 'it is quite hopeless to try to establish any kind of order in the infinite chaos of substances and procedures'.[12] This is a little exaggerated; if it were true Jung's work would have been impossible. The ramifications of alchemical symbolism seem completely otiose from a functional point of view. And perhaps they are. But behind the 'obscenely luxuriant growth of arcane imagery' lies the basic system of amalgamating philosopher's mercury and sulphur in 'salt', which gives a body to the others, and then 'putrefying' or 'mortifying' the mixture.[13] The resultant is then 'vivified' or 'regenerated'.[14] Sir Isaac Newton was of the opinion that it was essentially this process which was repeated in all the so-called seven steps of transmutation, though in fact each of the seven steps was given a different name.[15] Newton's view is probably correct: the different names of the seven steps seem to refer to the supposed effects of the repeated distillations. This fact accounts for the feeling of repetitiveness in diversity given by alchemical symbolism. Désirée Hirst's summary of the basic process is succinct and useful for our purpose:

> the general pattern of alchemic teaching never varies. It asserts the union of spirit, symbolized by the eagle, or by mercury, with the serpent or sulphur... This union forms the dragon, or winged serpent out of a conflict between opposites. The 'mortification', or death, of the dragon was necessary before that resurrection could take place which alone produces the 'philosophers' [*sic*] stone.[16]

Mercury is spirit, sulphur is soul; they are united, or 'married', in the dragon by salt, or body.[17]

The eagle and serpent are the subject of the illumination at the bottom of plate 15 of *The Marriage of Heaven and Hell* (Repro. *IB* 112). They represent the Marriage itself, with spirit and soul interpreted as Reason and Energy. However, at this stage in Blake's work there is a marked inequality in the status of the two terms. He has understood from Boehme 'the Contrariety and Combat in the Being of all Beings, how that one does oppose, poison and kill another'. And his statement that 'Without Contraries is no progression' (*MHH*3, E34) seems to indicate that he has also understood

> the Cure, how the one heals another, and brings it to Health; and if this were not, there were no Nature, but an eternal Stillness, and no Will; for the contrary Will makes the Motion, and the Original of the Seeking, that the opposite Sound seeks the Rest.[18]

Blake is thus following the Behmenist interpretation of the alchemical opposites.

But though Blake pays lip-service in *The Marriage* to the idea of the complementarity of the contraries, the spirit of that book is to support the claims of Energy and reduce the role of Reason to that of Energy's servant: 'Reason is the bound or outward circumference of Energy.' (*MHH*4, E34). But Blake's simple advocacy of energy had ceased by 1795. Instead he evolves a more orthodox alchemical conception in which the contraries of Reason and Energy (personified by Urizen and Luvah) are united in the Great Dragon, which appears in Blake as the 'triple Elohim', whose motives are wings and serpent; as the 'dark Hermaphrodite'; and as Satan, the Selfhood. These figures are phenomena of the same essence, the dual nature of which is exposed by the collusion of God and the biblical Satan in the Job illustrations, where the figures are opposed but complementary aspects of Blake's Satanic Selfhood, who is revealed in Job's dream (*Book of Job*, Plates III and XI).

The change in Blake's view of energy is well illustrated by the different appearance of the figure of Fire in the two versions of *The Gates of Paradise* (1793 and c.1818). Part of this is an alchemical emblem-book.[19] Plates 2–5 in both versions show the four elements. They represent creation as 'the separation of the elements', in alchemical phrase.[20] In the first version, however, Fire, as Energy, suggests the means of escape from the restrictions of the fallen world. The figure of Fire appears in the Notebook where the motto associates it with Milton's Satan: at this stage, then it represents the positive 'Messiah or Satan or Tempter' of *The Marriage* (Erdman and Moore, 1977 N91; 17, E40). The meaning of the sequence of four elements in *The Gates* in thus highly compressed: creation is seen as a fall through separation, but at the same time Blake wishes to suggest the means by which the restrictions of Reason can be overcome by Energy: that is why the emblem of the cupid hatching from an egg follows the emblem of Fire. The egg is the traditional symbol of the alchemical retort, which is seen as a microcosm: the Neoplatonic 'Mundane Egg', Blake's 'Mundane Shell'.[21]

But in the second version of *The Gates* 'Fire' is portrayed with horns and scales. He is identified as 'A dark Hermaphrodite':

> Blind in Fire with shield & spear
> Two Horn'd Reasoning Cloven Fiction

In Doubt which is Self contradiction
A dark Hermaphrodite We stood
Rational Truth Root of Evil & Good.

('The Keys of the Gates', 12–15, E268, taking the later version of 2.13)

To those nourished on the early symbolism of Orc and Urizen it may seem strange that Reason here should be associated with the expected attributes of Orc/Luvah. However, the word 'Hermaphrodite' gives the clue that 'Fire stands here for all the elements – '*We* stood' (emphasis added). But the sense in which the elements are thus represented is complex.

The Hermaphrodite, or 'Rebis', is a compound of Mercury and Sulphur. This is because, according to one train of alchemical symbolism, Mercury is feminine and Sulphur is masculine: they were sometimes known as the Red Man and his White Wife.[22] The Hermaphrodite is thus another name for that amalgam, also known as the 'dragon', which has to be 'mortified' or 'putrefied' in order that the Philosopher's Stone may be produced. The Hermaphrodite may be seen, for instance, in plates XXXIII and XXXVIII of Michael Maier's celebrated alchemical emblem-book, *Atalanta Fugiens*. In plate XXXIII the youthful Hermaphrodite is seen 'lying in the shadows' on a trestle cooking over a fire: 'Hermaproditus mortuo similis, in tenebris jacens, igne indiget'.[23] This is Blake's 'dark' Hermaphrodite, 'Blind in Fire'.

But why does Blake make the Hermaphrodite stand for the four elements, rather than the two principles of Mercury and Sulphur? In fact the two principles are very much there: they are the reason for the Hermaphrodite's 'Self contradiction'. (The third principle, salt, is here understood, rather than expressed, since it merely holds the other two together.) The horns which Blake added to the later emblem emphasize the dual nature of the Hermaphrodite, torn between fallen Reason and fallen Energy, 'Good and Evil'. It is the very principle of this separation which is wrong, the very knowledge of good and evil: the blind destructiveness of fallen Energy and the repressive rule of Reason are the two salient characteristics of Blake's Satan.

But the four fallen elements are also, as we have seen, part of the Hermaphrodite. The point is that the four elements appear as the three principles in the Hermaphrodite.[24] Or as Boehme expresses it in the *Clavis*:

The ancient wise men have called these three properties
Sulphur, Mercurius, and *Sal,* as to their Materials which were
produced thereby in the four Elements, into which this Spirit does
coagulate, or make itself Substantial.

The four Elements lie also in this ground, and are nothing
different or separate from it.[25]

Except in the notion of 'the triple Elohim' Blake does not pay much
attention to the fact that the principles are three. In this he is
following the tendency of most alchemical symbolism, especially in
the emblem-books. He is more interested, early and late, in the fundamental duality of Mercury and Sulphur, his Reason and Energy.
Though the four Zoas are crucial to the rationale of Blake's developed mythology, they somehow seem less integral to his vision than
the opposition of Urizen and Luvah, which is itself opposed to an
authentic third term, Los, who, as is known, is closely related to the
alchemical 'Archaeus' or 'Vulcan' (Percival, 1938: 204).

The change which has occurred between the first and second
versions of *The Gates of Paradise* is from a fairly narrow use of
alchemical sources to a wide and, so to speak, erudite use of them.
The change corresponds to Blake's ambivalent attitude towards
Energy after about 1795, and with his evolution of a new use of the
term Satan. The idea of the Hermaphrodite composed of two opposing principles which must be burnt permits Blake to find a symbolic
language which is both a continuation of his earlier themes and a
good vehicle for his sense that Urizen and Luvah are mutually
dependent parts of the same Satan. It is in the illuminations, however, that the emblems may seem overworked unless the reader has
a knowledge of the alchemical background; even if he does, they
may seem to be overloaded; but in this they follow the tradition of
alchemical symbolism.

We have mentioned that Urizen takes the place of the alchemical
Mercury or 'spirit'; but we have also seen that in the Hermaphrodite
Mercury is conceived of as female. The apparent contradiction is
merely a consequence of the luxuriant proliferation of alchemical
symbolism. Mercury was considered to be passive with respect to
sulphur, and was therefore sometimes portrayed as female – for
instance, as *Luna.*

But Mercury could also, of course, be portrayed as masculine, the
obvious example being Hermes. What concerns us here is his portrayal as an old man – 'Mercurius Senex'. This figure represents the

same amalgam as the Hermaphrodite, considered under the aspect of Mercury, which was often thought to be the most important principle in the work.

At the stage where the matter is putrefied it may be envisaged as an old bearded man, often a king, who is sickening and finally killed by the action of the alchemist's fire. This is the stage in which the matter blackens – the *nigredo*, or the melancholy stage: the old man is sometimes depicted as Saturn because of the association with melancholy.[26] Since the three principles are reflections of the Holy Trinity, and Mercury corresponds to the Father;[27] and since we have already seen that both Urizen and Luvah participate in the Hermaphrodite, it is a fair inference that Urizen is Mercurius Senex, the alchemists' Saturn, and the fallen image of Jehovah (Blake's Elohim).

But Blake's Satanic Selfhood can also be seen as an old man, indistinguishable from Urizen. Because Satan contains both Urizen and Luvah, Blake portrays him in either guise. Thus the figure with the tables of the Law on *Milton* 18 is identifiable as Urizen (*IB* 234). But he is also Satan, for Milton is striding forward to grapple with him, and beneath the design are the words 'To Annihilate the Self-hood of Deceit & False Forgiveness'. The Satan of Job's evil dream has the characteristics of Urizen, in that he possesses the long white hair and beard, and is pointing to the tablets of the law. The sepia drawing known as *Christ Trampling upon Urizen* (c.1808 *National Museum of Wales*) might equally well, then, be known as *Christ Trampling upon Satan*, for it draws on the tradition of Christ trampling upon the serpent.

The serpent was another word for the alchemical dragon. And in Boehme the serpent both stands for the three principles as represented in matter, and for Satan, the opposer of Christ. Christ is known by Boehme and his followers as 'the Treader upon the Serpent'. The Serpent in Boehme is the 'Self-hood'.[28] The 'Self-hood' is the cause of the desire of the knowledge of good and evil: in *The Epistles of Jacob Behmen* it is said that man has brought the will of the serpent into himself and each 'property' has entered into 'its selfehood . . . whence the lust, and Imagination to good and evil did arise in him'.[29] We should not, the letter continues, eat of the Tree of Knowledge of Good and Evil.

The iconography and meaning of Blake's Christ and Satan, then, are profoundly Behmenist. This is obvious from the work of the eighteenth-century English Behmenist, John Byrom, whom we have already mentioned as being interested in anti-Newtonian philosophers:

> Here *Christ*, the Serpent-bruiser, stands in Man,
> Storming the Devil's hellish, self-built Plan;
> And hence the Strife within the human Soul;
> *Satan's* to kill and *Christ's* to make it whole;
> As by Experience, in so great Degree,
> God, in his Goodness, causes you to see.
> . . .
> Still in its Self-hood [the soul] wou'd seek to shine,
> And, as its own, possess the Light divine.
> . . .
> Mov'd too by outward Reason, which is blind,
> And, of itself, sees nothing of this Kind.
> . . .
> The own Self-Will must die away, and shine,
> Rising thro' Death, in saving Will divine.[30]

The material forms of the three principles were created by Lucifer, 'the Great Prince out of the Center of Nature':

> For the Center [of Eternity] was *Sulphur, Mercurius*, and *Sal*, and it [the Center] was but a Spirit, but in the stern *Fiat* (in the stern fierce attraction) it came to be such hard Stones, Metals, and Earth, *all* according to the Forms of the Essences: It is *all* become material. . . .[31]

It is this infernal Trinity which Blake usually treats as a duality. It must go to *'Eternal Death'* – a Behmenist term for mortification. The bodily, or external, is then put off, and that which is not destroyed in the fire of Eternal Death is the 'raised Heavenly Spiritual Body'.[32] All these terms – 'Self-hood', 'Eternal Death', 'Spiritual Body' – are used by Blake. It should be clear that the borrowing is by no means superficial (where it might be claimed that his borrowing of Neoplatonic terms was superficial, or at least high-handed.)

As we have seen, it was really the duality of Urizen and Orc/ Luvah which interested Blake in the formation of his notion of Satan. (*I* should say the shadowy figure of Tharmas was associated with the third principle of salt or body.) In Blake's earlier work the duality is conceived of as an energetic principle on the one hand and a repressive principle on the other. But in the later work it is the principle of division itself which is wrong, and which vitiates them both. Urizen had always stood for the division himself: his dividers stand for the division between the instantaneous perception of the 'divine Nothing', and the time-bound process of creation. But Blake's organicist conception of consciousness becomes more profound in the later work, where he seeks a more representative embodiment of division in itself, and where Energy cannot escape the consequences of the subsequent repression.

The division comes from the human soul. Blake would have found an illustration of the divided soul in Plato's *Timaeus*, which he would have interpreted as showing the three principles. Here is the rational soul:

> But with respect to the most principal and excellent species of the soul, we should conceive as follows: that divinity assigned this to each of us as a daemon; and that it resides in the very summit of the body, elevating us from earth to an alliance with the heavens; as we are not terrestrial plants, but blossoms of heaven. . . In him therefore who vehemently labours to satisfy the cravings of desire and ambition, all the conceptions of his soul must be necessarily mortal.[33]

Hermes Trismegistus refers to the 'Strife and Dissension' which ensue if the animal and vegetable souls disobey the rational.[34] This is the 'Doubt' and Self contradiction' which the organic ('visionary') consciousness dispels.

Satan, then, 'is Urizen' (*Milton* 10:1, E104), and 'Luvah is named Satan' (*J* 49: 68, E199). The two halves work together:

> But the Wine-press of Los is eastward of Golgonooza, before the Seat
> Of Satan. Luvah laid the foundation & Urizen finish'd it in howling woe.

> (*Milton* 27:1-2, E124)

These two figures, combined and separately, afflict and torment Albion, as they do Job, with lack of energy and infirmity of purpose. This is the spiritual sickness into death, and in both cases its emblem may be 'sore boils' (*Job*, plate VI; *J* 43 [29]: 64, E192).

In the Job illustrations the two halves may appear to be separate –
drawing on the traditional iconography of God and Satan, or
blatantly quoted from Blake's earlier iconography of Urizen, and
Luvah. Or they may appear as a composite figure, as in Job's Evil
Dream (*Job*, plate XI). Here a cloven-hoofed deity, with long white
hair and beard, terrifies Job, who is lying on his bed. This is the
Satanic Selfhood, 'The lost Travellers Dream under the Hill' (E269).
A more innocuous-seeming, but far more truly vicious, sign of dis-
temper than boils, however, is 'self-imposition' (*Milton* 7: 21, E100).
This, the outward sign of 'self-contradiction', is one of the consequences of being riven by an internal line, dividing sick Jesus from
false Jehovah. Another feature of the Job designs is their tendency to
split the pictorial space between an upper and lower zone. This line
across the picture, sometimes appearing as a cloud-barrier, is the
line of internal division. Or this concept may be represented by putting Job himself across the middle of the design (plate XI again).

But if one accepts that this line of division is the ubiquitous condition of the fallen world, then it can be taken as a metaphor for all the
outlines of that world, and all the differences which constitute it: for
difference, in fact: indeed, for *différance*. But one of the chief differences that has to be conveyed by Blake's work is simply that
between those who see in this *hymeneal* line the seeds of hope, and
those who do not.[35] The former are capable, so to speak, of expelling
the line from centre to circumference, under the pressure of their
own vision and energy; the latter are imposed upon by it in their
very hearts. The former, when the Last Judgement is passed upon
them, at every moment, see the Last Judgement, which is 'Vision'
(E554): that is to say, it is the tissue of differences which constitute
the fallen world, including the difference, above all, between those
who see this as meaning hope and life, and those who do not. The
latter see only the law of division, confirmed for them, no doubt, by
the traditional iconography of Moses which, following an error in
Septuagint, gives him two horns. Thus Moses can be seen, receiving
his cloven fiction, in illustrations to Exodus such as those by
Holbein, where the scene looks very much like Satan colluding with
God to inflict misery on humanity, as in Job.[36]

Notes

1. Robert E. Schofield, *Mechanism and Materialism: British Natural Philosophy in an Age of Reason* (Princeton: Princeton University Press, 1970) p. 121.
2. Schofield (1970) p. 127.
3. E.A.H. [Hitchcock], *Remarks upon Alchemy and the Alchemist* (Boston: 1857) p. 106.
4. James Price, MD FRS, *An account of the Some Experiments on Mercury, Silver and Gold* (1782; 2nd edn. 1783).
5. J.H.S. Green, 'The Last Alchemist', *Discovery* 22 (Jan.1961) pp. 19, 21.
6. Green (1961) p. 21.
7. Isaac Frost, *Two Systems of Astronomy, the Newtonian and the System in Accordance with the Holy Scriptures* (1846). On earlier Muggletonian beliefs about astronomy and astrology, see Keith Thomas, *Religion and the Decline of Magic: Studies in Popular Beliefs in sixteenth and seventeenth century England* (London: Weidenfield & Nicolson, 1971) p. 378.
8. Schofield (1970) p. 99. See *The Private Journal and Literary Remains of John Byrom*, ed. Richard Parkinson, 2 vols. in 2 parts each (being vols. 32, 34, 40 and 44 of *Remains Historical and Literary Connected with the Palatine Countries of Lancaster and Chester* (Manchester Chetham Society, 1854, 1855, 1856, and 1857) vol. 1, pp. 397, 403, 405, 443.
9. Byrom (1855–7) vol. 2, pp. 23, 26, 131; vol. 2, pp. 573–8; vol. 2, p. 364.
10. See also Thomas (1971) p. 271; Christopher Hill, *The World Turned Upside Down* (1972; 2nd edn. Harmondsworth: Penguin, 1976) pp. 287–305; Henry J. Cadbury, 'Early Quakerism and Uncanonical Lore', *Harvard Theological Review* 40 (1947) pp. 204–5.
11. S. Foster Damon, 'De Brahm: Alchemist', *Ambix* 24 (July 1977) pp. 78–82.
12. Carl Jung, *Psychology and Alchemy* in *Collected Works*, trans. R.F.C. Hull, ed. Sir H. Read, M. Fordham and G. Adler, 20 vols (London: Routledge, 1953–79) vol. 12, p. 288.
13. Richard S. Westfall, 'Alchemy in Newton's Career', *Reason, Experiment and Mysticism in the Scientific Revolution*, ed. M.L. Righini Bonelli and W.R. Shea (London: Macmillan, 1975) p. 198, See also J.R. Partington, *A History of Chemistry*, 4 vols (London: Macmillan, 1961–70) vol. 2, pp. 142–8.
14. Ben Jonson, *The Alchemist: Subtle:* And When comes Vivification? *Face:* After Mortification (II.v.24–5).
15. Westfall (1975) pp. 201–2; Partington (1961) vol. 2, p. 137.
16. Désirée Hirst (1964: 164) identifies sulphur with body. But this is not the conception of the Paracelsian-Behmenist tradition which influenced Blake: 'Hermes says that mercury is spirit, sulphur is soul, and salt is body; metals are between spirit and body' (Partington (1961) vol. 2, p. 144, writing on Paracelsus).
17. The orthodox Christian use of the eagle-serpent symbolism is not the same as the alchemical: Christ came to be identified with the eagle and Satan with the serpent which has to be destroyed. In alchemical symbolism it is the amalgam of eagle and serpent which is destroyed and reborn in a new 'spiritual' form. Compare Rudolf Wittkower,

Allegory and the Migration of Symbols (New York: Barnes & Noble, 1977) pp. 31–2.

18. Jacob Boehme, *Works*, ed. William Law, 4 vols (1764–81) vol. 4, p. 12.
19. See Gerard Heym, 'Some Alchemical Picture Books', *Ambix* 1 (May, 1937) pp. 69–75, for a survey of some Renaissance emblem-books. I have not been able to find any alchemical *emblem-books* in the eighteenth-century.
20. Compare Walter Pagel, *Paracelsus: an introduction to philosophical medicine in the era of the Renaissance* (Basel and New York: J. Prager, 1958) pp. 91–2.
21. Compare H.J. Sheppard, 'Egg Symbolism in Alchemy', *Ambix* 6 (August, 1958) pp. 140–8.
22. Lapidus [Stephen Skinner], *In Pursuit of Gold: Alchemy in Theory and Practice* (London: Spearman, 1976) p. 26.
23. Michael Maierus, *Atalanta Fugiens, hoc est Emblemata Nova de Secretis Naturae Chymica* (Oppenheim, 1618), plates xxxiii and xxxviii. See also Satan in *Satan smiting Job with sore Boils* (c.1826; Tate Gallery) and compare with the winged hermaphrodite in Daniel Stolcius de Stolcenberg, *Hortulus Hermeticus* (Frankfurt, 1627) p. 109. See also the winged hermaphrodite shown in Jung (1968) p. 113.
24. Partington (1961) vol. 2, p. 204.
25. Boehme (1764–81) vol. 2, p. 21.
26. de Stolcenberg (1627) pp. 105, 157. See also Maierus (1618), plate cxxxiv.
27. See *Paracelsus His Aurora, & Treasure of the Philosophers. As also The Water-Stone of the Wise Men* (1659) pp. 125, 161, 164.
28. Boehme (1764–81) vol. 1, p. 222; vol. 4, p. 74.
29. [Jacob Boehme], *The Epistles of Jacob Behmen*, trans. J.E. [i.e. Ecliston] (1649) p. 112.
30. 'A Poetical Version of a Letter from Jacob Behmen', John Byrom, *Miscellaneous Poems*, 2 vols (1773) vol. 2, pp. 160–2.
31. Boehme (1764–81) vol. 2, p. 53.
32. Boehme (1764–81) vol. 2, pp. 53, 78; vol. 4, p. 58.
33. *The Cratylus, Phaedo, Parmenides and Timaeus of Plato*, trans. Thomas Taylor (1793) pp. 550–1.
34. *Hermes Mercurius Trismegistus, His Divine Pymander In Seventeen Books. Together with his Second Book Called Asclepius*, trans. J. Everard (1657) p. 3.
35. Compare Jacques Derrida, 'The Double Session', *Dissemination*, trans. Barbara Johnson (Chicago: University of Chicago Press, 1981) pp. 212–13.
36. Hans Holbein, *Historiarum Veteris Testamenti Icones* (1543) Exodus 33.

5

Blake and the 'Reasoning Historian'

ANDREW LINCOLN

Blake's declared hostility to 'The reasoning historian, turner and twister of causes and consequences, such as Hume, Gibbon and Voltaire' (*DC*, E543) might lead us to conclude that he learned little from Enlightenment historians. And the prophetic form of his narrative might seem to reinforce this conclusion. The historical perspective adopted by writers 'such as Hume, Gibbon and Voltaire' was secular, and tended to make social evolution seem partially dependent on impersonal causes. In contrast, Blake's mythical narratives consistently remind us of an eternal reality from which humanity has fallen, and they locate the mainspring of history in human consciousness, especially in limited visions of destiny. In this way they emphasize that the causes of historical change are spiritual, and they affirm the possibility of escape from fallen existence through a clarification of vision. But in spite of these differences, Blake's vision of history in some respects parallels that of the 'reasoning historians' of his age. He shares the philosophical historian's interest in exploring relationships between economic, social and religious developments, and he shares the 'conjectural' historian's interest in reconstructing the major stages of social evolution.[1] In this essay I shall argue that in *The Four Zoas* Blake adopts a number of ideas and patterns that had become familiar in historical writings in the latter half of the eighteenth century, and attempts to reconstitute them on the basis of spiritual causes.

I shall take as my example the account of the growth and collapse of Urizen's Universal Empire, in the seventh and eighth Nights of *The Four Zoas*. This is Blake's most complex and elaborate treatment of the development of commercial civilization. Unfortunately it is also one of the most difficult parts of the poem to discuss, because there are so many strands to the narrative, so many revisions, and so many textual problems. I want to make things easy for myself by passing over almost entirely that part of the narrative concerned with Golgonooza, Satan and Jesus, and by treating very selectively the context in which this material appears. Before I examine the narrative I shall consider very briefly some of the contemporary assumptions that seem relevant to Blake's enterprise. We do not know the full extent of Blake's reading among eighteenth-century historians. There is some evidence to suggest that he knew at least part of Gibbon's history of Rome in the early eighties.[2] Some of the writers referred to in his illuminated books had published influential historical works: Voltaire and Rousseau are introduced as portents of revolution in *The French Revolution* (1791) and *The Song of Los* (1795); Bolingbroke is denounced along with Hume and Gibbon in *Milton* (1804+).[3] Rapin and Echard are included among the historians mentioned in the *Descriptive Catalogue* in 1809 (E544).[4] Such references suggest that Blake's hostility to reasoning historians did not preclude an enduring interest in them. In this essay I shall refer to works by Hume, Gibbon and Rousseau, and to works by three authors that Blake does not mention in his writings – Adam Smith, Adam Ferguson and John Millar. In most cases I am concerned with ideas that would have been available to Blake in more than one source.

First, I want to consider assumptions about the place of war in civil society. The widely held view that civil government originates in a state of barbarism and war, and that it allows an escape from this state, naturally coexisted with a recognition that war is a continuing feature of civilized life. This paradox is emphasized dramatically in Rousseau's pessimistic view of civilization. In the *Discourse on Inequality*, the social contract that was intended to protect individuals from oppression is seen to lead inevitably to a disastrous intensification of war, because governments remain in a state of nature in their relations with each other, and the conflicts between them are necessarily more violent than those between individuals in the original state of nature:

> Political bodies, thus remaining in a State of Nature among themselves, soon experienced the Inconveniences which had obliged Individuals to quit it; and this State became much more fatal to those great Bodies, than it had been before to the Individuals which now composed them. Hence those national Wars,

those Battles, those Murders, those Reprisals which make Nature shudder and shock Reason; hence all those horrible Prejudices, which make it a Virtue and an Honour to shed human blood.[5]

Writers who took a more or less optimistic view of economic and cultural progress had to take a more accepting view of war, even if their conclusions in some ways paralleled Rousseau's. Adam Smith's account 'Of the Expense of Defence' in *The Wealth of Nations* offers a detailed analysis of how social development influences the conduct of war, and it soberly demonstrates the high military cost of economic growth. As society advances, the progress of manufactures and improvements in the art of war demand the professionalization and, increasingly, the mechanization of warfare. Smith argues that it is only by means of a standing army – often seen as an instrument of government tyranny – 'that the civilization of any country can be perpetuated; or even preserved for any considerable time'.[6] He accepts this prospect with equanimity, maintaining that war is 'certainly the noblest of the arts', even if with the 'progress of improvement it necessarily becomes the most complicated among them' (II: 697). The contemporary awareness of the close relationship between war and progress seems to have been reinforced by the tradition of civic humanism mediated by Machiavelli and his successors which continued to influence political theory throughout the eighteenth century.[7] In this tradition, the health or virtue of the state is seen to depend on the military commitment of the citizen, and the soldier is often seen as a type of the virtuous citizen in his acceptance of discipline and self-sacrifice for the universal good. The influence of this tradition can be seen in Gibbon's history of Rome, in which the fortunes of the state are closely related to the personal willingness of citizens to bear arms. In this account there is an essential difference between the motives of the barbarian and of the civilized soldier, seen for example in Gibbon's comments on the ancient British tribes, who 'possessed valour without conduct, and the love of freedom without the spirit of union'.[8] If the civil state brings to war a new sense of purpose, war itself could be seen to give a sense of purpose to the state. In Adam Ferguson's *History of Civil Society*, war is an essential stimulus to progress as it gives cohesion and direction: 'Without the rivalship of nations, and the practice of war, civil society itself could scarcely have found an object, or a form'.[9] In Enlightenment histories the progress from primitive to civil society is repeatedly shown to entail a new commitment to warfare, a commitment that is often moralized.

If progress gives a new significance to war, it is sometimes also seen to generate internal conflict. This idea assumes an important place in Hume's *History of England*, in which the seventeenth-century struggle between king and commons is seen as an inevitable consequence of the progress of commerce and of the arts, which allowed the love of liberty to acquire new force, and therefore produced a new attitude to government.[10] English history provided a particular example of what was taken to be a general principle. The Scottish historian John Millar, for example, in his essay *On the Origin of Ranks*, argues in general terms that commercial expansion will always tend to produce an opposition between the sovereign and the people, because it furnishes the means of tyranny and oppression, notably the much feared standing army, at the same time as it inspires the people with ideas of independence.[11] The necessity for internal conflict is a subject that Hume returns to in several of his essays. In 'Of the Origin of Government' he asserts that: 'In all governments, there is a perpetual intestine struggle, open or secret, between AUTHORITY and LIBERTY; and neither of them can ever absolutely prevail in the contest.'[12] In 'Of Superstition and Enthusiasm' the religious dimension of the conflict is singled out, and the balance of power seems to tilt more decisively against liberty. Hume associates superstition with priestly power, and with antagonism to civil liberty, while enthusiasm is a friend to liberty. Of course, Hume is not an advocate of enthusiasm, which he sees as responsible for 'the most cruel disorders in human society'. But 'its fury is like that of thunder and tempest, which exhaust themselves in a little time, and leave the air more calm and pure than before', while superstition 'steals in gradually and insensibly . . . Till at last the priest, having firmly established his authority, becomes the tyrant and disturber of human society, by his endless contentions, persecutions, and religious wars.'[13]

The acceptance of war and contentions as ineradicable aspects of civil society does not necessarily imply a pessimistic view of progress. Indeed, Hume's *History of England* demonstrated that conflict could have a liberalizing effect on the state. But the connections that are being made here, between economic development and the increased potential for violence, are typical of the contemporary awareness that civilization can generate powerful destructive forces that must be contained if progress is to continue. And in some writers we can see a paradoxical view of progress, in which the forces that promote social development are the same as those that undermine it.[14]

This paradox appears very clearly in some discussions of the consequences of economic development for the ordinary worker. Adam Smith, for example, who is usually regarded as an economic optimist, warned his readers candidly of the negative effects that could arise from progress. In *The Wealth of Nations* he notes that in barbarous societies of hunters, shepherds, and even of husbandmen, before the improvement of manufactures and the extension of foreign commerce, 'Invention is kept alive' by the variety of occupations, and by the demands they make on the individuals involved. In contrast, the division and specialization of labour, which is the driving force of economic development, can result in 'mental mutilation', as the labourer is given 'no occasion to exert his understanding, or to exercise his invention'. When this happens, Smith says, the labourer 'generally becomes as stupid and ignorant as it is possible for a human creature to become'. Far from enlightening and enlivening the members of society, economic development could, it seems, undermine the 'intellectual, social, and martial virtues' of the vast majority, unless preventative measures could be devised.'[15] Smith's views on this subject were reformulated by his pupils Ferguson and Millar. Ferguson's comment that 'manufacturers prosper most where the workshop may . . . be considered as an engine, the parts of which are men' was later quoted approvingly by Marx.[16]

The most elaborate examination of the paradoxical relationship between growth and decay was probably that offered by Gibbon. In his 'General Observations on the Fall of the Empire in the West', Gibbon saw the decline of Rome as

> the natural and inevitable effect of immoderate greatness. Prosperity ripened the principle of decay; the causes of destruction multiplied with the extent of conquest; and, as soon as time or accident had removed the artificial supports, the stupendous fabric yielded to the pressure of its own weight.

In practice, of course, his account showed that the principle of decay was rather difficult to identify. But his notorious presentation of the role of religion in the decline of the empire provides a vivid example of how an activity that initially promotes social development can eventually undermine it. In Gibbon's account the pagan religions served the interests of the state by fostering civil obedience and tolerance:

> The various modes of worship which prevailed in the Roman world were all considered by the people as equally true; by the philosopher as equally false; and by the magistrate as equally useful. And thus toleration produced not only mutual indulgence, but even religious concord.

But eventually Christianity rose from among these religions, and with its otherworldly vision of destiny, its preoccupation with sinfulness, and with its fanatical and dogmatic followers, it helped to turn attention away from the former interests of Rome, and to sap the strength of the empire: 'The clergy successfully preached the doctrines of patience and pusillanimity; the active virtues were discouraged; and the last remains of military spirit were buried in the cloister'.[17]

Gibbon explains that 'the conquests of Rome prepared and facilitated those of Christianity'. The drive for unification in the empire provided the conditions in which the new religion could flourish. His account even creates an implicit parallel between Rome's extension of privileges to all within its jurisdiction, and Christianity's promise of divine favour which is, as Gibbon has it, 'universally proposed.'[18] Paradoxically, in Christianity the spirit of union appears in a form that could undermine the citizen's commitment to the political interests of the state.

Blake's own account of the growth and collapse of commercial civilization appears to incorporate a number of the ideas that have been outlined here. But they are transformed by the distinctive perspective of his myth, which attempts to show that all historical developments are produced by mental operations – that all effects have spiritual causes. The ideology that governs the commercial civilization in his myth is seen as an anterior development: the idea of a unified social order emerges before that order can be realized, when reason (or Urizen) begins to assume a dominant position in human consciousness. This means that before I can begin to examine the particular features of Urizen's empire, I shall have to say something about the assumptions that govern them.

In Blake's history of empire, the bases of social unity are religion (the web that holds Urizen's world together) and law, both of which are ostensibly motivated by pity. It is Urizen's pity that urges him to liberate the bound Orc from what he sees as the torments of natural appetite – not by unbinding Orc's chains, but by educating him into an acceptance of law. As the sequence unfolds, the constraints of law are seen to be inadequate in themselves: social unity requires an emotional commitment – a spirit of unity – which supplements law as an instrument of control. In Blake's myth, this spirit has to be created by the prophet, who presents an image of human destiny in a collective form, a form that will persuade the individual that fulfilment is to be found within a unified community, through a love that transcends self-interest. Under the aegis of fallen reason, this is the work of the reasoning and reasonable part of the prophetic consciousness, the Spectre of Urthona. I shall argue that Vala, as the Shadowy female, is the symbol of this spirit of union, this communal love. She becomes the focus for Blake's own version of the paradox considered by contemporary historians, in which the forces that allow civilization to develop are the same as those that undermine it. She is the emotional force that allows fallen reason to develop commerce and industry, to control religion, to channel energy and skills more closely into the arts of war; and she is the power that eventually leads to the collapse of the civilization she has helped to inspire.

Here we begin to encounter the sometimes confusing nature of Blake's terminology. As the Shadowy female, Vala is born after a dialogue between the Spectre of Urthona and his female counterpart, the Shadow of Enitharmon. Vala is brought into being as a product of this dialogue, because she embodies an attempt to reconcile contraries, or negative and positive views of love. The Shadow of Enitharmon's account of human origins provides the ethical basis of the new vision of love. She presents love in negative terms, as a seductive and disruptive power that must be restrained and punished.[19] But the sense of moral outrage that cries out for the punishment of sinful love is itself seen as an expression of a fierce repressed passion: in her view Vala must be 'subjected to the rage' of Orc. The Spectre's account of the fall provides the spiritual basis of the new vision of love. In his account love is also seductive, but ideally it is also a unifying power.'[20] His vision of a prelapsarian 'Universal Manhood', a community united in love, provides an ideal that can govern future action: he aspires to 'unite again in bliss' (*FZ* 84: 35, E359). However, if love assumes a redemptive role in his vision, it is not a spontaneous emotion but an abstract, spiritual ideal that represents a comforting escape from the disturbing fury of natural passion: he seeks to bring down 'soft Vala' to the embraces of the terror Orc, in order to 'destroy' the body.

As the product of this conferring between the two sides of the prophetic mind, then, Vala embodies two contrary views of love, one fearful, one hopeful. As an expression of the Shadow of Enitharmon's fear, she is the sinful and seductive power of love that must be resisted and punished if reasonable social order is to be maintained. As an expression of the Spectre's hope, she promotes his vision of a loving unity to be achieved through self-denial. The two views complement each other in their repressive intent. Embodying both, Vala can provide a justification not only for the suppression of natural energy, but also for its expression in violent forms. She provides a justification for the retributive violence that underpins law, and for the martial spirit that must shape and defend the state. The spontaneous passion that she represses characteristically finds release in war – the only arena in which the libidinous fury of natural energy can be formally sanctioned by civilized society.

The new emotional basis of social development seems to be epitomized in the seduction of Orc by Vala. This action recalls the revolutionary myth in the 'Preludium' of *America*, but in its new context the myth seems to have a quite different significance. It is the female rather than Orc who makes the first move, embracing his fire 'that he might lose his rage' (*FZ* 91: 4, E363). After Orc has risen to embrace her, and to punish her, the maintenance of social order is no longer simply a matter of restraining individual energies by law; it becomes a dynamic process, an energetic striving to realize abstract social and religious ideals.

The immediate result of Orc's rising is the state of universal warfare. War has always been a feature of fallen experience in Blake's myth, but now it is no longer simply an expression of barbarous appetite.[21] As in contemporary histories, it is moralized, governed by ideology, and becomes essential to the development of the social order. Subsequently its destructive power is enhanced by increasing mechanization (*FZ* 100: 28–31; 102; 14–22, E373, 374). The second result is that energy is now absorbed by a more sophisticated technology which begins to displace traditional craftsmanship: the simple workmanship of the hour-glass and the water-wheel are destroyed because they are like the workmanship of the shepherd and the ploughman, and they are replaced by

intricate wheels invented Wheel without wheel
To perplex youth in their outgoings & to bind to labours
Of day & night the myriads of Eternity. that they might file
And polish brass & iron hour after hour laborious workmanship
Kept ignorant of the use that they might spend the days of
　　wisdom
In sorrowful drudgery.

(FZ 92: 26–31, E364)

The development of oppressive and dehumanizing forms of manufacture here is comparable to the process discussed by Smith and
others, which transforms the labourer into a mere component of the
industrial mechanism. But here the transformation is not simply
the result of material developments. The seduction of Orc by the
shadowy female provides the reorientation of desire that makes
such a development possible.

The birth of Vala, then, is initially seen as a triumph for Urizen, as
it provides the emotional basis for material expansion, allowing him
to build 'First Trades & Commerce ships & armed vessels' (*FZ* 95:
25, E360), the mechanisms of commerce, and then to develop a religion which will give the confused ideology of love its appropriate
institutional form: the temple in the image of the human heart
(*FZ* 96: 1–18, E361).

As we have seen, one of the consequences of material expansion
discussed by Hume and others is internal conflict. And here, once
the foundations of commercial civilization are laid, so a conflict
arises between priestly authority and libertarian enthusiasm, sym-
bolized in the opposition between the Prester Serpent on one hand,
and Tharmas and Los on the other. Los rises to become for the first
time in this poem a prophet of revolution, who eagerly foresees the
overthrow of Kings and Princes in an apocalyptic bloodbath (*FZ* 96:
19–27, E361). This opposition is presented in terms that recall in several respects Hume's conception: the priest as the tyrant and disturber of human society by his endless contentions and religious
wars (see *FZ* 98: 22–9, E363), the enthusiast as one whose anarchic
fury is like that of the thunder and tempest which exhaust themselves in a little time. Tharmas, who appears to embody the instinctive reaction to authoritarian control, is soon seduced by Vala,
and – adopting her rhetoric of sin and love – is 'Wood and subdud'
by her (see *FZ* 94: 24–6, 54–5, E366–7).[22]

A dominant idea in Blake's conception of the unfolding social order is that all activities within it, whether they are directed towards the expansion of commerce and state control, or against it, are at once influenced by and tend to propagate the influence of Vala. If Vala allows war to be moralized and motivated by social ideals, military conflict in turn strengthens her influence, which thrives on the hopes and fears aroused by war. If she promotes religious indoctrination, that indoctrination in turn draws 'the myriads of perturbed spirits thro the universe' into her irresistible vortex.

In the progress of Vala Blake describes a process that parallels the progress of religion in Gibbon's account of Rome. What is at first a convenient instrument of state power eventually assumes a form that challenges and triumphs over that power. Ironically, it is while Urizen reads the words of his sacred books in his temple that Vala begins to challenge him (*FZ* 102: 23–103: 20, E375). In her speech to him the ideal of Universal Manhood, which initially provided a justification for the pursuit of Universal Empire, appears in a form that reveals the gulf between the ideology and the practices of the state. Vala speaks of a blissful state remove from the 'terrors' of desire, a state of brotherhood and love in eternal fields where 'we should live . . . as those who sinned not'. But this otherworldly vision, which negates the material basis of empire, is accompanied by an appeal to liberalize the state ('We are all servants to thy will . . . relent/ Thy furious power be our father & our loved King'). The challenge at once denies and confirms the power of the state, and thus offers a rationale for state religion.

In the poem as we now have it, the confrontation between Urizen and the Shadowy female is followed by the complex and much revised sequence describing the descent, judgement and crucifixion of Jesus (*FZ* 103: 32–106: 17, E376–81). The sequence shows how institutional Christianity emerged from an attempt to neutralize the fundamental opposition between a religion of love and a civil government based on the rule of law. The elevation of Christianity into a state religion is seen as a particular manifestation of an archetypal process, in which Urizen is finally seduced by Vala and begins to judge his own activities by her values. The result of this seduction is that Urizen embraces a vision of destiny that negates the basis of his imperial ambitions. In the light of Vala's otherworldly vision of happiness and brotherhood, the will that drives civilization is finally recognized as a manifestation of the same natural appetite it seeks to suppress (*FZ* 107: 19, E382). The course of human destiny is no longer seen to depend on the development of reasonable methods of social control. Instead it is felt to be determined by the struggle of the defective individual will for repentance. Blake's account of Urizen's empire ends with a state in which all activities are thus nullified by a stony stupor (*FZ* 107: 35, E383), a state that corresponds to the condition of sleep described in *Europe*, where humanity is bound in the power of Enitharmon for 'Eighteen hundred years' after the birth of Christ.

In some respects, then, Blake's view of 'causes and consequences' seems to parallel that of contemporary historians. His vision of history as a sequence of sudden revelations and grotesque transformations, full of sound and fury, may seem remote from their ostensibly impartial analyses of historical progress. But it can be seen an attempt to engage with and contain such analyses – to wrest the discourse of history from the grasp of those whose vision was confined to the fallen world, and who made historical change appear dependent on impersonal processes. We have become used to the idea that Blake's mythical history is influenced by his response to contemporary events, and we have learned much about the patterns of his narratives by studying their sources in the Bible and in other mythologies. I would suggest that Blake's mythical history can also be seen as the most extraordinary product of the eighteenth-century tradition of philosophical history, and that we have something to learn about his work from the reasoning historians whom he regarded as his spiritual enemies.

Notes

1. The conjectural or theoretical method was used by writers who sought to outline the major stages of social evolution, reconstructing the unknown from the known by developing hypotheses about physiological, economic, or cultural phenomena. Among the best-known examples of this method are Hume's *The Natural History of Religion* (1757), Rousseau's *A Discourse Upon the Origin and Foundation of the Inequality among Mankind* (1755), and Adam Smith's *Wealth of Nations* (1776).

2. G.E. Bentley Jr. notes that in the early fragment 'then She bore Pale desire' the reference to the fall of the Roman Empire, 'A sacrifice done by a Priestly hand', apparently echoes the comparable view developed in Gibbon's *The History of the Decline and Fall of the Roman Empire*, vols 1–3 (1776, 1781), see Bentley (1977) p. 439. See also Erdman (1977) p. 72 for links to *King Edward III* in Blake's *Poetical Sketches* and for the influence of Gibbon on *Jerusalem* see pp. 468–9.

3. Henry St. John, Earl of Bolingbroke, was the author of, among other works, *Letters on the Study and Use of History*, (privately printed 1735, 2nd edn 1752). His *Remarks on the History of England* were published as a single volume in 1743 and reprinted c. 1780.

4. *The History of England, from the first entrance of Julius Caesar and the Romans (to the conclusion of the reign of James the Second, and establishment of King William and Queen Mary)*, by Laurence Echard (or Eachard, 3 vols, 1707–18) was popular until eclipsed by Paul Rapin-Thoyras's *History of England as well Ecclesiastical as Civil*, trans. N. Tindal, 15 vols (1728–31). Until the mid-century, Rapin's *History* was widely regarded as 'the best and most important general history of England' (Duncan Forbes, *Hume's Political Philosophy* (Cambridge: Cambridge University Press, 1975) p. 233).

5. John James [*sic*] Rousseau, *A Discourse Upon the Origin and Foundation of the Inequality among Mankind* (1761) p. 139. The idea that nations remain in a state of nature in their relations with each other is explained by John Locke in *The Second Treatise of Government* (Bk II, 14).

6. Adam Smith, *An Inquiry into the Nature and Causes of the Wealth of Nations* (1776), eds R.H. Campbell, A.S. Skinner and W.B. Todd, 2 vols (Oxford: Clarendon Press, 1976) vol. 2, p. 706.

7. See J.G.A. Pocock, *The Machiavellian Moment* (Princeton, NJ: Princeton University Press, 1975), chaps x–xiv.

8. Edward Gibbon, *The History of the Decline and Fall of the Roman Empire*, ed. J.B. Bury, 7 vols (1776–88, reprinted, London: Methuen, 1909–14), vol. 1, p. 4.

9. Adam Ferguson, *An Essay on the History of Great Britain* (1767), ed. Duncan Forbes (Edinburgh: Edinburgh University Press, 1966) p. 24.

10. Hume explains that the rise of commerce and the arts had the effect of redistributing wealth from the barons to the gentry. As a consequence 'the spirit of liberty was universally diffused'. David Hume, *The History of Great Britain*, 2 vols (Edinburgh, 1754) vol. 2, pp. 124, 161–2.

11. 'So widely different are the effects of opulence and refinement, which, at the same time that they furnished the king with a standing army, the great engine of tyranny and oppression, have also a tendency to inspire the people with notions of liberty and independence. It may thence be expected that a conflict will arise between these two opposite parties . . . ' John Millar, *The Origin of the Distinction of Ranks* (1779), p. 289.

12. David Hume, *The Philosophical Works*, eds Thomas Hill Green and Thomas Hodge Gross, (a reprint of the new edition, 1886) 4 vols, (Aalen: Scientia Verlag, 1964) vol. 3, p. 116.

13. Hume (1964), vol. 3, p. 149.

14. Pocock suggests that this paradoxical view of the history of civilization is 'Machiavelli's unintended legacy to Western thought', J.G.A. Pocock 'Between Machiavelli and Hume: Gibbon as a Civic Humanist and Philosophical Historian', *Edward Gibbon and the Decline and Fall of the Roman Empire*, edited by G.W. Bowerstock, John Clive, Stephen R. Grauband (Cambridge, Mass., and London, 1977) (103–19), p. 105.

15. Smith (1776) vol. 2, pp. 782–3.
16. Karl Marx, *The Poverty of Philosophy* (London: Lawrence & Wishart, 1956) p. 110. See also Forbes (1966) pp. 182–3.
17. Gibbon (1909–14), vol. 4, ch. 38, p. 173; vol. 1, ch. 2, p. 31; vol. 4, ch. 38, p. 175.
18. Gibbon (1909–14) vol. 2, ch. 15, p. 60; vol. 2, ch. 15, p. 7.
19. In the Shadow of Enitharmon's account of the fall, Man succumbs to the influence of Vala 'melting in high noon Upon her bosom'. Vala subsequently assumes a 'double form', as Luvah (her male counterpart) emerges and confers with Urizen 'To bind the father & enslave his brethren'. In this account, then, Man is enslaved first by delight and then by the will to power, both of which are derived from Vala (*FZ*83: 7–32 E358–9).
20. In the Spectre's account of the fall, he loses his creative power when 'the gentle passions' emerge to stand befoe the eyes of Man as a 'female bright'. This may suggest the seductive power of love, but paradoxically the Spectre's vision of Universal Manhood also seems dominated by the gentle passions. It is a vision of 'mild fields' in which Tharmas is 'mild' and Luvah is 'sweet melodious'. The Spectre's hopes rest on a 'soft Vala' (*FZ*84: 1–35 E359).
21. War is seen as a horrifying expression of natural appetite, for example, in Night VI (*FZ*70: 30–36 E347).
22. Before the two parts of Night VIIB were transposed into their present order, the seduction of Tharmas by Vala preceded, and perhaps initiated, the rebellion of Tharmas. In either order, this seduction brings Tharmas into the power of Vala's confused idealism.

6

'Among the Flocks of Tharmas': *The Four Zoas* and the Pastoral of Commerce

PHILIP COX

This account of *The Four Zoas* attempts to historicize the poem by providing a reading of the roles of Tharmas and Urizen in the context of earlier eighteenth-century philosophical, economic and poetic texts. The intention is not to be prescriptive nor to circumscribe the many potential and possibly contradictory interpretations that can be applied to these two Zoas or, indeed, to the poem as a whole. Blake's mythic figures are constantly in a state of flux, forever being transformed in response to their immediate dramatic context within a poem, or, particularly within *The Four Zoas*, to Blake's shifting attitude towards contemporary political events.[1] However, it is the critic's inevitable task to fix this state of flux during the act of critical commentary. The reading offered here, then, necessarily fixes the roles of Tharmas and Urizen in this way but does so in the knowledge that the roles thus defined constitute only one aspect of the wider dynamics of the poem. My initial emphasis is a generic one and my starting point is John Dyer's georgic poem *The Fleece* which was first published in 1757.

The Fleece celebrates the English wool trade and vital to this celebration is the prominence of London. The description of the city at the end of the Third Book is a vivid illustration of this:

> See the silver maze
> Of stately Thamis, ever chequer'd o'er
> With deeply-laden barges, gliding smooth
> And constant as his stream: in growing pomp,

By Neptune still attended, slow he rolls
To great Augusta's mart, where lofty trade
Amid a thousand golden spires enthron'd,
Gives audience to the world: the strand around
Close swarms with busy crowds of many a realm.
What bales, what wealth, what industry, what fleets!
Lo, from the simple fleece how much proceeds![2]

The Thames is central in all such descriptions of London, not simply because of its geographical centrality but because the river was the commercial centre and the source of trading wealth. Dyer records this distinction by elevating the name to the obselete but poetical 'Thamis'. The 'stately' river rolls through the countryside and into the city with 'growing pomp' like a monarch on a royal progress. Once in the city, however, the notion of regality and royalty is transferred from the geographically specific river to the more abstract 'trade'. It is Trade which 'gives audience to the world'. Trade which presides over, not just England, but an entire commercial empire and whose throne is London itself with its 'thousand golden spires'. What seems to have happened here, tacitly, is that the power traditionally associated with the monarchy has been newly bestowed upon the ruling forces of commerce. This is just one example of the unacknowledged tension in the poem between the interests of an established ruling aristocracy and those representing the more recent commercial power of the private trader. It is important to be aware of this, for, although Dyer frequently appeals to images of stability and unity, he is essentially depicting a society in a state of economic change.[3]

Pastoral and georgic are normally used in opposition to city life and yet Dyer's present ideological purpose makes it necessary to present a harmonious bond between these two opposites, for trade is centred upon the city. The problem is exacerbated by the fact that the first book ends with a section overtly written in the form of an eclogue. This eclogue portrays Damon and Colin at a sheep-shearing celebration. The shepherds themselves are explicit in their criticism of city life – Colin, for example, describes the beautiful scenery of his home countryside and remarks:

Far nobler prospects these,
Than gardens black with smoke in dusty towns,
Where stenchy vapours often blot the sun:

> Yet flying from his quiet, thither crowds
> Each greedy wretch for tardy-rising wealth,
> Which comes too late . . .

(Dyer, 1761: 82).

It is by no means unusual for the eclogue to criticize both cities and the busy pursuit of wealth, yet it does, in the present poem, work counter to Dyer's avowed celebration of London as a centre of commerce. The most interesting aspect of this eclogue scene for the present discussion, however, is the way in which the landscape opens out at the end of the Book:

> near at hand the wide
> Majestic wave of Severn slowly rolls
> Along the deep-divided glebe: the flood,
> And sailing bark with low contracted sail,
> Linger among the reeds and copsy banks
> To listen; and to view the joyous scene.

(Dyer, 1761: 85)

At one level Dyer is recording here a moment of transition in society and in the poetic response to social change. The river leads outward to the commercial world that has recently been attacked by the shepherds. The trading bark acts as a more pointed reminder of the economic links between the countryside and the world of city trade. Yet the impression is not one of intrusion or violent, exploitative greed. The boat lingers, listens and partakes of the 'joyous scene'.[4] Commerce is in this image harmoniously fused with the rural environment. In poetic terms, Dyer's treatment of trade is seen as no longer antithetical to the world of the eclogue. Although its borders have been enlarged, the countryside can still be referred to in terms of nymphs and swains and pastoral shepherds called Damon and Colin.

In a sense this marks the appropriation of the pastoral mode for the ends of commercial interest. The effect of trade upon the life of rural areas can, it appears, be dealt with in terms of traditional pastoral. This is in evidence, for example, in the description of pastoral love in the third Book. It is important to remember that economic change in the structure of the countryside had altered marital relationships. Maxine Berg notes the hypothesis that:

income earning activities such as handicraft production outside of agriculture released the traditional social controls on marriage – inheritance and patriarchal control . . .[5]

In the present poem Dyer records the encroachment of commercial interest upon marriage but does so in the language of a love-pastoral that looks back through Pope to Virgil. He addresses the industrious 'nymph' at her loom and directs her attention to the 'amorous youth':

> And th'amorous youth, delighted with your toils,
> Quavers the choicest of his sonnets, warm'd
> By growing traffic, friend to wedded love.

> (Dyer, 1761: 128)

There is something absurd to the modern ear in these traffic-warmed sonnets, but the underlying issues are serious enough. The conventional form used in the poem suggests a desire for stability and yet its use ironically reveals the enormous social changes that occasion such a desire. With a perhaps questionable mixture of love and the desire for financial gain, the youth turns his attention to industry:

> The am'rous youth with various hopes inflam'd,
> Now on the busy stage see him step forth,
> With beating breast: high-honour'd he beholds
> Rich industry. First he bespeaks a loom . . .

> (Dyer, 1761: 128)

The loom comes to symbolize indirectly the marriage of love and commerce: the energy of youthful love is transformed into the motivation which causes the machine to be built. In this unintentional travesty of pastoral love, Dyer shows how the encroachment of commercial interest transforms individual relationships.

In *The Fleece*, Dyer attempts to create a myth to which newly emergent commercial society and empire can relate. His poem implicitly reveals the precariousness of this undertaking. Underlying tensions between government and merchants, and between both of these and the exploited rural areas, can be discerned. Dyer

uses pastoral poetry in a way which effectively hides transformations taking place within the developing commercial society. His
aim is to achieve a seamless continuity between a propagandist use
of pastoral and the epic aspirations of expanding commercial
empire. Overall it can be said that the pastoral innocence depicted
as being the basis of the wool trade gives a moral justification for the
empire which grows out of it.

The Four Zoas, like *The Fleece*, centres its attention upon a unifying
entity ultimately referred to by Blake as Albion. Having recognized
this, though, it has to be remembered that it is not with Albion
proper that Blake begins the action of his epic but with one constituent part of the Eternal Man – Tharmas:

> Begin with Tharmas Parent power. darkning in the West.

> (FZ 4: 6, E301)

The prominence thus given to Tharmas would seem to suggest that
he has a crucial importance in the poem as a whole. At this early
point in the narrative Tharmas has already moved a long way
towards his fallen state. For the most part it is only through various
retrospective accounts that the reader is able to piece together an
understanding of the prelapsarian Tharmas. In the Second Night,
for example, Los laments nostalgically to Enitharmon:

> I know thee not as once I knew thee in those blessed fields
> Where memory wishes to repose among the flocks of Tharmas

> (FZ 34: 39–40, E323)

Tharmas is here seen as the guiding shepherd of a Blakean arcadia.
It is with such pastoral innocence that Dyer begins *The Fleece* and
which he merges into the modern epic world of commercial empire.
It is useful to bear this in mind when reading Blake's account in
Night the First of Tharmas's final downfall.[6]

The setting of the opening argument between Tharmas and his
emanation Enion is in many ways a pastoral one which has been
deprived of its original innocence. Tharmas and Enion appear as
fallen versions of Adam and Eve in that both the Zoa and his
emanation are in the process of losing their prelapsarian vision.
Tharmas employs pastoral imagery in an attempt to describe Enion

and only reveals the extent to which he has become alienated from
the positive implications that such imagery offers:

> Sometimes I think thou art a flower expanding
> Sometimes I think thou art a fruit breaking from its bud
> In dreadful dolor & pain & I am like an atom
> A Nothing left in darkness yet I am an identity
> I wish & feel & weep & groan Ah terrible terrible

> (FZ 4: 41–5, E302)

Images of growth and development appear to Tharmas only in terms
of 'dolor & pain'. He attempts to assert his own 'identity' at the
expense of Enion and, paradoxically perhaps, this results simply in
an awareness of his own isolated insignificance. Blake is depicting
the psychology of 'experience', showing how a certain analytic rationality is completely unable to understand the state of innocence:

> Why wilt thou Examine every little fibre of my soul
> Spreading them out before the sun like Stalks of flax to dry
> The infant joy is beautiful but its anatomy
> Horrible Ghast & Deadly nought shalt thou find in it
> But Death Despair & Everlasting brooding Melancholy.

> (FZ 4: 29–33, E302)

One should perhaps note in passing here how the language of
weaving – albeit of flax – has already entered into the depiction of
this fallen psychology.

In *The Fleece* it was noted how Dyer linked the private lives of
'nymph' and 'swain' with the growing influences and demands of
commercial expansion. The private demands of pastoral and those
of individual relationships were seen as dependent upon the
public events of empire. It is not simply that public events affect
private actions: there is, in addition to this, a closer reciprocity of
motivation. The private argument between Blake's two protag-
onists also has a public significance in a similar way. After the
bitter dispute between Tharmas and Enion, the Shepherd of
Eternity stoops his 'innocent head' and sinks down into the sea, 'a
pale white corse'. His Sceptre, however, emerges and is woven by
Enion in her looms:

Wondering she saw her woof begin to animate. & not
As Garments woven subservient to her hands but having a will
Of its own perverse & wayward Enion lovd & wept

Nine days she labourd at her work. & nine dark sleepless nights
But on the tenth trembling morn the Circle of Destiny Complete
Round rolld the Sea Englobing in a watry Globe self balancd
A Frowning Continent appeard Where Enion in the Desart
Terrified in her own Creation   viewing her woven shadow
Sat in a dread intoxication of Repentance & Contrition

(*FZ* 5: 20–8, E302–3)

In psychological terms this marks the separation of the lovers.
Tharmas asserts his own 'identity' and emerges in spectrous form
apart from Enion, 'Frowning' in terrible opposition to her desires.
Yet this version of Tharmas is as much the work of Enion as her
partner himself. Her over-jealous fears and ruthless analysis of his
hidden desires make the Spectre, in part at least, 'her own
Creation'. She repents at the irrevocable split that she has occasioned but it is too late.

In addition to this private reading, however, there are additional
possible public interpretations of the episode. Enion's act parallels
the divine act of creation in Genesis. She too creates a world, a
projection of her own fallen psyche and that of Tharmas. It is possible to see this new world in relation to the commercial empire
created by Dyer in *The Fleece*. At one level of interpretation the
passage can be seen to provide an analogue for the process whereby
the produce of rural areas is converted into an economic commodity. The rural worker is losing control over his or her own work. No
longer does the product appear 'subservient' to the wishes of the
producer, it seems to possess a will of its own, yet a 'will' which
lacks any comprehensible motivation, it is 'perverse & wayward'.
Thus the produce of rural labour comes under the influence of
market forces, the exigencies of trade.[7] Ironically, these 'perverse &
wayward' forces come to be seen as the 'Circle of Destiny', the
unquestioned rule by which life in this fallen world is regulated.
Like Urizen in *The Book of Urizen*, the Circle of Destiny is 'self
balanc'd' (*BU* 4: 18, E72), financial necessity pays heed to nothing
but its own furtherance. There is a movement in the passage from
the rural worker out towards a global awareness in the same way

as, in *The Fleece*, Dyer follows the woollen cloth on its voyages in the trading ships. Blake, however, describes the creation of a fierce trading nation or empire. What emerges is a 'Frowning Continent', a nation which becomes aggressive in the protection of its trade. Yet, during this process, Enion is revealed to be apart from her creation in an (exploited) desert, still feeling a misplaced love but also an ineffectual sense of 'Repentance & Contrition'. What is perhaps particularly significant in this intellectual allegory is the fact that the product is in one sense the original rural worker, Tharmas the shepherd. As Dyer's poem transformed the shepherds into part of the commercial trading process, so Blake converts the pastoral ideal, in the form of Tharmas, into an element of global empire. Whereas Dyer maintained that the shepherds could keep their innocence, Blake shows that this is impossible. In the pastoral love episode discussed in the analysis of *The Fleece*, the 'swain' is changed into a loom owner and the building of the loom is seen as a symbol of union between himself and his 'nymph'. In the political and economic reading of the present poem, Tharmas is transformed into an agent of exploitative trade, divorced from Enion who remains in the poem as the voice of the exploited rural areas that Tharmas has left behind. The Spectre created in Enion's looms is 'insane & most Deformd'. (*FZ* 5: 38–9, E303). After a short while he begins to assert his authority:

> soon in masculine strength augmenting he
> Reard up a form of gold & stood upon the glittering rock
> A shadow form winged   & in his depths
> The dazzlings as of gems shone clear, rapturous in fury
> Glorying in his own eyes . . . .

> (*FZ* 6: 4–8, E303).

Again, in terms of individual psychology, this represents the fallen Tharmas attempting to assert his oppressive and intrusive 'identity' over Enion. Yet this private psychology is part of the mass psychology of the nation as a whole.[8] At a national level, then, this can be seen as the pride and fury of emergent empire glorying in itself, dazzling with the 'gems' of conspicuous wealth. Its authority, literally in the above passage its support, is 'gold', financial advantage.

This spectrous side of the fallen Tharmas is, however, only one aspect of his character and it is not the one that Blake dwells upon at

length. More common throughout *The Four Zoas* is the portrayal of
Tharmas crying out helplessly for his lost emanation:

> O fool fool to lose my sweetest bliss
> Where art thou Enion ah too near to cunning too far off
> And yet too near. Dashd down I send thee into distant darkness
> Far as my strength can hurl thee wander there & laugh & play
> Among the frozen arrows they will tear thy tender flesh
> Fall off afar from Tharmas come not too near my strong fury
> Scream & fall off & laugh at Tharmas lovely summer beauty
> Till winter rends thee into Shivers as thou hast rended me
>
> So Tharmas bellowd oer the ocean thundring sobbing bursting
> The bounds of Destiny were broken & hatred now began
> Instead of love to Enion . . .

(FZ 45: 1–11, E330).

Tharmas's variable behaviour in the above passage makes it easy to
see why so many commentators have found his role hard to define.
It was seen earlier how, when Tharmas asserted his 'identity', he
was simultaneously aware of his own solitude. On his own he was
a mere 'atom'. His spectrous side represents the dominance of
'identity' whereas Tharmas as he normally appears within the
poem exhibits a coexistent aimlessness and formlessness. The
present passage shows the Zoa suffering on the horns of a self-
created dilemma. He needs Enion to give him purpose and a sense
of fulfilment yet, at the same time, he is wary of the apparent threat
she presents to the autonomy of his newly dominant 'identity'. He
thus alternates between love for his discarded rural emanation and
cruel destructive hatred. There is a further political and social
dimension to this fluctuation, however. It is possible to see such
contradictory behaviour as being analogous to an ideology (such as
Dyer's) which celebrates pastoral beauty – 'lovely summer beauty'
– whilst at the same time ruthlessly exploiting the actual rural
landscape, turning it into the 'winter' of Enion's 'desert'. It is significant that the 'Bounds of Destiny' are here described as 'broken'.
It has been observed how the original 'Circle of Destiny' was in
itself 'perverse & wayward'. When this circle is broken the chaotic
forces of which it is composed come to the fore and Tharmas is
revealed in raging, 'hardly definable' chaos. Again this can be seen to

reflect the ambiguity of Tharmas's individual psychology. Underlying the forceful, masculine assertion of the Spectre is a helpless uncertainty, a fearful combination of conflicting emotions. However, these emotions are cruelly destructive when unleashed. At a national level, Blake indicates the hidden aspect of the 'Frowning Continent' that the supporters of trade presented to the public. He suggests that a commercial empire is in fact founded upon forces which have a chaotic, sea-like incoherence analogous to that presented by Tharmas.

Tharmas is driven solely by self-interest, a love of self rather than a love of Enion. It is useful to recall that much eighteenth-century thought placed self-love at the centre of a theory of morality. Thus Pope, in *An Essay on Man*, can write that:

> God loves from Whole to Parts: but human soul
> Must rise from Individual to the Whole.
> Self-love but serves the virtuous mind to wake . . .[9]

Popean 'self-love', which could so easily be transformed into institutionalized selfishness, was, for Blake, anathema. He could never claim in the Popean sense that 'true SELF-LOVE and SOCIAL are the same' (IV.396). All social good, according to this theory, could be traced back to a root of apparent selfishness. Lawrence Nihell, Bishop of Kilfenora, in his book *Rational Self-love* (1770), could write of this questionable virtue in terms which anticipate the imagery associated with the fallen Tharmas:

> SELF-LOVE, thus philosophically understood, is to Human Nature what the *Gale* is to the *Navigator*, a *Force* or *Impulse*, which bears us through Life; and without the Help of which Man must have languished in a State of Inaction, and Inutility to Himself and the World . . .[10]

It was precisely upon this motivation of self-love that trade or commerce was seen to be founded in much writing of the period. Josiah Tucker, for example, writes in his *The Elements of Commerce and Theory of Taxes* (1755) that

> a lasting and extensive *National Commerce* is no otherwise to be obtained, than by a prudent Direction of the Passion of Self-Love to its *proper objects*.[11]

Tucker sees self-love as a force which can be controlled and manip-
ulated. For Blake, on the other hand, 'self-love', at a national or individual level, leads to disunity and uncontrolled chaos. This, it will
be noticed, is in direct opposition to the accepted Albion myths of
order and harmony.

This is an important observation, especially since it has become
usual to place commerce solely within the domain of Urizen. Yet
any discussion of the role played by Tharmas in *The Four Zoas* has to
accommodate an understanding of Urizen and of the relationship
that exists between these two Zoas.

Throughout the poem the forces of Urizen and Tharmas are
oppositional and yet at the same time mutually dependent. They
share a relationship that is analogous to that between the ruling
court aristocracy and the interests of the merchants in Blake's early
play 'King Edward the Third'. Trade, as has been seen, was founded
upon the impulse of 'self-love' and it was almost an eighteenth-
century commonplace that government and the nation could suffer
whilst trade prospered. The *British Merchant* of 1713, for example,
discusses 'General Maxims of Trade':

> There are General Maxims of Trade, which are assented to by
> everybody. That a trade may be of benefit to the Merchant, and an
> injury to the Body of the Nation, is one of these Maxims . . .[12]

The trading instinct is one that has to be controlled and harnessed,
as was seen from the earlier quotation from Tucker. In the present
poem the worlds of Urizen and Tharmas exist dialectically in a
similar way. The ordered tyranny of Urizenic government relies
upon the existence of the chaotic and arbitrary 'laws' of competitive
trade embodied in the nebulous Tharmas. Tharmas is similarly
reliant upon Urizen. The spectrous Tharmas who in the first Night
of the poem emerged as a 'Frowning Continent' from the looms of
Enion was at his most Urizenic. In order to assert his 'identity' he
needs the tyrannical 'will' of Urizen. Similarly, trading empires need
the support of a strong home government.

This reciprocity of the forces of Tharmas and Urizen is suggested
in the second Night of the poem where Urizen creates his universe,
the 'mundane shell'. At times the descriptions recall the poeticizing
of 'mundane' labour in such poems as *The Fleece*:

> Sorrowing went the Planters forth to plant, the Sowers to sow
> They dug the channels for the rivers & they pourd abroad

The seas & lakes, they reard the mountains & the rocks & hills
On broad pavilions, on pillard roofs & porches & high towers
In beautious order . . . (*FZ* 32: 16–33; 3, E321)

Dyer's depiction of rural labour, particularly in the episode concerning the love-lorn 'swain', frequently takes on a mythic quality. Individual labour is elevated to a constituent part of the overall Albion myth. Dyer in effect creates a new world where each act reflects or contributes to the development of the encompassing empire. In the present episode from Blake's poem, Urizen is portrayed as actually creating a new world where all is similarly directed towards one end. Like Dyer's version of England, the ordered universe of Urizen's 'mundane shell' looks out on the prospect of commercial expansion. This is tellingly conveyed by a reference to Tharmas:

For many a window ornamented with sweet ornaments
Lookd out into the World of Tharmas, where in the ceaseless
        torrents
His billows roll where monsters wander in the foamy paths

(*FZ* 33: 5–7, E321)

Discussing this section, Wilkie and Johnson note that the 'fragile construct' of Urizen's world looks out upon the 'oceanic chaos of the unorganised instinctual reality represented by Tharmas' (1978: 52). At a political level, this 'unorganised instinctual reality' can be seen to be reflected in the aggressive self-interest of the merchant classes who, despite their self-love, have a necessary relationship with the 'fragile construct' of strictly ordered government. The seas of Tharmas in the above passage are rough but, at the same time, they are crossed with 'foamy paths' which, it could be argued, represent at one level the established routes of trading vessels. Thus the 'monsters' of Tharmas can be interpreted as his ships. In this way Blake can be seen to be glancing ironically at fashionable names for ships in the British fleet. The writer of a letter in the *Gentleman's Magazine* of January 1797 notes the number of ships named after ancient heroes and proceeds to comment that

Not satisfied with human beings, we have impressed into our service all the monsters of those fabulous times, such as the *Minotaur, Centaur, Cerbus, Hydra* and *Harpy* . . . (LXVII: 27)

Blake's text brings out the full aggressive significance of this, notably classically inspired, taste for naming ships. There are, moreover, significant poetic precedents for the association of monsters and ships. An example is provided by one of Edward Young's two Odes which were collectively entitled *Sea-Piece* (1737). In 'Ode the First: The British Sailor's Exultation', Young describes the preparation of a British fleet for war:

> Hear, and revere. – At Britain's nod.
> From each enchanted grove and wood,
> Hastes the huge oak, or shadeless forest leaves;
> The mountain pines assume new forms,
> Spread canvass wings, and fly through storms,
> And ride o'er rocks, and dance on foaming waves.
>
> She nods again: the labouring earth
> Discloses a tremendous birth;
> In smoking rivers runs her molten ore!
> Thence monsters, of enormous size
> And hideous aspect, threatening rise,
> Flame from the deck, from trembling bastions roar.
>
> These ministers of fate fulfil,
> On empires wide, an island's will,
> When thrones unjust wake vengeance . . .[13]

In Blake's early drama 'King Edward the Third' there is some doubt as to whether the merchant ships, their 'ministers of fate', will fulfill the 'island's will'. In *The Four Zoas* as a whole the 'monsters' of Tharmas have a similarly ambivalent relationship with Urizenic government. In the present scene, however, the presence of Urizen's 'window' indicates that, at this early stage of the narrative, the forces of Urizen and Tharmas work together in relative harmony.

In *Imperium Pelagi*, Young describes an analogous harmony and fellow-feeling between the forces of government and those of trade and proceeds to describe an entire cosmic system founded upon the dynamics of commerce:

> Kings, merchants are in league and love;
> Earth's odours pay swift airs above,
> That o'er the teeming field prolific range,

> Planets are merchants, take, return,
> Lustre and heat; by traffic burn:
> The whole creation is one vast Exchange.

(vol. II p. 357)

One should perhaps keep this stanza in mind when reading the account of Urizen's creation of the stars:

> Each took his station, & his course began with sorrow & care
>
> In sevens & tens & fifties, hundreds, thousands, numberd all
> According to their various powers. Subordinate to Urizen
> And to his sons in their degrees & to his beautious daughters
>
> Travelling in silent majesty along their orderd ways
> In right lined paths outmeasured by proportions of number
>   weight
> And measure. mathematic motion wondrous. along the deep

(FZ 33: 18–24, E322)

Underlying this description of the Urizenic cosmic system is another account of the foamy paths of the world of Tharmas. Ships too travel majestically along pre-ordained routes, following their 'course in the vast deep' – the word 'deep' here surely signalling the ocean as much as the sky.[14] Moreover, the connection between stars and ships is far from being an arbitrary one, for navigators depended upon the guidance of the stars to determine the 'foamy paths' taken by their vessels. This connection is expressly made by Young in the passage quoted earlier – 'Planets are merchants'. Thus, in an earlier reaction to Blake's Urizenic world, commercial activity is combined with the scientific measurement of the stars and planets:

> And many said We see no Visions in the darksom air
> Measure the course of that sulphur orb that lights the darksom
>   day
> Set stations on this breeding Earth & let us buy & sell
> Others arose & schools Erected forming Instruments
> To measure out the course of heaven.

(FZ 28: 18–21, E318)

Like the stars in the passage quoted above, the merchants must first of all establish their 'stations' from which to trade. In general, the link between the sea or commerce and the stars appear to have been common in eighteenth-century thought. The writer of the letter to the *Gentleman's Magazine* quoted earlier, observes that:

> As our mariners direct their course through the ocean by observations on the heavenly bodies it might not be improper to borrow some names from these celestial objects. Two constellations, the *Orion*, and the *Twins* (*Pylades* and *Orestes*), have been distinguished.

> (LXVII: 30).

Discussing the stars in relation to commercial Britain, Young observes in *Imperium Pelagi* that:

> These are her friends, a marshall'd train
> A golden host and azure plain,
> By turns do duty, and by turns retreat:
> They may retreat, but not from her;
> The star that quits the hemisphere
> Must quit the skies, to want a British fleet.

> (vol. II: 354)

The expected order of things, then, in this eighteenth-century vision was a harmonious cooperation between the sea and stars, commerce and government, Tharmas and Urizen.

However, in *The Four Zoas*, the relationship is not always as ordered or harmonious. A revealing confrontation takes place between Tharmas and Urizen at the beginning of the sixth Night. The ensuing dispute ends with Urizen plagued by Tharmas's 'monsters' which in the earlier scene had appeared subservient to his aims:

> he strove
> In vain for hideous monsters of the deeps annoyed him sore
> Scaled & finnd with iron & brass they devourd the path before
>   him
> Incessant was the conflict

> (FZ 69: 25–8, E346)

Tharmas's monsters resemble even more closely here the monstrous warships of Young's *Sea-Piece*. The actual confrontation between the Zoas is in itself pertinent to the present discussion. The fallen Tharmas, despairing at the chaotic aimlessness of the life he has to lead, suggests to Urizen a mutual suicide pact. Such a pact would be, after all, only the grim reverse side of a relationship founded upon a mutually dependent competitive antagonism. Tharmas addresses Urizen:

> Withhold thy light from me for ever & I will withhold
> From thee thy food so shall we cease to be & all our sorrows
> End

> (*FZ* 69: 15–17, E346)

Tharmas intends to fulfil the terms of his suggested agreement even if Urizen fails to agree to them. The friendly proposal becomes a threat. This is significant, for even in desperation they have no real accord. Wilkie and Johnson, who interpret this passage primarily in terms of its psychological significance, note that:

> Urizen's compulsive need for order and control and Tharmas's chaotic helplessness – potentially of mutual benefit – have become self-contained and self-perpetuating states of being. (1978: 125).

This is a perceptive comment but it fails to appreciate how, in the fallen world of *The Four Zoas*, the 'mutual benefit' of cooperation has itself an ambivalent aspect. In the present episode Tharmas, as always, acts solely to his own advantage, according to the dictates of 'self-love'. From a psychological perspective, Wilkie and Johnson see Tharmas as threatening to 'cut off' Urizen's 'intellect' from 'instinctual nourishment' (1978: 126). At a political and economic level this is a reversal of the relationship envisaged by Young in his 'Ode to the King' – a prefatory poem to *Ocean: An Ode* (1728):

> At his proud foot
> The sea, pour'd out,
> Immortal nourishment supplies,
> Thence wealth and state,
> And power and fate,
> Which Europe reads in George's eyes.

> (vol. II: 145)

Tharmas's threat, then, can be seen as analogous to the withdrawal of profits from 'nourishment' (or 'food' as Tharmas calls it – or any of the other products supplied by trade) as an act of defiance by merchants in opposition to a hostile government.

In reading *The Four Zoas* as a psychodrama it is usual to interpret Tharmas as a selfish yet unorganized instinctive power and Urizen as an oppositional force of ordered rationality. What this essay has attempted to show is how this individual psychological approach can be related to the mass psychology of the eighteenth-century commercial empire, the 'Albion' of Dyer's poem. *The Fleece* attempts to hide the disunity within mercantile expansionism and central to this attempt is the role played by genre. In Dyer pastoral and georgic perform an ideological function in that they imply that the dynamics of a contemporary commercial society can be conveyed through literary forms that originated in an earlier period. Whilst writing about a society which is in a radical state of flux, Dyer suggests through his use of genre that there is an essential continuity between past and present. It is this implicit denial of discontinuity that *The Four Zoas* engages with. Tharmas, the shepherd of eternity, is far removed from his pastoral role throughout most of the poem and it is precisely this difference that is crucial to our understanding of his status. Written at the end of the century, Blake's text deconstructs Dyer's myth and foregrounds the tensions inherent within it. Dyer's pastoral masks the vicissitudes of nascent capitalism whereas Blake's radically transformed shepherd highlights the enormous social, pyschological and artistic upheavals produced by economic change.

Notes

1. While Erdman in the third edition of *Blake: Prophet Against Empire* (1977: 295n) has rejected the precise political allegory he advocated in the first edition, he still acknowledges the presence of 'certain salient historical allusion or sources' in the poem (E818).
2. John Dyer, *Poems* (1761) p. 152.
3. In 1725 Daniel Defoe noted 'How many noble seats, superior to the palaces of sovereign princes, in some countries, do we see erected within a few miles of this city by tradesmen, or the sons of tradesmen, while the seats and castles of the ancient gentry, like their families, look worn out and fallen into decay – *The Complete English Tradesman* (1745; reprinted New York: Burt Franklin, 1970) vol. I, p. 244–5. The growing power of the mercantile class can be registered by the increasing num-

ber of the country's trading vessels. Rude notes that: 'England's merchant navy increased from 3300 ships with a tonnage of 260 000 in 1702 to 9400 ships with a tonnage of 695 000 in 1776 . . . by 1800 her carrying capacity had risen to five or six times what it had the been the century before', George Rude, *Europe in the Eighteenth Century, Aristocracy and the Bourgeois Challenge* (London: Weidenfield & Nicolson, 1972) p. 59.

4. See John Barrell, *English Literature in History 1730–1780: An Equal, Wide Survey* (London: Hutchinson, 1985) pp. 98–9, for a further discussion of this scene and (with Harriet Guest) 'On the Use of Contradiction: Economics and Morality in the Eighteenth-Century Long Poem', *The New Eighteenth Century: Theory, Politics, Literature*, eds Felicity Nussbaum and Laura Brown(London: Methuen, 1987) pp. 121–43.

5. Maxine Berg, *The Age of Manufactures 1700–1820* (London: Fontana, 1985) p. 80.

6. The textual status of the first two Nights is extremely confused. What the Erdman edition calls 'Night the [Second]' was never so named by Blake. It was, however, twice prefixed with 'Night the First' although on both occasions this seems to have been rejected. At one point 'Night the First' seems to have ended on page 9 below line 33. As Erdman publishes the text it concludes after page 8 line 15. However, it is followed by pages 19–20 before 'Night the [Second]' appears on page 23. See Erdman's account on E824–28.

7. 'The rural, industrial labourers were both tied to the community and yet, just as surely, rootless. Their affiliations were, in a sense, international, for it was on this, larger stage that the vicissitudes of their lives were worked out. Their wages were determined not with reference to local prices but with reference to the international value of their production', D. Levine, *Family Formation in An Age of Nascent Capitalism* (London: Academic Press, 1977) p. 14. Berg elaborates upon this analysis (1985) p. 131: 'They became more and more subject to commercial and not just harvest fluctuations, and they faced periods of enforced idleness as a result of changes in fashions, interruptions in foreign trade, and an economic cycle moving increasing to the boom–slump pattern that would come to dominate industrial capitalism. Merchant employers controlled the rural workers' access to markets; against the backdrop of international markets they could force wages down below those customarily acceptable to urban workers, and even below subsistence'.

8. For more on the complex interrelation of private and public psychology, see Wilhelm Reich, *The Mass Psychology Of Fascism*, trans. Vincent R. Carfagno (New York: Farrer, Strauss & Giroux, 1970).

9. *The Poems of Alexander Pope*, ed. John Butt (London: Methuen, 1965) iv. 11. 361–3, p. 546.

10. L. Nihell, *Rational Self-Love: or, A Philosophical and Moral Essay on the Natural Principles of Happiness and Virtue* (1770) p. 3.

11. Quoted in Stephen Copley (ed.) *Literature and the Social Order in Eighteenth-Century England* (London: Croom Helm and Methuen, 1984) p. 114.

12. J. Smith, *Chronicon Rusticum-Commerciale: Or. Memoirs of Wool &tc.* (1741) p. 108.

13. The *Poetical Works of Edward Young* (Aldine Edition), 2 vols (1891) ii, p. 376–77.

14. 'The word 'deeps', found so frequently in Blake's poetry, carries the meaning of both a terrestrial sea and interplanetary or interstellar space' (Worrall, 1981: 274).

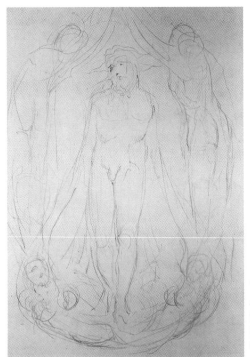

1 William Blake.
A Watcher surrounded by
four Daughters of Men.
Pencil drawing, inscribed
'Book of ENOCH'.

2 William Blake.
A Watcher seducing
one of the Daughters
of Men. Pencil drawing,
inscribed 'from
the Book of Enoch'.

3 William Blake.
Two phallic males
descending to one of
the Daughters of Men.
Pencil drawing,
inscribed 'From the
Book of Enoch'.

4 William Blake.
A spectrous female rising
above a recumbent form; a
figure looking on, apparently
in horror. Pencil drawing,
inscribed 'B of Enoch'.

5 William Blake.
Two figures, perhaps
before the throne of
'one whose countenance
was as snow, and whose
garment as a shining sun'.
Pencil drawing, inscribed
'Book of Enoch'.

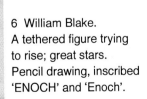

6 William Blake.
A tethered figure trying
to rise; great stars.
Pencil drawing, inscribed
'ENOCH' and 'Enoch'.

7 William Blake.
The temptation of
Eve. Pen and water-
colour illustration to
John Milton, *Paradise
Lost* ix, 780–4.

8 William Blake.
Mirth and her Com-
panions. Illustration to
John Milton, *L'Allegro*,
line engraving.

7

Blake, Democritus, and the 'Fluxions of the Atom': Some Contexts for Materialist Critiques

MARY LYNN JOHNSON

Blake the intemperate antimaterialist is a sitting duck for *au courant* projects with 'historicizing' in the title. But too often the living critic, in exposing the timebound and material underpinning of a dead poet's achievement, fails to acknowledge what John Dunn has called the 'arrogance of ideological explanation', or 'the claim to understand another's thinking more deeply than he does himself, without being in a position to provide true descriptions of almost any of it'.[1]

Our generation's presumption of temporal superiority ought itself to be historicized, along with claims of intrinsic compatibility between materialist philosophies and progressive political positions. In Blake's hands, an ultra-idealist radical Christian critique could be just as politically astute as a materialist one, a tool wielded as effectively against the rationalist dogma of French *philosophes* and their deflationary ridicule as it was against the oppressive pieties of Anglican Tories. In scientific paradigms as well, the distorting lens of hindsight has foreshortened our perspective on materialist thought, exaggerating its prominence in a 'triumphal progress of discoveries along the royal road of truth'[2] – the Whiggish view of science, as it has been called. To appreciate more fully the cultural tensions that gave currency to Blake's antimaterialist polemic, we need a 'thicker' account of the varieties of materialism he must actually have known.[3]

On page 9 of his Notebook Blake brings four natural philosophers together for a comprehensive reprimand – consolidating, as Donald

Ault has noted, 'the whole sweep of scientific history . . . in an inter-connected set of images':

> Mock on Mock on Voltaire Rousseau
> Mock on Mock on tis all in vain
> You throw the sand against the wind
> And the wind blows it back again.
>
> And every sand becomes a Gem
> Reflected in the beams divine
> Blown back they blind the mocking Eye
> But still in Israels paths they shine
>
> The Atoms of Democritus
> And Newtons Particles of light
> Are sands upon the Red sea shore
> Where Israels tents do shine so bright.

(Ault 1974, p. 54; E477–8)

When Blake wrote these lines, probably around 1803, the key text on the fundamental structure of matter was still, a century after its first publication, Newton's famous speculation in Query 31 at the end of the *Opticks* (1704) that God probably 'form'd Matter in solid, massy, hard, impenetrable, moveable Particles'.[4] Ault suggests that in consolidating scientific error Blake is 'exerting his peculiar archetypal vision of history and implying that Democritus, Plato, Aristotle, Lucretius and Newton were all asking the same questions and that their solutions are merely historically conditioned recurrences of the same "Satanic" doctrines' (Ault, 1974: 54). In the case of Democritus, Lucretius and Newton, it takes no 'peculiar archetypal vision' to see that they, along with Bacon, Locke and Voltaire, were not only asking the same questions but getting the same answer: atoms, moving randomly in a void, are the ultimate constituents of everything we see in nature. The line of continuity in atomistic philosophy is clear enough to us today, but in his own time Newton chose *not* to acknowledge his place in the Dem-ocritean tradition. Thus in forging a link between 'the atoms of Democritus' and 'Newtons particles of light' Blake was actually recovering a heritage that Newton himself had sought to conceal, if not altogether to efface.

Hoping to gain the widest possible acceptance for those specific principles of physics which he could support experimentally, Newton repeatedly avoided taking a position on either the basic components of matter or the composition of light. In his published and unpublished work on optics, beginning in 1664, when the fluid theory of light was the dominant paradigm, Newton revealed his preference for the corpuscular hypothesis only indirectly, almost covertly.[5] Not until 1706 did he associate himself in print with particles of light, in a query appended to the first Latin edition of the *Opticks*: 'Are not Rays of Light very small Bodies emitted from shining Substances, and refracted by certain attractions whereby Light and other Bodies mutually act on one another?' (Query 21; substantively included in the second [1718] and subsequent English editions as parts of Queries 29 and 30). From these hints and a scattering of related comments in the Queries, eighteenth-century theorists went on to apply to light particles the Newtonian laws of motion and the effects of attraction and repulsion, and the particulate hypothesis became fully (though not absolutely) institutionalized by the middle of the century.

Newton was equally guarded in writing of the classical atomistic philosophers. His fullest reference to 'the oldest and most celebrated Philosophers of *Greece* and *Phoenicia*, who made a *Vacuum*, and Atoms, and the Gravity of Atoms, the first Principles of their Philosophy' appears in the *Opticks*, Query 30, in a review of arguments against aether. Newton came closest to acknowledging his real affinity with Democritus and his successors in a private manuscript, the so-called Classical Scholia, though even here he did not allude to the atomistic aspect of their philosophy. It is not known why Newton withdrew this manuscript, after having carefully prepared it for publication; his authorship did not come to light until 1834 (too late to confirm Blake's suspicions), and the full text was not published until 1984. Nor is there an explanation of why, having withdrawn it, he leaked the material through his disciple David Gregory, who with Newton's full knowledge quoted and paraphrased it without attribution in the Preface to his own text popularizing Newton's theories published in 1702. Gregory's private notes provide a clue: at one time, Newton planned to 'demonstrate at length the agreement between his philosophy and that of the Ancients', showing that the 'philosophy of Epicurus and Lucretius is the true and ancient one, wrongly twisted towards atheism by the ancients'.[6] It seems likely that despite Newton's attraction to the explanatory power of atomism, its elegance and economy in accounting for complex phenomena, he did not wish to risk having his science impeded by the theological baggage that atomistic philosophy still carried. His suppression of the Classical Scholia is consistent with his other suppressions, discovered over the past twenty years, of writings with heterodox overtones.

The association between atomism and atheism goes back to antiquity: atheism was the standard charge against Democritus and his shadowy mentor Leucippus, co-founders of the atomistic system in the fifth century BC; against Epicurus, its developer and refiner in the fourth century BC; and against Lucretius, its inspired evangelist in the first century BC. That is probably why the works of the atomists, except for Lucretius' *On the Nature of Things*, have come down to us only in paraphrased snippits such as those preserved by Aristotle and Diogenes Laertius.[7] According to Aristotle, Democritus' atoms differ from each other in only three respects – shape, position and order – but (like letters of the alphabet) they are capable of combining in an infinite variety of ways, to produce everything that has ever existed or ever will exist. The atoms must be hard and impenetrable; otherwise they would have worn away over time. They must be infinitesimally small but finitely divisible; otherwise they would have even smaller subparts. Equally important is the void in which the atoms move: it permeates the entire universe and every object in it, just as the atoms do. Without the void there would be no universe – no empty space in which atoms might collide at random, over aeons, to form the cosmic whirl which gives rise to new worlds. Atoms are being, the void is non-being; the two change places constantly, as atoms move into new positions and leave atom-sized vacancies behind them. Atoms themselves have no sensory qualities; visual perception occurs when effluences of atoms, called idols, stream off objects (as they do constantly), compress the air between themselves and the eye, and form an imprint of concentrated atoms which enter the moist interior of the eye and generate the images we perceive. Perhaps the most often-cited dictum of Democritus has to do with this separation between primary and secondary qualities: 'By convention colour, by convention sweet, by convention bitter: in reality atoms and the void'.

The rediscovery and rehabilitation of ancient Greek atomistic philosophy, after centuries of Christian efforts to suppress and discredit it, occurred almost simultaneously at several sites in seventeenth-century Europe, with the French philosopher-priest

Pierre Gassendi, biographer of Epicurus, being its pioneering Christianizer and scientific modernizer, and Blake's abomination Bacon one of its chief exponents. In order to provide a function for God, and to restore immortality and immateriality to the soul, Gassendi denied the atoms everything that had made them so compelling in the Democritean formulation – infinitude, independent existence, and motion – reducing matter to a dust-heap of inert, energyless identical minute objects.[8] Descartes, abhorring a vacuum, adopted corpuscles but managed to preserve the plenum by devising a complicated arrangement of vortices to allow for their movement. In England there was less squeamishness about the void, and Robert Boyle promoted a Christianized corpuscular philosophy in the scientific community through the Royal Society. Newton's later association with atomism, despite his personal reticence on the subject, ensured that by the time Blake wrote, thinkers of virtually every political stripe and religious persuasion could be found among its proponents. As Gabriel Moked has recently revealed, for example, even the arch-idealist High Church monarchist Berkeley was something of an atomist: in *Siris* (1744), the work Blake annotated (c. 1820), Berkeley fully accepts Newton's particles of light and cites approvingly his terse reference to the atomists of antiquity.[9]

Blake does not say where he got his information about classical atomism, but the heavily documented entry on 'Atomical Philosophy' in Rees's *Cyclopaedia* (1802–20), filling four closely written columns, shows that it was easy enough to come by. Thomas Creech's 1682 translation of Lucretius was reprinted at least five times, and Dryden's 1685 translation of five selections was even more popular.[10] Cicero's *On the Nature of the Gods*, which is contemporary with Lucretius' *On the Nature of Things* and is perhaps the most concentrated source of anti-Epicurean arguments from antiquity, first appeared in English in 1683 and went through ten British editions in the eighteenth century and 18 editions between 1801 and 1836; Blake knew this work, at least by reputation, well enough to depict it in *Night Thoughts*, design 199. And the connection between mockery and atomism may have occurred to Blake as he prepared his commercial engraving of a portrait bust of Democritus as 'Laughing Philosopher' for Lavater's *Essays on Physiognomy* (1789–98); the atomist, known for his contemptuously amused detachment from human follies, illustrates Lavater's theory of the effects of 'Mockery' on the countenance (I, 160). In Rees's *Cyclopaedia* Democritus is identified as a 'Derider' (XII, s.v.).

Twice in his later prophecies Blake uses a key phrase of Ciceronian origin, well known in English, which captures the primal horror of random movement in a vacuum: the 'fortuitous concourse' of atoms (*concursus fortuitus* in *On the Nature of the Gods* I: xxiv, 66; echoed, for example, in Locke's *Essay Concerning Human Understanding*, IV; xx, 15). This phrase, adapted to chaotic psychological situations, appears in *The Four Zoas*, as Luvah laments 'that we all go to Eternal Death / To our Primeval Chaos in fortuitous concourse of incoherent / Discordant principles of Love & Hate' (27: 11–13 E318), and again in *Jerusalem*, when Albion's 'Spectrous Chaos', who identifies himself as the 'Rational Power', declares that 'that Human Form / You call Divine, is but a Worm seventy inches long / That creeps forth in a night & is dried in the morning sun, / In fortuitous concourse of memorys accumulated & lost' ([29] 33: 5–8 E175). Blake's scores of references to a boundless 'void', 'vacuum' or 'non-entity', often in association with 'chaos', and characteristically modified by terms such as 'abominable', 'abhorred', 'abstract', 'awful', 'horrible', 'Newtonian', 'Satanic', or 'soul-shuddering', seem more consonant with the void in classical atomism than with the one God fills with creation in Genesis. And his image of 'Rock & Sand . . . / Justling together in the void' (FZ 16: 5–7; E309) evokes the random collisions of classical atomism. It should also be noted that both Newton and Democritus opened a void *within* objects, in the undetectably minute intervals between atoms, or 'pores' as Newton called them, and perhaps this notion of an inner void also finds its way into Blake's numerous representations of the hollowness of the fallen psyche (e.g. *J* 5: 56–7 E148).

Blake treats Democritus' atoms and Newton's even more minute particles of light as interchangeable airborne granular bodies which, seen aright, become jewel-like sands on the Red Sea shore (Nicolson 1946: 166–8; Ault 1974: 55, 142–7). Each component of this complex of images has multiple resonances in the science, philosophy and history of atomism. The main line of continuity from Democritus to Newton is the notion of atoms as tiny hard bodies, aptly compared to grains of sand: as Frye has remarked, from the reductive perspective of materialist philosophy all nature appears a mere sandstorm. The metaphor of sand probably derives from Lucretius' comparison of atoms in motion to motes dancing in a sunbeam (II, 129), a figure so well known that in sixteenth-century English usage 'atom' and 'mote' were synonymous, as Leopold Damrosch Jr observes in his searching reading of 'Mock on' (Damrosch 1980: 99). The classical atomists had explained perception as the result of the bombardment of atoms upon the senses, and in both the Cartesian and the Newtonian formulations light is also discontinuous: so sandy particles, conveyed by other sandy particles, enter the eye as sandy particles.

The idea of interchangeability between atoms and light–particles can be extrapolated from Newton's own words, 'Are not gross Bodies and Light convertible into one another . . .?' (Query 30). Newton's followers applied the same laws of motion to both kinds of particles, and within a very few years, in effect, 'Light had become matter';[11] it was then but a short step for associated explanatory metaphors, such as the comparison of light particles to sandlike projectiles, to migrate from mechanics to optics. For Blake, a particularly convenient non-technical source of scientific information on both light-particles and atoms would have been William Nicholson's *An Introduction to Natural Philosophy* (1782), a work for which he had engraved the title-page vignette. This straightforward and readable 'account of the present state of Natural Philosophy', intended for 'such as possess very little mathematical knowledge' (vii), covers areas of controversy as well as consensus; the book was published by Joseph Johnson, and Blake may even have known the author.[12]

The prevailing notion of light and its perception, from Newton's time to Blake's, is summarized in the following excerpt from the entry on 'Optics' in the *Encyclopedia Britannica* (1771):

> Light consists of an inconceivably great number of particles flowing from a luminous body in all manner of directions, and these particles are so small, as to surpass all human comprehension. . . . Dr Niewentynt has computed, that there flows more than 6,000,000,000,000 times as many particles of light from a candle in one second of time, as there are grains of sand in the whole earth, supposing each cubic inch of it to contain 1,000,000. These particles, by falling directly upon our eyes, excite in our minds the idea of light.[13]

For these impressive figures the encylopedist, William Smellie, relies on *The Religious Philosopher* (1718–19), by the Dutch theologian Bernard Nieuwentijdt, whose staggering calculation, meant to strike awe into the hearts of atheists, is given in the original as $418,660 \times 10^{39}$.[14] A large superstructure of further calculation and theoretical speculation was erected upon Dr Nieuwentijdt's shaky figures, most notably limits on the size and velocity of the particles, in relation to the delicacy of the eye, and projections over time of loss of mass in what was called the 'wastage' of light particles from the sun. Although William Nicholson does not cite Nieuwentijdt, he reasons from astronomical measures of the velocity of light, in comparison with known velocities of ordinary bodies, that 'if the particles of light were equal in mass to the two millionth part of a grain of sand, we should be no more able to endure their impulse than that of sand shot point blank from the mouth of a cannon'.[15]

The opening salvo of 'Mock on', a sardonic challenge to Voltaire and Rousseau to go ahead and mock all they want, at first appears unrelated to the question of atomism. Alicia Ostriker cites Job's words to his comforters, 'Suffer me that I may speak; and after that I have spoken, mock on' (Job 21:3; Ostriker, 1977: 959n). Blake is addressing the continuing currency, a quarter-century after both philosophers' deaths in 1778, of their attacks on conventional Christianity. In mending 'mockers eye' to 'mocking eye' in his Notebook, Blake makes clear that the mockery of Voltaire and Rousseau consists not so much in what they say as how they see; as with the biblical hypocrite who fails to perceive the mote in his own eye, their blindness is self-induced. Possibly Blake is also recalling the legend that Democritus blinded himself in order to concentrate on his philosophy. Blake's sandstorm metaphor for the reductionist technique of mockery that Voltaire perfected – seizing upon isolated absurdities – calls to mind Hobbes's remark that 'by casting atomes of Scripture as dust before mens eyes, [commentators] make everything more obscure than it is; an ordinary artifice of those that seek not the truth, but their own advantage' (*Leviathan*, III, 43). Voltaire's besetting error, as Blake emphasized in the three versions of the poem on 'The Gray Monk' and elsewhere, is to sneer at inspiration and vision and mock the divine spirit within humanity.

Rousseau appears in 'Mock on' not as an atomist, or even as a mocker, but in his usual capacity as Voltaire's inseparable sidekick in Blake's formulaic denunciations of French materialism (*J* 54: 16–18; 66: 12–15; E203, 218). On historical grounds, it is really Voltaire alone who belongs in the poem. Voltaire introduced Bacon, Newton and Locke to his compatriots through his compatriots through his *Philosophical Letters* of 1734 (which had appeared in English the year before as *Letters on the English Nation*). With the English publication of *The Elements of Sir Isaac Newton's Philosophy* (1738) and

The Metaphysics of Sir Isaac Newton, or, A Comparison of the Opinions of Sir Isaac Newton and M. Leibniz (1747), Voltaire became the foremost popularizer of Newton's thought on both sides of the Channel, and he was probably the main source of Blake's inaccurate equation of Newtonian science with mechanism and atheism[16] (Christiansen, 1982: 141–61).

If Voltaire had done no more than make Diderot aware of Bacon, he would have had a large share in transmitting the English scientific revival of atomism to France, and that in itself would have been enough to call down Blake's indignation upon him. Diderot and d'Alembert made Bacon the guiding genius of the French *Encyclopedia* (1751), leading their English translator (1752) to express the hope that this new attention would 'raise a Desire in the *English* Reader to consult those admirable Works; which certainly hitherto have been too much neglected in *England*'. Nineteenth-century admirers of Bacon – Coleridge, for example, who called him the 'British Plato' – sought to liberate Bacon from what they regarded as his misappropriation by French materialists.[17] But for Blake, the philosopher's sympathetic portrayal of the ancient atomists gives him away. In annotating Bacon's essay 'On Atheism', Blake does not comment directly on the claim that the school of 'Leucippus, and Democritus and Epicurus . . . doth demonstrate Religion', since randomness cannot produce order without a 'divine Marshall', but this sophistic argument must have prompted his characterization of Bacon at the end of the essays as 'An Atheist pretending to talk against Atheism' and the marginal note: 'Bacon was a Contemplative Atheist Evidently an Epicurean' (E626). On a blank leaf near the beginning of the *Essays* he sums up Bacon's philosophical position: 'Every Body Knows that this is Epicurus and Lucretius & Yet Every Body Says that it is Christian Philosophy. how is this Possible?' (E620). Also in the annotations to Reynolds Blake equates 'Epicurean or Newtonian Philosophy' with atheism (E660), and he has the Daughters of Albion, weaving human existence from stony fibres, call 'the Rocks Atomic Origins of Existence; denying Eternity / By the Atheistical Epicurean Philosophy of Albions Tree' (*J* 67: 12–13; E220). In this passage Blake is perhaps recalling, in addition to the primary biblical source, Diderot's epithet for the *Encyclopedia* itself, 'the tree of human knowledge', and d'Alembert's homage to Bacon in the Preliminary Discourse.

In 'Mock on', Blake turns the imagery of scientific and philosophical materialism against itself, infusing atomistic images of light, colour, and sand into a reworking of events from the Exodus.

Voltaire, in describing Newton's separation of white light into particle-streams of colour, had emphasized 'how prodigiously small the Rays of Light must be, which, containing in them all Colours from the Sun, penetrate a Pore of a Diamond', and had speculated that the 'solid Parts' of each separate ray of colour 'must be so many Atoms perfectly hard'.[18] Blake reunites these fissioned rays and transmutes them into the 'beams divine' of the pillar of cloud and fire, opposing atomistic physical perception to holistic spiritual vision. He picks up the biblical narrative at the point where the strong east wind has been blowing all night to turn the Red Sea to dry land in preparation for the crossing; this is the moment when the angel who has been leading the children of Israel moves the pillar of cloud behind the company, where it becomes 'a cloud and darkness' to the Egyptians, while giving 'light by night' to the Israelites (Exod. 14: 20–2). When the sands are 'blown back' in the third stanza to blind the mockers while also illuminating 'Israels paths', Voltaire and Rousseau are placed in the position of the Egyptian pursuers; the divine radiance is visible only to the eyes of faith. By the end of the poem the wind is no longer blowing; the sands have come to rest not in the desert but on the Red Sea *shore*, indicating that the children of Israel have already passed through the parted waters and are safely encamped in their tents on the farther bank.

The Red Sea shore comes up again in another unexpected twist of intertwined allusions. In an anecdote that Blake must have known because it is so widely repeated (appearing first in Diogenes Laertius, who quotes earlier sources, and continuing into the encyclopedias and classical dictionaries of Blake's time), Democritus himself is supposed to have gone as far as the Red Sea in his restless search for knowledge. And if Blake ever happened to look up 'Atomical Philosophy' in Rees's *Cyclopaedia* (III, s.v.), he would have come upon the opinion of the Cambridge Platonist Ralph Cudworth 'that neither Democritus, nor Protagoras, nor Leucippus, was the first inventor of this philosophy; and our reason is, because they were all three of them atheists'. Cudworth alleges 'historical probability for the opinion that . . . the first inventor of this atomical philosophy was one Moschus, A Phoenician, who according to Strabo, lived before the Trojan war, and who has been supposed by some persons to be the same with Moses the Jewish lawgiver'. As incredible as it now seems, the widely-repeated claim that Moses was the first atomist was taken seriously in Newton's time and persisted even into the middle of the next century.[19]

Moses is also linked to atomism through Hutchinsonianism, a cobbled-together system of Christian materialism meant to overthrow Newton and establish Moses as the fountainhead of scientific knowledge. In *Moses's Principia* (1724) and a score of subsequent books, John Hutchinson expounded an atomistic model that he claimed was derived directly from the revealed word of God – the first chapter of Genesis in the original Hebrew, stripped of conventional supratextual markings. In Hutchinson's view, Newtonian matter, since it requires the presence of God to fill the void and keep the system running, is not material enough, whereas the Hutchinsonian counter-system allows no contact whatsoever between God and matter. Derived from typologically and etymologically significant Hebrew ur-words, Hutchinson's primordial atoms of fire, light and air, corresponding to the Trinity, are perpetually interchanged: the sun emits particles of light that travel outward in all directions until they congeal to establish the cosmic boundary, the firmament, at which point they grow heavy, give rise to the other elements, and gravitate back to the sun. As an alternate view of matter, Hutchinsonianism provided a rallying point for High Churchmen alienated from the Latitudinarian wing that gained power after the Glorious Revolution.[20] Among the system's influential proponents were Duncan Forbes, Lord President of the Scottish Sessions, and George Horne, vice-chancellor of Oxford University, later Bishop of Norwich. Hutchinson's ideas interested both John Wesley and Coleridge; whole grammars and lexicons of Hutchinsonian Hebrew were available; pamphlets and tracts flew back and forth between Hutchinsonians and Newtonians; the *Gentleman's Magazine* carried almost a half-century's worth of correspondence on the subject, and books of Hutchinsonianism continued to appear well into the first third of the nineteenth century.[21]

At the point where Blake entered the philosophical and scientific debate on matter, the atom had become far less inert, and even less substantive, than it had been in Newton's time, and the nature of light had become more problematic. Geoffrey Cantor has identified as many as four competing theories of light in the late eighteenth and early nineteenth centuries – two with a corpuscular basis: Newton's projectile theory and various fluid theories, including Hutchinson's; and two with a wave basis: the vibration theories of Euler and of Thomas Young, and the undulatory theory that Augustin Fresnel was to advance in 1815.[22] By the end of the eighteenth century dynamic alternatives had arisen, in both atheist and Christian formulations, to the hard-body theory of the atom. The atheist Holbach, in his *System of Nature* (1781), restored to atoms the energy and independent motility Gassendi had denied them; and the dissenting Unitarian minister and scientist Joseph Priestley went even further: in *Disquisitions Relating to Matter and Spirit* (published by Joseph Johnson in 1777), he proposed reactivated, ultrafine atoms as the substance of the soul. As John W. Yolton has shown,[23] Priestley's project arose out of an intense controversy generated by a passing remark of Locke's: that for all we know, God may have 'given to some Systems of Matter fitly disposed, a power to perceive and think' – it being no more difficult, Locke says, to 'conceive, that GOD can, if he pleases, superadd to Matter a Faculty of Thinking' than that he can superadd the soul to the body (*An Essay Concerning Human Understanding*, IV, iii, 6). Blake knew Priestley's work and reputation well enough to group 'd^r Priestley' with 'Bacon & Newton' in 'The Everlasting Gospel' (E519) and perhaps, as traditionally argued, to draw upon him for the character 'Inflammable Gass' in *An Island in the Moon*.

In his argument for the materiality of the soul, Priestley became the strongest voice in England to propose that the atom is an interplay of forces rather than a minute solid. Holding that 'matter is not that *inert* substance that it has been supposed to be; that *powers of attraction* or *repulsion* are necessary to its very being, and that no part of it appears to be *impenetrable* to other parts', Priestley seeks to remove 'the *odium* which hath hitherto lain upon matter, from its supposed necessary property of *solidity, inertness, or sluggishness*'. Quoting liberally from his own *History of Discoveries Relating to Vision, Light and Colours* (1772), Priestley develops the argument that matter has 'no properties but those of *attraction and repulsion*' and thus 'ought to rise in our esteem, as making a nearer approach to the nature of spiritual and immaterial beings' (p. 17). Blake's dictum in *The Marriage of Heaven and Hell* that 'Attraction and Repulsion' are 'necessary to Human Existence' (*MHH* 3, E34) may rest not only upon Newton's well-known use of these terms but also upon the new twist given them by Priestley. But for Priestley, objects are mostly void; the reason we cannot put our hand through a table is not because the table is solid but because the surface atoms of our hand and of the table mutually repel each other. Here Priestley, as he acknowledges, is modifying a theory that the Croatian priest and scientist Roger Joseph Boscovich had advanced in 1758, the notion that atoms are mathematical points without mass, with each atom the centre of a field that is alternately attractive and repulsive at varying distances; all chemical and physical properties of matter can be explained as interactions among these forces. Although Boscovich himself objected strenuously to the theological uses to which Priestley put his theory, Priestley, quoting his earlier book, insisted that his only departure from Boscovich's original theory 'would be to suppose the force of the sphere of repulsion next to any of the *indivisible points* . . . not to be absolutely *infinite*, but such as may be overcome by the momentum of light' (p. 23). William Nicholson, among others, found persuasive Priestley's argument that if 'we know that a sphere of repulsion exists as the proximate cause of our ideas of impenetrability and extension, why should we add to this an extended atom existing in the center of the sphere of repulsion?' (p. 29).[24]

Priestley finds grist for his mill in Newton's account of the passage of light through solids:

> When light is reflected back from a body on which it seems to strike, it was natural to suppose that this was occasioned by its impinging against the *solid parts* of the body; but it has been demonstrated by Sir Isaac Newton, that the rays of light are always reflected by a *power of repulsion* acting at some distance from the body. Again, when part of a beam of light has overcome this power of repulsion, and has entered any transparent substance, it goes on in a right line . . . without the least interruption and without a single particle being reflected, till it comes to the opposite side; having met with no solid particles in its way, not even in the densest transparent substances, as glass, crystal, or diamond . . .
>
> Now these facts seem to prove, that such dense bodies as glass, crystal, and diamonds, have no solid parts, or so very few, that the particles of light are never found to impinge upon them . . . and certainly till some portion of light can be shewn to be reflected within the substance of a homogenous transparent body . . . there must be all the reason in the world to believe, that no such resisting particles exist. All the phenomena may be explained without them, and indeed cannot be explained with them. (pp. 14–15).

To establish an atomic basis even for divine light, and for divinity itself, Priestley goes back to the decree of the council of Constantinople in 381 on *'uncreated light'* emanating from the divine essence 'which is, as it were, his garment, and which appeared at the trans-figuration of Christ'. He argues that the bishops 'must have believed God to have been a luminous substance; for it is impossible that a visible, and consequently a corporeal light, should be an emanation from a pure spirit' (p. 185). As a corollary, he cites a fourteenth century dispute in the Greek church on the question of how the light of the transfiguration, if uncreated and immaterial, could have been seen by bodily eyes.

Assisting with the de-solidification of the atom was the continuing popularity of what Arnold Thackray, borrowing a metaphor from Priestley, has termed the 'nutshell theory of matter'.[25] The Oxford lecturer John Keill had suggested, in the seventeenth century, that if we consider the ease with which the particles of light pass between the atoms in a window, and if we allow for the necessary void in spaces between particles, 'the quantity of matter in a piece of glass might have no greater proportion to the bulk of the glass than a grain of sand to the earth'. In *Letters on the English Nation*, Voltaire states that Newton, 'examining the extreme porosity of bodies, each part having its pores, and each part of those parts having its own . . . shows that there is no certainty that there exists a single cubic inch of solid matter in the universe, so remote is our intelligence from conceiving what matter is',[26] and the idea was widely repeated, by William Nicholson among many others. Priestley turns this concept back upon the proponents of solidity, wondering why, if there is so little solid matter in the universe, 'it did not occur to philosophers sooner, that perhaps there might be nothing for it to do after all, and that there might be no such thing in nature' (p. 17). In a private notebook Berkeley had already speculated that 'Matter tho' allow'd to exist may be no greater than a pin's head'.[27]

After Priestley, the history of the atom flows through two separate channels – speculative philosophy on the one hand and experimental science on the other, so that by 1841, when Marx completed his doctoral dissertation on Democritus and Epicurus, the philosophical atom was entirely distinct from the physical one.[28] In 1800 Volta announced the discovery of the pile, or battery, and Humphry Davy, assisted by the young Michael Faraday, put electrical energy to immediate use in isolating new chemical elements in his vastly popular lecture-demonstrations at the newly established Royal Institution in London. Though religious affiliation, political commitment and scientific orientation cannot be neatly correlated,[29] it is noteworthy that many English atomists of Blake's time were dissenting Christians. Both Davy, an Anglican, and Faraday, a member of an obscure Scottish sect, the Sandemanians, eagerly explored German nature-philosophy and made their way from Boscovichean point-atoms to dynamic force-fields. In 1803 the Quaker chemist John Dalton, who like Priestley was associated with a dissenting academy and shared his curiosity about Boscovichean short-range inter-atomic forces, gave his first series of lectures on his theory of atomic weights; later that year, according to a reviewer for the *Literary Journal*, in his general lecture series at the Royal Institution, he mentioned his 'very curious theory of *atoms'*. Dalton's *New System of Chemical Philosophy*, which appeared in separate parts in 1808, 1810, and 1827, is often considered the starting point for modern scientific investigation of the atom; the big drawback of the system, and the main reason Davy rejected it, was that it required a different atom for each element.[30] At exactly this time, in a series of papers written between 1799 and 1804, Thomas Young advanced the vibration theory of light, a precursor of the wave theory, to deal with anomalies that could not be explained by the Newtonian projectile model of granular particles of light. Young, too, was a dissenter, a Quaker who had studied at Göttingen, Leyden, Edinburgh and Cambridge universities.[31]

To us, it may appear quaint and eccentric that Blake, railing against the Newtonian calculus of fluxions in 1827, the last year of his life, declared the atom 'A Thing that does not Exist'. But I believe he chooses his metaphor purposefully, blurring the distinction between 'atom' and 'point', in full cognizance of the atom's controversial scientific and philosophical status. In rejecting the atom, he is not really concerned with what matter is composed of but with defending the integrity of singular, uncompromisable units of meaning in art and life. The immediate stimulus for his impassioned anti-atomistic diatribe was a discouraging sales report on the Job designs from his old friend George Cumberland:

> I know too well that a great majority of Englishmen are fond of The Indefinite which they Measure by Newtons Doctine of the Fluxions of an Atom. A Thing that does not Exist. These are Politicians & think that Republican Art is Inimical to their Atom. For a Line or Lineament is not formed by Chance a Line is a Line in its Minutest Subdivision Strait or Crooked It is Itself & Not Intermeasurable with or by any Thing Else Such is Job but since the

French Revolution Englishmen are all Intermeasurable One by Another Certainly a happy state of Agreement to which I for One do not Agree. God keep me from the Divinity of Yes & No too The Yea Nay Creeping Jesus from supposing Up & Down to be the same Thing as all Experimentalists must suppose[.] (E783)

For Blake, a true line can be only the firm, assured stroke of an artist, not some abstraction generated from a random succession of vanishing quantities in motion, as in the popular understanding of Newton's fluxional calculus. In graphic design, Blake's indivisible unit of meaning is the incised line, not the flicked-on dot or stipple that renders merely the illusion of a line in reproductive engraving; in society, his inviolable unit is the unique individual person in community, not an undifferentiated populace of docile subjects, or a mass market for commodified commercial art. Blake's concern about the intermeasurability of unique non-mechanical units must have been common at the time: in 1824, only a few years before the date of this letter, England had brought its 900-year-old profusion of local measurements under the central system of the imperial standard.[32] The French system weights and measures was also in transition, and Blake's reference to the French Revolution may have something to do with the post-Revolutionary scientific adoption of the metric system, in place of units like the English foot and the biblical cubit, both of which are based on the human body.

Blake's remarks are also thoroughly in keeping with the awkward status of the fluxional calculus in England. Newton's distinction between 'moments' and 'limits' had never been well understood, even among mathematicians, and terminology of the fluxionists was extremely loose.[33] Berkeley's *The Analyst* (1734) scorned Newton's fluxions as *'ghost of departed quantities'* and scoffed that 'he who can digest a second or third fluxion . . . need not, methinks, be squeamish about any point in Divinity'.[34] Even Voltaire, as Newton's champion, described fluxions as 'the art of numbering and measuring exactly something the very existence of which cannot be conceived'.[35] By the end of the century, English mathematicians, wedded to the clumsy notation and kinetic-geometric basis of Newtonian fluents, were becoming aware of their increasing isolation; lacking the Leibnizian analytical calculus, they were unable to follow Continental advances made possible by the use of multivariate functions, and their work had become irrelevant abroad. The 1799 publication of Laplace's

Celestial Mechanics, which was almost completely incomprehensible in England, finally broke the hold of fluxional calculus upon the English scientific community and paved the way for change in the educational system.[36]

Blake's querulous letter to Cumberland also makes sense in the context of the atom's uneasy status in natural philosophy. Only a year before Blake declared the atom nonexistent, Sir Humphry Davy had announced in his 1826 presidential address to the Royal Society that 'the term atom can only have the meaning "equivalent"' – that is, a unit of chemical proportion rather than a hard material entity.[37] Because the atom could not be verified experimentally, scientists no less than philosophers questioned its existence for the rest of the nineteenth century, with physicists moving only slowly from the concept of an indestructible particle to that of a nexus of forces, and with chemists finding the table of affinities a far better predictor of observable reactions than Dalton's atomic weights.

Nearly 200 years after Blake's writings on the atom, as superconducting supercolliders yield traces of ever-more-elusive subparticles and we look back before time to find the origin of matter in a singularity inconceivably smaller than Berkeley's pinhead, we continue in our own fashion to pursue the question raised in Blake's 1794 preludium to *Europe*: 'Then tell me, what is the material world, and is it dead?' Until all the experimental results are in, perhaps the Fairy's answer will suffice: 'I'll . . . shew you all alive / The world, when every particle of dust breathes forth its joy'. (*Europe* iii: 17–18, E60).

Notes

1. John Dunn, 'Practising History and Social Science on "Realist" Assumptions', *Action and Interpretation*, eds Christopher Hookway and Philip Pettit (Cambridge: Cambridge University Press, 1978) p. 169.

2. G.S. Rousseau and Roy Porter, 'Introduction', *The Ferment of Knowledge: Studies in the Historiography of Eighteenth-Century Science*, eds G.S. Rousseau and R. Porter (Cambridge: Cambridge University Press, 1980) p. 1.

3. As G.N. Cantor points out in 'The Eighteenth Century Problem', *History of Science* 20 (1982) pp. 44–63, matter theory was not 'a discrete country on the eighteenth century map of knowledge' but was woven into 'writings on mechanics, electricity, optics, theology, and epistemology' (p. 60). For Blake's response to the Newtonian strand, see Ault (1974) and Peterfreund (1990a).

4. Isaac Newton, *Opticks*, 4th edn (1730), ed. I. Bernard Cohen (New York: Dover, 1952) p. 400.
5. For further discussion, see Casper Hakfoort, 'Newton's Optics: the Changing Spectrum of Science', *Let Newton Be!*, eds John Fauvel et al., (Oxford: Oxford University Press, 1988) pp. 81–99.
6. See Paolo Casini, 'Newton: the Classical Scholia', *History of Science* 22 (1984) pp. 1–58, for the entire text; the Gregory quotation is from Casini (1984) p. 23n.
7. The most convenient compilation of surviving fragments of Democritus' thought appears in *Early Greek Philosophy*, trans. Jonathan Barnes (Harmondsworth: Penguin, 1987) pp. 244–88. For a readable modern account of classical atomism, see Cyril Bailey, *The Greek Atomists and Epicurus* (Oxford: Oxford University Press, 1928), and for particular application to Blake see Glausser (1991).
8. For a fuller account, see Lynn Sumida Joy, *Gassendi the Atomist* (Cambridge: Cambridge University Press, 1987).
9. Quoted by Gabriel Moked, *Particles and Ideas: Bishop Berkeley's Corpuscularian Philosophy*, (Oxford: Oxford University Press, 1988) p. 100.
10. For further discussion of cultural dissemination in Britain, see Thomas Franklin Mayo, *Epicurus in England, 1650–1725* (Dallas: Southwest Press, 1934); Robert Kargon, *Atomism in England from Harriot to Newton* (Oxford: Oxford University Press, 1966); Howard Jones, *The Epicurean Tradition*, (London and New York: Routledge, 1989); Richard W.F. Kroll, *The Material Word: Literate Culture in the Restoration and Early Eighteenth Century* (Baltimore: Johns Hopkins University Press, 1991).
11. G.N. Cantor, 'Weighing Light: the Role of Metaphor in Eighteenth-Century Optical Discourse', *The Figural and the Literal: Problems of Language in the History of Science and Philosophy, 1630–1800*, eds Andrew E. Benjamin et al (Manchester: Manchester University Press, 1987) pp. 124–46 (132).
12. The personal acquaintance is suggested in Rodney M. and Mary R. Baine, 'Blake's Inflammable Gass', *Blake Newsletter*, 10: 2 (1976) pp. 51–2; the vignette with Blake's signature is identified in Christopher Heppner, 'Another "New" Blake Engraving: More About Blake and William Nicholson', *Blake Newsletter*, 12: 3 (1978–79), pp. 193–7. Quotations from William Nicholson, *An Introduction to Natural Philosophy* refer to the 3rd edn (Philadelphia, 1788).
13. *Encyclopaedia Britannica: or, A Dictionary of Arts and Sciences. Compiled upon a New Plan . . .*, 3 vols, (Edinburgh, 1771; facs. Chicago: Encyclopaedia Britannica, c. 1968). Competing theories of light in this period are presented in G.N. Cantor, *Optics after Newton: Theories of Light in Britain and Ireland, 1704–1840* (Manchester: Manchester University Press, 1983); and challenged (with a reference to Blake) in Robert Palter, 'Some Impressions of Recent Work on Eighteenth-Century Science', *Historical Studies in the Physical Sciences* 19: 2 (1989) pp. 357–401.
14. Cantor (1987) p. 134.
15. Nicholson (1788) p. 213. For more on the 'ballistic' metaphor for the transmission of light, see Cantor (1987) pp. 135–9.

16. John Lockman's often reprinted translation of *Lettres Philosophiques* (1734), published in England a year *before* the French original as *Letters Concerning the English Nation* (1733), is the text Blake would have known; quotations here refer to Voltaire, *Letters on England*, trans. by Leonard Tancock (Harmondsworth: Penguin, 1980).

17. See Richard Yeo, 'An Idol of the Market-Place: Baconianism in Nineteenth Century Britain', *History of Science*, 23 (1985) pp. 251–98 (254–56).

18. [François Marie Arouet] Voltaire, *The Elements of Sir Isaac Newton's Philosophy*, trans. John Hanna (1738; facs. London, Frank Cass, 1967) p. 107.

19. See Danton B. Sailor, 'Moses and Atomism', *Journal of the History of Ideas* 24 (1964) pp. 3–46.

20. C.B. Wilde, 'Hutchinsonianism, Natural Philosophy and Religious Controversy in Eighteenth Century Britain', *History of Science* 18 (1980) pp. 1–24 (2).

21. For further details of Hutchinsonianism, see Wilde (1980); Albert J. Kuhn, 'Glory and Gravity: Hutchinson vs. Newton', *Journal of the History of Ideas*, 22 (1961) pp. 303–22; G.N. Cantor, 'Revelation and the Cyclical Cosmos of John Hutchinson', *Images of the Earth*, ed. L.J. Jordanova and Roy Porter (Chalfont St Giles: British Studies in the History of Science, 1979) pp. 3–22.

22. See Cantor (1983) pp. 129–46. For further discussion see Jed Z. Buchwald, *The Rise of the Wave Theory of Light* (London and Chicago: University of Chicago Press, 1989) and Eugene Frankel 'Corpuscular Optics and the Wave Theory of Light: The Science and Politics of a Revolution in Physics', *Social Studies of Science* 6 (1976) pp. 141–84.

23. John W. Yolton, *Thinking Matter: Materialism in Eighteenth-Century Britain* (Minneapolis: University of Minnesota Press, 1983) pp. 107–26.

24. This reference (p. xxxviii) and all subsequent quotations from Joseph Priestley refer to *Disquisitions Relating to Matter and Spirit and The Doctrine of Philosophical Necessity Illustrated* (1777; facs. New York: Garland, 1976).

25. Arnold Thackray, *Atoms and Powers: An Essay on Newtonian Matter-Theory and the Development of Chemistry* (Cambridge, Mass.: Harvard University Press, 1970) pp. 53–67.

26. Voltaire (1734/1980) p. 84.

27. As cited by Yolton (1983) p. 125n.

28. 'Difference Between the Democritean and Epicurean Philosophy of Nature' [Doctoral Dissertation, Berlin University, 1841], trans. Dirk J. and Sally R. Struik, Karl Marx and Frederick Engels, *Collected Works*, 1 (New York: International Publishers, 1975) p. 50. (For the whole dissertation, favouring the greater individualism of Epicurus, see pp. 25–105). See also Marx's 'Notebooks on Epicurean Philosophy' (1939), trans. Richard Dixon, in the same volume, pp. 403–509. For an interpretation of Marx's mature thinking on this issue, see Gideon Freudenthal, *Atom and Individual in the Age of Newton: On the Genesis of the Mechanistic World View' Boston Studies in the Philosophy of Science*, vol. 88 (Boston: D. Reidel, 1986).

29. See Simon Schaffer, 'Priestley's Questions: an Historiographic Survey', *History of Science* 22 (1984) pp. 151–83; and Robert E. Schofield, 'Joseph Priestley: Theology, Physics, and Metaphysics', *Enlightenment and Dissent* 2 (1983) pp. 69–81. Peterfreund (1990b) makes brief reference to Boscovich.

30. For further details on the debate surrounding hard-body and point-force atoms, see David M. Knight, *Atoms and Elements: A Study of Theories of Matter in England in the Nineteenth Century* (London: Hutchinson, 1967) pp. 16–59; Wilson L. Scott, *The Conflict Between Atomism and Conservation Theory, 1644–1860*, (London: Macdonald, 1970) pp. 185–211; Trevor H. Levere, *Affinity and Matter: Elements of Chemical Philosophy 1800–1865* (Oxford: Clarendon Press, 1972) pp. 23–106; and P.M. Heimann and J.E. McGuire, 'Newtonian Forces and Lockean Powers: Concepts of Matter in Eighteenth-Century Thought', *Historical Studies in the Physical Sciences* 3 (1971) pp. 235–57.

31. See Cantor (1983) p. 129.

32. Ronald Edward Zupko, *Revolution In Measurement: Western European Weights and Measures Since the Age of Science* (Philadelphia: American Philosophical Society, 1990) pp. 70–112. See also Peterfreund (1989).

33. Niccolò Guicciardini, *The Development of Newtonian Calculus in Britain 1700–1800* (Cambridge: Cambridge University Press, 1989) pp. 38–61.

34. Quoted in Cantor (1988) pp. 211, 214. Berkeley's resistance to the calculus is also discussed in relation to Blake in Nurmi (1957) pp. 208–9, Curtis (1972) pp. 462–3, and Ault (1974) pp. 102–3.

35. Voltaire (1734/1980) p. 86.

36. Guicciardini (1989) p. 141.

37. Humphry Davy, 'Discourses of the President, Anniversary, 1826', *Collected Works* II (London, 1840) pp. 96–7. Davy's objections are further discussed in Gerd Buchdahl, 'Sources of Scepticism in Atomic Theory', *British Journal of the Philosophy of Science* 10 (1960) pp. 120–34 and L.A. Whitt, 'Atoms or Affinities? The Ambivalent Reception of Daltonian Theory', *Studies in the History and Philosophy of Science* 21 (March 1990) pp. 57–89.

8

Innovative Reproduction: Painters and Engravers at the Royal Academy of Arts

D.W. DÖRRBECKER

And as usual, I could not help noticing how superior the copies were to the original. . . . and the copies are always the handsomest.[1]

At least where the self-conscious pictorial representation of their own social standing was at stake, even British architects, sculptors, and painters from the mid-eighteenth century onwards had finally secured for themselves and for their professions an elevated position among the *artes liberales*. In the young Joshua Reynolds's self-portrait, dating from the late 1740s, the painter's gaze is no longer that of a humble artisan, but is directed from his easel towards the sphere of his respectable and well-established patrons.[2] Clothed in an elegant frock coat, the painter has charged his own facial expression with his social ambition. It seems telling that Reynolds never again chose to picture himself with the tools of his trade.

Probably in the late 1770s, he produced another self-portrait. It was designed to be hung in the Assembly Room of the Royal Academy, of an institution, that is, of which Reynolds had become the first President about a decade earlier. Here, the formal references in the handling of light and colour go to Rembrandt, while the emulation of Michelangelo, whose overshadowed portrait bust appears to rest upon the shining presence of the proud painter's hand, supplies a keynote for the iconographic programme. No longer does the viewer encounter the fashionable, almost coxcomb dress of the earlier portrait; instead, the President of the Royal Academy is now seen in the dignified attire of a Doctor of Civil Law. Subsequent to his acceptance by the court, from which he had received a knighthood, the University of Oxford, in 1773, had bestowed an *honoris causa* doctorate upon this British prince of painters.[3]

Thus, the Academy self-portrait may stand for the most important social and ideological achievement of British high-brow artists during the eighteenth century, their arrival at a social position which Reynolds himself had addressed in a number of passages of his *Discourses*. Even in one of the very first sentences of his first annual lecture he had pointed out that the 'value and rank of every art is in proportion to the mental labour employed in it, or the mental pleasure produced by it. As this principle is observed or neglected, our profession becomes either a liberal art, or a mechanical trade'.[4]

Manual labour, work which requires one's entire physical strength, would from now on be derided by the President and his Royal Academicians. The business of the engravers entailed being bowed over copper plates for days, weeks and months, straining their eyes over the magnifying-glass while laboriously laying their mezzotint grounds, cutting their strokes, their dots and flicks, their worm lines, dots and lozenges. Artisans such as Valentine Green, whose job it was to transfer the formal self-portrait of the President of the Royal Academy to copper, were seldom deemed fit for 'good society'.[5] Seemingly rather indolent, the engravers had missed their connection; or, to be more precise, it had been seen to that they could not possibly get it. It is the success and failure in securing such social acceptance and the meaning of both for our own current approach towards the results of artistic labour, with which my slightly polemical paper is concerned.[6]

The functioning of 'corporate bodies' such as the academies of art was well understood by contemporaries; in the early 1820s, William Hazlitt defined them as:

> more corrupt and profligate than individuals, because they have more power to do mischief, and are less amenable to disgrace or punishment. They feel neither shame, remorse, gratitude, nor good-will. The principle of private or natural conscience is extinguished in each individual (we have no moral sense in the breasts of others), and nothing is considered but how the united efforts of the whole (released from idle scruples) may be best directed to the obtaining of political advantages and privileges to be shared as common spoil. Each member reaps the benefit, and lays the blame, if there is any, upon the rest. . . . 'Self-love and social' here

look like the same; and in consulting the interests of a particular class, which are also your own, there is even a show of public virtue.[7]

Consequently the issue of the control of representation was particularly acute in an era dominated by images printed from wood or metal plates and prior to the multiple media innovations of the twentieth century. During the pre-photographic centuries, printed reproductions of all sorts of pictures possessed a media value which can alone be compared to that of the similarly political consequence and authority of the word printed from movable type. And in some respects it may actually have been more important still, given the large percentage of illiteracy of those centuries.[8]

This simple insight is sufficient to demonstrate that as yet too small an intellectual investment has been made in the investigation of the genre of printed images, their production, distribution, and reception. This situation is no historical 'accident', and it cannot be 'excused' as such. It is unquestionable that in this field the history of art has inherited the hierarchy of the artistic and technical discriminations between the various genres that stem from particular and determinable conflicts of opposed interests, conflicts which have been encoded in certain figures of speech, and which can be decoded both in terms of the sociology of art and of politics.[9] If the intellectual position and status that is attributed to any research in the history of reproductive engraving is to change from what it is at present, one of the prerequisites must be the critique of the normative axioms which the academic discipline of the history of art has – consciously or unconsciously – first borrowed from the academic theory of only one of the parties, and an interested one for that, and which it now naively seems to accept as its own.

Following this preliminary outline, I wish to continue with a truism, before attempting a historical reconstruction of the ideological tenets that were at stake in the engravers' claims for their admission to full membership in the Royal Academy. Such a reconstruction may be of use (if not an absolute requisite) where one wants to trace and to eradicate the petrifaction of the historical quarrel between academicians and engravers in the language of current art historical discourse.

First then, something that we all know equally well, something that in one form or the other, in ourselves or in others, we have all experienced. It should serve for a backdrop against which the historical reconstruction will stand out in full relief. Upstarts, parvenus, are generally inclined towards unsocial, socially irrational behaviour. It therefore comes as no surprise to find that painters, sculptors and architects, once their professions had achieved 'nobility', once their social climbing from the ties of the guilds of 'mere' craftsmen had been crowned by success, were quick to withdraw those ladders that had proved instrumental in gaining access to the new and socially elevated station of the modern 'artist'.

During the second half of the eighteenth and the first decades of the nineteenth century, in a relatively short period of time, the social sub-system of the visual arts[10] in Britain and, especially, in the British metropolis underwent a series of vehement and truly radical changes. Unlike in Italy, France, the Netherlands, or the German-speaking countries, the stages of this development were here compressed into the course of only a few decades. From the guild organization of artistic labour they lead to its modern structure which is dependent on an anonymous art market, the economic weight of which was then much more substantial than is commonly known today.[11] The controversy between the 'elevated' arts of invention and that of the reproductive engravers was to turn into a conflict which centred on the academy as an institution of the most eminent sociological importance. This had not been the case in the other European countries. It meant, however, that the debate concerning 'original invention' and 'slavish reproduction' gained momentum not just for the sphere of economic machinations, but also achieved some relevance in the public discourse of aesthetics.[12] Furthermore, the British example seems particularly important on account of the many technical inventions of British engravers of the late eighteenth and early nineteenth century which resulted in the international reputation of engravers such as Strange, Sharp and Woollett.[13]

What are the results yielded by an examination and study of the sources relating to the 'engravers' battle' for academic recognition? Fairly concisely, they may be summed up like this. The establishment of an academy of arts in the British Isles came late. Much later than on the Continent. Well into the eighteenth century, the social status of British artists (and especially of those who were working in the provinces)[14] had remained more or less the same as that of any other artisan. When, on 5 November 1759, a congregation of artists at the Foundling Hospital aired their demands for instituting an academy as a place for exhibitions and for the education of artists, all the various media of the visual arts were represented. In consequence, the assembly referred to itself as 'a general meeting of all Artists in the several branches of Painting, Sculpture, Architecture, Engraving, Chasing, Seal-cutting and Medalling'.[15] Here then, the engravers were still accepted as the fourth estate among the society of artists. When only two years later Hogarth – of all people – designed the frontispiece for the catalogue of the 1761 exhibition of the Society of Artists of Great Britain, he subscribed to a reduction of these 'several branches' to the three major 'arts of design'.

It is this reduction and the canonization of painting, sculpture and architecture as the sole representatives of true 'art' that marks the beginning of the continuous struggle between the professions of the painter and the engraver. The memorandum of 28 November 1768, which was addressed to the king only two weeks before the official 'Instrument of Foundation' for the Royal Academy was signed by George III, similarly speaks of 'We, your Majesty's most faithful subjects, Painters, Sculptors, and Architects of this metropolis',[16] even though the document was also signed by Francesco Bartolozzi, at that time possibly London's most renowned and best-paid engraver. This isolation of the art of engraving from the so-called arts of 'invention' is then cemented with the first paragraph of the 'Instrument of Foundation' where the term 'artist' was defined by an interpolation saying that it was to be understood as applying exclusively to the professions of the painter, sculptor or architect.[17]

The exclusion of engravers was not agreed upon by the 36 founding members of the Academy without some inside opposition. Therefore, a compromise was offered to the refused class of artisan-artists on whose future cooperation depended the economic career of more than one of the painters. Six Associate Engravers of the Royal Academy were to be admitted, yet these were to be without any influence upon either the administration of the Academy itself, or upon its politics. The Academicians agreed upon this number of associate engravers as early as 19 January 1769, that is within only five weeks of the establishment of their new institution.[18] However, this offer of a compromise did not precisely seem a generous one. One may sympathize with the unwillingness of the engravers to accept it when measuring the six places for associate engravers against the number of 40 full members and further 20 Associate Royal Academicians from the ranks of the painters, sculptors and architects. Furthermore, the engravers were infuriated by the fact that any ARA had more than just a decent chance to become eventually a full member, while to engravers such advancement was to remain continually blocked.

Small wonder then, that the suggested compromise fuelled the fire rather than extinguishing it as had been intended. All the important and well-established engravers then working in London seem to have shared the view that the acceptance of the title of an Associate Engraver would mean humiliation rather than elevation. Robert Strange, one of the foremost victims of the expulsion of engravers from the Academy, commented on this move in his *Inquiry into the Rise and Establishment of the Royal Academy of Arts* of 1775: 'The remedy became worse than the desease. To save appearances with the public, they [the Academicians] now resolved to admit a certain number of engravers; but still to bring, as much as possible, the art into contempt. Care was therefore taken, that the *mode of admission* should effectually *exclude* every engraver, who has any of that conscious pride, which the better artists always possess.'[19] And it is with satisfaction that the pamphleteer remarks upon the 'considerable time [that] past [*sic*] before they could make any proselytes to their new association. Every artist of this profession, who had either spirit or abilities, entertained the utmost contempt for their proposal.'[20]

As early as January 1769 the General Assembly of the Academicians had also decided not to admit 'copies' of any kind to its exhibitions. Even without such 'non-original' works, the latter were indeed crowded by pictures and visitors alike.[21] The anti-copy rule proved to be of the utmost importance for the social discrimination between the academically approved representatives of the arts and the artisan engravers.[22] The academical argument concerning the different status of an 'original' and a 'copy', and therefore the different status appropriate for their respective producers, still loomed large over the refusal by the General Assembly in 1809 and 1812 of the elder Landseer's memoranda in favour of the admission of engravers to full membership in the Royal Academy.

In the Council's reply to Landseer, it was pointed out that as with earlier petitions of the engravers the Academicians agreed:

That all the Fine Arts have claims to admiration and encouragement, and honourable distinction, it would be superfluous to urge . . . but, that these claims are not all equal has never been denied [one may add: not even by the engravers themselves – DWD], and the relative pre-eminence of the Arts has ever been estimated accordingly as they more or less abound in those intellectual qualities of Invention and Composition, which Painting, Sculpture and Architecture so eminently possess, but of which Engraving is wholly devoid; its greatest praise consisting in translating with as little loss as possible the beauties of these original Arts of Design. With such an important difference in their intellectual pretensions as Artists, it appear'd to the framers of this Society that to admit Engravers into the first class of their Members, would be incompatible with justice and a due regard to the dignity of the Royal Academy.[23]

For a long time this was to remain the last word. And from Strange's *Inquiry* of 1775 it becomes evident that this was indeed a strategy followed from the very beginnings by that self-elected body of the 'first class' of artists:

Our academicians . . . therefore said, – that engravers were man [sic] of no genius, – servile copiers, – and consequently not fit to instruct in a royal academy. . . . In short every odium, that could be devised, was thrown upon this art; and those who professed it were held out to the public, as too contemptible to merit the attention of this establishment.[24]

The engravers were unable to refute the central argument of the Academicians which, idealistically and in an axiomatic manner, presupposes the higher claims of the 'design' as the 'original'. At the same time, however, the painters were at a loss to ward off the corresponding argument of the reproductive engravers. Time and again, from Strange's treatise onwards, it was insisted that the academy was made up only to a minimal extent of history painters as that class of artists which, according to its own theory, best represented the 'innovative' arts. The militant exponent of the losing fraction of artist endorsed this in a somewhat malicious note which testifies to the incompatibility of the two models of discourse that were employed by the competing parties:

I shall, indeed, so far agree with the royal academicians, that engravers in general are not qualified to instruct in an academy, no more than portrait painters, landscape painters, miniature painters, coach painters, &c. of which this academy is chiefly composed. It is well known that in all academies, properly regulated, the task of instructing is reserved for historical-painters and sculptors only: so that in reality . . . there are few of our royal academicians who are properly qualified to instruct, or capable of drawing a figure, with either propriety, taste or elegance.[25]

Let me attempt to clarify the issues here at stake in both theory and practice from a variety of interpretative vistas. For the sake of brevity, I shall concentrate on Sir Joshua Reynolds and his earliest opponent in this question, Sir Robert Strange.

At the very beginning there is the quest for the contribution of the visual arts to the self-definition of society. Such self-definition, during the eighteenth century, employed the new understanding that was then first applied to the word 'nation'. Only three weeks after the Royal Academy had been established, on 2 January 1769, Reynolds opened the first of his academical *Discourses*, addressed to the upper classes of the public, with the following sentences:

An Academy, in which the Polite Arts may be regularly cultivated, is at last opened among us by Royal Munificence. This must appear an event in the highest degree interesting, not only to the Artists, but to the whole nation. . . . An Institution like this has often been recommended upon considerations merely mercantile; but an Academy, founded upon such principles, can never effect even its own narrow purposes. If it has an origin no higher, no taste can ever be formed in manufactures; but if the higher Arts of Design flourish, these inferior ends will be answered of course.[26]

In one of his subsequent speeches, in 1790, Reynolds returned to this polarity between 'considerations merely mercantile' and a view towards the improvement of 'manufactures' on one side – which had probably been inspired by the founding in 1648 (and Colbert's subsequent managing) of the Académie Royale at Paris – and the 'higher' ends of the 'Arts of Design' on the other:

The Art which we profess has beauty for its object: this it is our business to discover and to express; but the beauty of which we are in quest is general and intellectual; . . . but which he [i.e. the artist] is yet so far able to communicate, as to raise the thoughts, and extend the views of the spectator; and which, by a succession of art, may be so far diffused, that its effects may extend themselves imperceptibly into publick benefits, and be among the means of bestowing on whole nations refinement of taste: which, if it does not lead directly to purity of manners, obviates at least their greatest depravation, by disentangling the mind from apetite, and conducting the thoughts through successive stages of excellence, till that contemplation of universal rectitude and harmony which began by Taste, may, as it is exalted and refined, conclude in Virtue.[27]

The British engravers answered such idealist conceptions of the contribution made by the visual arts to the education of public taste, and thereby to social virtue with a retort rooted in middle-class ideologies. Thus, Strange concluded the open letter which serves as an introduction to his *Inquiry* by characterizing his trade as 'a profession, which has been honoured in the most civilized countries: a profession which is now a credit and advantage to this kingdom in particular, as well as an ornament to the arts in general.'[28] With the first of Reynolds' *Discourses* in mind, he then begins his pamphlet with some patriotic confessions that seem to answer those of the President of the Academy:

The progress of the fine arts cannot but attract the attention of every lover of his country. Connected with various branches of manufactures, they become objects of importance in a commercial kingdom.[29]

The mercantile and materialist reasoning in which the development, even of the arts, is seen as dependent upon economic factors, is antithetically opposed to the intellectual self-definition of the members of the Academy who, in order to justify their own sacrosanct position, constantly had recourse to the venerable tradition of the *artes liberales*.

There was good reason for the Academicians to declare and define their own working processes as being intellectually more elevated than those of the 'servile copiers'. They knew all too well that in the end – and despite the hierarchical subordination of the 'arts of manufacture' under those 'of design' which had been proclaimed by their President – they could not easily falsify the engravers' claims that the reputation and financial success of a painter depended to a large extent on the services of the engravers. In order to illustrate this fact, one may refer to James Barry's 'Lear and Cordelia', a picture painted for Boydell's 'Shakspeare Gallery', and to Francis Legat's engraving which was the *raison d'être* for the commissioning of the oil.[30] Legat's dexterity, the varied patterns of his strokes, cut in the manner of Strange, gives an idea of the high quality of the 'translations' of paintings into prints that were executed by reproductive engravers at the end of the eighteenth century. From Hogarth onwards, it had been the latter, and not the painters, who had opened up a modern British art market for the first time, and, more particularly, a market for history and subject paintings by British artists. Without them that genre of painting which held the foremost rank in the academy's theoretical hierarchy might well have remained an entirely fictional one.[31]

There can be little doubt that the public reputation of numerous members of the British Royal Academy, and their chances to secure new and ever more commissions, was measured until well into the nineteenth century by their ability to find a ready market for reproductions of their paintings at one of London's numerous print shops. On this economic front it made little difference whether the reproductive engravings came in the form of large-scale 'furniture prints', or in that of a small-sized book illustration.[32] Also, it was no secret at all that the income of an artist such as Thomas Stothard RA stemmed almost exclusively from commissions for book illustrations, and that Joseph Mallord William Turner RA, just as Henry Fuseli RA, earned a vital share of their profits by working for the publishers of illustrated books.[33]

On the art market then, the representatives of the 'Arts of design' had to rely on the cooperation of that 'lower' class of artisans, the engravers. In addition, some of the engravers who in the manner of Strange concentrated on the reproduction of old master paintings, demonstrated that they themselves could do quite well without the Academicians' current supply of 'original inventions'. Yet of course, it was not just the painter who was partly dependent upon the engraver and his employer, the print or book publisher. The dialectical structure of eighteenth- and nineteenth-century print culture also dictated that the latter had to take pains to sign the most renowned representatives among the painters to supply them with the designs for reproductions.

In 1775 Strange had informed his readers that 'No body knew better, or has more experienced, than Sir Joshua Reynolds the importance of engraving: and especially in a country where the arts, yet in their infancy, were now to be improved by a school of painting.' Even though, according to Strange, the painters at the Royal Academy were found 'totally insensible of what could not but affect their own reputation': and accordingly he had

> appeal[ed] to their understandings, whether perpetuating the merit of their works to posterity, supposing them to be men of abilities, must not, in a great measure, depend upon the perfection of engraving, an art, which they meant to disgrace by this exclusion? . . . Since the memorable area of the revival of the arts, in the fifteenth century, I know no painter, the remembrance of whose works will depend more on the art of engraving than that of Sir Joshua Reynolds. This was not the case with the great masters, Titian, Rubens, Vandyke &c. Their works have stood the test of ages, . . .[34]

In their durability they may be contrasted to the works of the President and his colleagues whose paintings (mostly on account of their use of bitumen as a ground) had begun to deteriorate even during the painters' lifetimes.

Reynolds's constant use of the notions of 'limitation' and of 'copying' marks another factor that seems of the foremost importance for an understanding of the implications of the historical quarrel between painters and engravers, and for the deconstruction of its consequences in modern art historical thought. It is these concepts which mediate between academical art theory and academical teaching and production practices. According to the founding president of the Royal Academy, the unfaltering imitation of the canonized works of the old masters paves the way to every possible excellency in modern art. And it is this road that has to be followed by genius and by merely talented artists alike if they ever want to produce original inventions of their own.[35] It is the practice of imitation, the constant study and the discriminate selection of the excellencies of the old masters which for Reynolds characterizes the intellectual and scholarly activity of the painter and as such legitimizes his claims for representing one of the liberal arts. Therefore, he informed his audience that to

> derive all from native power, to owe nothing to another, is the praise which men, who do not much think on what they are saying, bestow sometimes upon others, and sometimes on themselves: and their imaginary dignity is naturally heightened by a

supercilious censure of the low, the barren, the grovelling, the servile imitator.[36]

The vocabulary employed in this rebuke to the older, pre-Winckelmann literature of art, in which 'almost all imitation, which implies a more regular and progressive method of attaining the ends of painting, has ever been particularly inveighed against with great keenness, both by ancient and modern writers,'[37] is interesting in two respects. On one side, it is clearly reminiscent of the phrasing which was used during the foundation period of the Royal Academy through to 1812 in order to describe the qualitative distance between the so-called 'innovative' arts and the trade of the engravers which was then said to be concerned with mere 'servile imitation' of the inventions of others.[38] On the other side, Reynolds's claims for artistic imitation (however distinct from the practice of 'servile copying'), in accordance with the views of Sir Robert Strange, implicitly acknowledge that the nation's visual culture determined both the initial training at the Royal Academy Schools and the ultimate education of the public taste. And, to be sure, the President himself never attempted to conceal the extent to which his own innovative ideas were actually indebted to the contents of his well-filled print portfolios.[39]

The reproductive engravers asserted that by making accessible the works of the old masters, just as those of the contemporary painters, they too, and in a large measure, were involved in fulfilling the academical programme for the education of public taste. Moreover, they proudly maintained that on account of the 'democratic' character of their art, which was within the financial reach of a much wider public than that of the painters, his work made the engraver a 'member of [the state] virtuously useful, and [he] contributes in his sphere to the general purpose and perfection of society,'[40] exactly that which Reynolds had claimed for the academical painter in the ninth of his *Discourses*.

At least indirectly, these extravagant claims were not only endorsed within the discourse of contemporary art criticism, but also pictorially in a painting by Nathaniel Hone. His satirical account of the 'original inventions' of the President of the Royal Academy, when submitted for exhibition at the Royal Academy in 1775 under the title 'The Pictorial Conjuror, Displaying the Whole Art of Deception', was to cause what until then must have been the biggest scandal at the newly-founded academy surrounding any single work.

Hone, an enemy of Reynolds prior to Blake, went to some pains with his art historical research when working on the programme for his painting. Today, with Panofsky, one may describe his composition with the alternative title of 'Problems in Reynolds: Mostly Iconographic'. There is no need to go into much detail here, yet a few hints at Hone's pictorial attack on the President's claims at inventiveness may not be out of place.[41]

Hone's magician bears the likeness of Reynold's favourite model, George White, draped in the manner of Rembrandt. If this is a hint at the President's source for the handling of light, shade, colouring and decorum in his paintings, and his reliance on the tradition of seventeenth-century Dutch 'naturalism', then the whirlwind of reproductive engravings that the 'Conjuror' has set into motion by a touch of his wand is an outspoken reference to the numerous borrowings of motifs from the works of the old masters (mostly of the Italian sixteenth-century school) which, during the past years, the President had implanted into his 'original inventions'. As has been demonstrated by diligent twentieth-century art historians, every single one of the reproductive prints illustrated in Hone's painting had indeed been employed in one of the productions of Reynolds's genius. No doubt, the Royal Academy's first President knew very well what he was speaking about when stating that 'nothing can come of nothing'.[42]

For any estimate of the innovative potential inherent in reproductive prints, it is crucial to be aware of the radical changes that eighteenth-century engravers had introduced to their medium. From the standard seventeenth-century practice of the mixed-media plate, prepared by etching and then finished with the graver in the line manner, the way leads towards a rich spectrum of methods of laying the lines themselves. In addition, alternative modalities of representation could be achieved by the use of the mezzotint and aquatint, the stipple and crayon techniques which could also be employed in numerous and complex combinations.

Each newly perfected tool, the roulette or the chalk-roll, the matting-wheel or the mace-head, and every new working process of the engraver, has to be seen as the equivalent of a parallel revision of the viewing conventions of the users of printed images. The engravers developed a precise vocabulary of parameters for the visual translation of the material and tactile qualities as well as the colour of physical reality.[43] Where modern art historians and connoisseurs, when faced with eighteenth-century reproductive

engravings, are wont to bemoan the 'loss of identity' in the
individual 'handwriting' of the engravers, they overlook the
engravers' own intentions. For the latter, such 'loss' meant a gain: it
allowed them to supply the public with an increased amount of
'rationalized' truth, of almost scientific 'intermeasurability' of the
messages of their images.[44]

Starting out from similar thoughts in 1806, John Landseer in his
third lecture on *The Art of Engraving* drew the following conclusions:

> Now, Engraving is no more an art of copying Painting, than the
> English language is an art of copying Greek or Latin. Engraving is
> a distinct language of Art: and though it may bear such resemb-
> lance to Painting in the construction of its grammar, as grammars
> of languages bear to each other, yet its alphabet and idiom, or
> mode of expression, are totally different . . . An Engraving there-
> fore – that of the death of General Wolfe, for example, is no more a
> copy of Mr. West's picture, than the same composition, if sculp-
> tured or modelled in low relief, would be a copy. In both cases
> they would be, not copies, but translations from one language of
> Art, into another language of Art.[45]

By introducing the concept of 'translation' then, it became possible
for Landseer and his contemporaries to seize upon the paradox of
an 'original reproduction'.[46]

Despite Landseer's repeated attempts (including his 1806 lectures
which were published the following year and his memoranda of
1809 and 1812) to push the Academicians from inside the institution
to credit the work of outstanding engravers with full membership,
the old agreement concerning the 'slavish' character of reproductive
engraving remained effective well beyond the mid-century. It was
only in 1928 that the engravers at the Royal Academy were able to
secure the final privilege of a quorum. At that time the art of engraving had actually lost all contact with the reproduction of images,
that is, with what had previously stigmatized it for the adherents of
the bourgeois academic understanding of art, and it had therefore
also lost all its former economic importance.[47]

In historical terms this means that the painters had actually
succeeded in defending their differing claims to rank of the producers of 'original' inventions and those of 'servile' copies. They
held their position up to that point in history when the trade of
reproductive engraving had died at the hands of the various photo-

graphic processes, and when the body of engravers that remained was made up almost exclusively of *peintre-graveurs*.[48] Again, Hazlitt's brilliant attack on societies and other corporate bodies may serve to sum this up – and without keeping tongue in cheek:

> Age does not improve the morality of public bodies. They grow more and more tenacious of their idle privileges and sense-less self-consequence. They get weak and obstinate at the same time. . . . They become more attached to forms, the more obsolete they are . . .[49]

The engravers' struggle for official recognition as artists at the London Royal Academy may seem just another chapter from history, an unhappy one like so many others, of no particular importance, and here not even told for the first time. Its result, however, is still with us, and that is why the 'engravers' battle' for academic status is of importance even today.

Art history as a separate discipline came into being at approximately the same time as the Royal Academy. And it has, probably often without even knowing it, perpetuated a classification of the various genres of the visual arts that had clearly been shaped under the influence of considerations which did not just follow any arbitrary set of abstract aesthetical values, but which had been the consequence of distinct interests in social status and economic power. Therefore, and in conclusion, it is necessary briefly to address the issue of the zombie existence of the past conflict in present art historical research and, more particularly, the language of such research.

The present collection of articles is intended to supply a kind of neohistoricist answer to the 1982 Santa Cruz 'Blake and Criticism' conference and the *Critical Paths* leading Blakeans towards 'the Argument of [deconstructive] Method' (Hilton and Vogler, 1986; Miller et al., 1987). Therefore, it seems appropriate to round off this historical sketch with at least a few hints at the lasting impact of the past debate on present-day procedures in art historical discourse.

Just as John Landseer, when delivering his lectures on *The Art of Engraving* to his audience at the Royal Institution during 1806, and before the time when slide projectors became generally available in lecture theatres and class-rooms, art historians were literally burdened down by our heritage of printed images. In the manner of Jacob Burckhardt, each of the professors must have been dragging

huge portfolios to the auditorium which contained whatever reproductions they had laboriously assembled over the years.

Such a physical burden was combined with the more intellectual
awareness of the insufficiency of all reproductions wherever a
discussion of the real thing was at stake (that is, where the engraved
reproduction is not itself the subject of the scholarly discourse). This
awareness may have been similar to that of the limitations of teaching art history by means of slides that many colleagues in art-history
departments will share today, and it may have contributed to the fact
that even at the end of the twentieth century art history, as it is
taught at most of our universities, disclaims the inheritance of reproductive engraving as part of its canon. Rather, in its business of historical interpretation it still prefers to seize upon exactly that sort of
material that had previously been 'nobilitated' by the ranking system
of eighteenth-century academies of art – upon 'original inventions'
that is. Though by now most artists seem to have given up on any
such hierarchies of subject-matter, working materials, or production
techniques, art-history still treads that trodden path of academicism.

Writing in 1951, Paul Oskar Kristeller remarked that the decisive
importance of the eighteenth century for the history of aesthetics and
art criticism had then been generally acknowledged.[50] All of the
changes and differences of opinion during the past two hundred
years presuppose a set of basic assumptions that have come to us
from that classical century of modern aesthetics. It was only then that
terms such as taste and perception, genius, originality, and creative
imagination were given their present meaning. Furthermore, it has
frequently been pointed out that even the notion of 'art' and the
related idea of the 'fine arts' were coined only during the eighteenth
century. It may be added that this is also the case with terms such as
'society' (meaning bourgeois society), 'state', and 'nation'.

Not just terminologically, but also ideologically the 'modern
system of the literature of art' has preserved the basic structures of
discourse that had been brought into being by a series of academic
and political controversies between artists. Thus, the familiar social
conflict that I have described in some detail, can also tell us about
the genesis of a series of terminological preconceptions which are
of central importance for the understanding of both art and art
history since the eighteenth century. The social history of art will
here have to be understood either as a process that involves the
criticism of ideologies and their linguistics or it will not be understood at all.

Art historians are used to measuring and describing the innovative potential of any given work by its distance in the treatment of subject-matter and form from those buildings, sculptures, or paintings that can be considered as the artist's own models, as the particular tradition that they were working in. Today, many artists search for new forms by consciously distancing themselves from tradition, and the measure of such distance will be described and remunerated on the art market under the label of 'originality'. The engravers of the eighteenth century, however, made their inventions in the service of the best possible approximation of what they found and saw in the designs they were to reproduce, no matter what the technique that had been used to produce their models. It was this thrust of their inventions toward the production of what we have learned to term a 'facsimile' that stigmatized the products of their inventiveness as mere 'copies'.

In case the classification of art historical categories remains dependent upon the creative processes employed by the artists themselves, and I see no reason to object to this, it would seem about time – centuries from Dürer's copies after Mantegna and the copies of Rubens after Titian, or just a few decades from Picasso's 'translations' of Velázquez and Bacon's 'reproductions' of Van Gogh – to scrutinize and radically rethink its notions of 'original' and 'copy'.

Notes

1. Mark Twain [Samuel Langhorne Clemens], *The Innocents Abroad: or, The New Pilgrims' Progress*, vol. 1, Author's National Edition: The Writings of Mark Twain 1 (1889; St. Clair Shores, Mich.: Scholarly Press, 1977) pp. 247–8. In revising the conference paper for publication, and on account of the printing space allotted to each of the contributors to the present volume, I had to abridge text and notes alike. In particular, the visual material that accompanied the original paper in the form of a series of slides, and its discussion had to be sacrificed.
2. See Joshua Reynolds's 'Self-Portrait Shading the Eyes' of c. 1747–49 (London, National Portrait Gallery), reproduced in Nicholas Penny, ed., *Reynolds*, exh. cat. (London: Royal Academy of Arts, in association with Weidenfeld & Nicolson, 1986) no. 13.
3. The self-portrait 'Sir Joshua Reynolds, DCL', c. 1773–80 (London: Royal Academy of Arts), is reproduced in Penny 1986, no. 116. See Fritz Saxl and Rudolf Wittkower, *British Art and the Mediterranean*, 2nd edn (London: Oxford University Press, 1969) 67.7, who identify the bust as a copy of Daniele da Volterra's portrait of Michelangelo.

4. Sir Joshua Reynolds, *Discourses on Art*, ed. Robert R. Wark, 2nd rev. edn (New Haven, Conn. and London: Yale University Press, for the Paul Mellon Centre for Studies in British Art, 1975) p. 57.

5. See Valentine Green's mezzotint after Sir Joshua Reynolds, 'Sir Joshua Reynolds, DCL', 1780 (London: British Museum Print Room) in Penny, 1986, no. 117.

6. For the history of the conflict between Academicians and engravers, see Celina Fox, 'The Engravers' Battle for Professional Recognition in Early Nineteenth Century London', *London Journal* 2 (1976) pp. 3–31, and John Gage, 'An Early Exhibition and the Politics of British Printmaking, 1800–1812', *Print Quarterly* 6 (1989) pp. 123–39.

7. William Hazlitt, 'On Corporate Bodies', essay XXVII in *Table Talk: or, Original Essays*, ed. P.P. Howe, *The Complete Works of William Hazlitt* 8 (1931; New York: AMS Press; and London: Frank Cass, 1967) p. 264. In the same essay the Royal Academy is described as 'a kind of hospital and infirmary for the obliquities of taste and ingenuity – a receptacle where enthusiasm and originality stop and stagnate', p. 269.

8. '. . . what is the use of that art of Engraving, of which Printing is the proper termination? The answer will be short: – It disseminates every valuable discovery in mechanical, chemical, agricultural, architectural, and astronomical, Science: It renders the scenery of remote countries, the distinguished features of our own, or the more delightful ideal scenery of highly gifted imaginations, familiar to every class of the community: By multiplying the vivid beams of embodied Intellect, which emanate from the mind of the poetic Painter, it becomes the radiance of his glory, and the organ of public instruction: It diffuses the fame, with the portraits, of the patriotic and illustrious: It consecrates and embalms the memory of the brave.' – John Landseer, *Lectures on the Art of Engraving. Delivered at the Royal Institution of Great Britain* (London: Longman, Hurst, Rees, and Orme, 1807) p. 280. For much the same sentiments, one may turn to the relief and inscription of Banks's monument to Woollett on the Western walls of the cloisters of Westminster Abbey: 'WILLIAM WOOLETT: / BORN AUGUST XXII.^{D}MDCCXXXV, / DIED MAY XXII.^{D}MDCCLXXXV: / INCISOR EXCELLENTISSIMUS / [tablet with Banks's relief, showing an engraver surrounded by a number of allegorical figures that are described in what follows] / T. BANKS, R. A. / SCULP.^{T} / THE GENIUS OF ENGRAVING / HANDING DOWN TO POSTERITY / THE WORKS OF PAINTING, SCULPTURE, AND ARCHITECTURE: / WHILST FAME IS DISTRIBUTING THEM / OVER THE FOUR QUARTERS / OF THE GLOBE.' The monument was commissioned in 1791 and erected the following year; see C.F. Bell, ed., *Annals of Thomas Banks, Sculptor, Royal Academician* (Cambridge: Cambridge University Press, 1938) p. 82.

9. For a similar statement see, for example, Werner Busch, *Joseph Wright of Derby: Das Experiment mit der Luftpumpe: Eine Heilige Allianz zwischen Wissenschaft und Religion*, Kunststück: Fischer Taschenbuch 3941 (Frankfurt am Main: Fischer Taschenbuch Verlag, 1986) p. 9.

10. For the theoretical concept of artistic and intellectual sub-systems see Pierre Bourdieu, *Zur Soziologie der symbolischen Formen*, trans. Wolfgang Fietkau, Suhrkamp Taschenbuch Wissenschaft 107 (Frankfurt am Main: Suhrkamp, 1974) pp. 76–86 and passim.

11. One may think of the example of William Woolett's reproductive engraving after Benjamin West's 'Death of Wolfe' (1771). Issued by John Boydell in 1776, by 1790 this print had earned its publisher the enormous sum of £15 000. Economically even more important was the well-known project of the Shakespeare Gallery, for which see Winifred H. Friedman, *Boydell's Shakespeare Gallery*, Outstanding Dissertations in the Fine Arts (New York and London: Garland, 1976); and Sven H.A. Bruntjen, *John Boydell, 1719–1804: A Study in Art Patronage and Publishing in Georgian London*, Outstanding Dissertations in the Fine Arts (New York and London: Garland, 1985). The economics of the British print culture are also dealt with in two exhibition catalogues that bear upon various aspects of my paper: see David Alexander and Richard T. Godfrey, *Painters and Engraving: The Reproductive Print from Hogarth to Wilkie* (New Haven, Conn.: Yale Center for British Art, 1980), and Brenda D. Rix, *Pictures for the Parlour: The English Reproductive Print from 1775 to 1900* (Toronto: Art Gallery of Ontario, 1983). Contemporary sources documenting the profits of the export trade in British prints can be found in William T. Whitley, *Artists and Their Friends in England 1700–1799*, vol. 2 (London and Boston: Medici Society, 1928) 72. For an important early critique of the links between the art of engraving and the commercial interests of the publishers see Landseer, 1807, xi–xxii, 295–304, 309–19, and passim. The same criticisms, put forward in a less obliging manner, loom large behind the attack on the 'Monopolizing Trader', on 'Booksellers & Trading Dealers' in Blake's draft of c. 1810 for a 'Public Address': see E576, and, with useful commentary on the background, Read, 1981.

12. For the politically concrete meaning of terms such as 'liberal arts' or of 'slavish and servile copying', see Barrell, 1986. For some wider contexts in which these terms were embedded see Michael Meehan, *Liberty and Poetics in Eighteenth-Century England* (London: Croom Helm, 1986) and Gerald Newman, *The Rise of English Nationalism: A Cultural History. 1740–1830* (London: Weidenfeld & Nicolson, 1987).

13. One may think of Winckelmann's statement that Strange is 'außer allem Zweifel der größte Künstler unserer und vielleicht aller Zeiten in seiner Kunst' (here quoted from Carl Justi, *Winckelmann und seine Zeitgenossen*, 4th edn, vol. 2 [Leipzig: Koehler & Amelang, 1943] p. 166), of the estimate of Strange as 'unquestionably the best engraver England ever produced' (John Thomas Smith, *Nollekens and His Times*, vol. 2 [London: Henry Colburn, 1828] p. 247), or of Raimbach's recollections of a visit paid in 1802 to the studio of the French engraver Bervic: 'His apartment in the Louvre was hung round with Woolett's [*sic*] finest landscapes, of which he spoke in raptures as miracles d'harmonie' (Abraham Raimbach, *Memoirs and Recollections of the late Abraham Raimbach, Esq. Engraver*, ed. M.T.S. Raimbach [London: Frederick Shoberl Junior, 1843] pp. 53–4 n. 73).

See also Richard and Samuel Redgrave, *A Century of Painters of the English School*, vol. 1 (London: Smith, Elder, 1866) p. 463, etc.

14.　For questions relating to the development of the British art world outside London, see Trevor Fawcett, *The Rise of English Provincial Art: Artists, Patrons and Institutions outside London, 1800–1830*, Oxford Studies in the History of Art and Architecture 12 (Oxford: Clarendon Press, 1974).

15.　Here quoted from Sidney C. Hutchison, *The History of the Royal Academy 1768–1968* (London: Chapman & Hall, 1968) p. 35.

16.　Hutchison, 1968, p. 43.

17.　'I.　The said Society shall consist of forty Members only, who shall be called Academicians of the Royal Academy; they shall all of them be artists by profession at the time of their admission, that is to say, Painters, Sculptors, or Architects, . . . ' (here quoted from Hutchison 1968, p. 209). That besides Bartolozzi another engraver numbered among the founding members was thought to be of little consequence; for both an elegant, though somewhat hypocritical way out was used by admitting them as a painter (Bartolozzi) and as a sculptor (Yeo) respectively. Just as the rule itself, the exception of Bartolozzi's inclusion among the founding members of the Academy fuelled the attacks on the institution and on Bartolozzi himself in Robert Strange, *An Inquiry into the Rise and Establishment of the Royal Academy of Arts* (London: E. & C. Dilly, J. Robson, and J. Walter, 1775) pp. 113–14 (for the personal disagreements between the two engravers see pp. 20–41).

18.　See Hutchison, 1968, p. 53.

19.　Strange, 1775, p. 124 (the emphasis is part of the original text).

20.　Strange, 1775, p. 126.

21.　Some visual proof for this assertion is provided by Pietro Antonio Martini's engraving after John Henry Ramberg, 'The Exhibition of the Royal Academy, 1787'; or by Richard Earlom's mezzotint after Charles Brandoin, 'The Royal Academy Exhibition of the Year 1771', published in 1772, and by various similar pictorial representations of the annual exhibitions.

22.　The following rule applied to the annual exhibitions: 'No Picture copied from a Picture or Print, a Drawing from a Drawing; a Medal from a Medal; a Chasing from a Chasing; a Model from a Model, or any other species of Sculpture, or any Copy be admitted in the Exhibition' (here quoted from Hutchison 1968, p. 54). For the prehistory of the conflict produced by this regulation see also Strange 1775, pp. 42–52.

23.　Here quoted from Hutchison 1968, pp. 89–90; for Landseer's new advance see also John Evan Hodgson and Fred A. Eaton, *The Royal Academy and Its Members 1768–1830* (London: John Murray, 1905) p. 297.

24.　Strange, 1775, pp. 117–18.

25.　Strange, 1775, pp. 118–19.

26.　Reynolds, 1975, p. 13: for the functioning of the arts in the self-definition of the nation which evidently was of such vital importance to Reynolds see the discussion in Barrell, 1986.

27.　Reynolds, 1975, p. 171.

28. Strange, 1775, pp. 58–9.

29. Strange, 1775, p. 60.

30. See James Barry's painting 'King Lear Weeping over the Dead Body of Cordelia', 1786–87 (London: Tate Gallery), which is discussed by William L. Pressly, *The Life and Art of James Barry,* Studies in British Art (New Haven, Conn. and London: Yale University Press, for the Paul Mellon Centre for Studies in British Art, 1981) pp. 234–5, no. P29, and Francis Legat's engraving after Barry's oil, first published in 1792, and then issued as part of the *Collection of Prints, from Pictures Painted for the Purpose of Illustrating the Dramatic Works of Shakspeare, by the Artists of Great Britain,* vol. 2 (London: John & Josiah Boydell, Shakspeare Gallery, 1803 [1805] pl. XL.

31. Writing in retrospect during the 1850s, Charles Robert Leslie commented: 'But for engraving . . . Hogarth must have confined himself to portraits on which he might have starved, for he was never popular as a portrait painter. But when the prints of 'The Harlot's Progress' appeared, 1200 copies were immediately subscribed for. This was the beginning of the patronage produced for painting by engraving', *Autobiographical Recollections,* ed. Tom Taylor, (1860; Wakefield, W. Yorks.: EP Publishing, 1978) vol. I, p. 214.

32. A short introduction to eighteenth-century 'furniture prints' can be found in David Alexander, *Affecting Moments: Prints of English Literature Made in the Age of Sensibility 1775–1800* (York: University of York, 1986) pp. 2–4. On British book illustrations of the eighteenth and nineteenth centuries see Edward Hodnett, *Image and Text: Studies in the Illustration of English Literature* (London: Scolar Press, 1982), and (to my taste by far the better book) Richard D. Altick, *Paintings from Books: Art and Literature in Britain, 1760–1900* (Columbus: Ohio State University Press, 1985). For an account of some of the economic speculations involved, readers may want to turn to Bentley, 1980.

33. For a recent case study see Shelley M. Bennett, *Thomas Stothard: The Mechanisms of Art Patronage in England circa 1800* (Columbia: University of Missouri Press, 1988).

34. Strange, 1775, pp. 120–1.

35. 'Invention, strictly speaking, is little more than a new combination of those images which have been previously gathered and deposited in the memory: nothing can come of nothing: he who has laid up no materials, can produce no combinations'. However, two pages later Reynolds warns 'How incapable those are of producing any thing of their own, who have spent much of their time in making finished copies . . . ' (1975, pp. 27–9). In Henry Fuseli's 'Lecture VII: On Design' academic terms such as 'original' and 'copy' are used to perpetuate ideas about the social position of the 'humble copyist' or the 'noble rank of an artist'; see *Lectures on Painting by the Royal Academicians,* ed. Ralph N. Wornum (London: Henry G. Bohn, 1848) pp. 491–2.

36. Reynolds, 1975, p. 95.

37. Reynolds, 1975, p. 95.

38. Once more, see Strange, 1775, pp. 117–18, and the Minutes of the General Assembly for 1812 as cited by Hutchison 1968, pp. 89–90.

39. The same function was to be served by the library of the Academy; its holdings were particularly strong in print publications, offering a rich harvest for the students' and members' stock of ideas. See paragraph XX in 'The Instrument of Foundation' of the Royal Academy of Arts (cited in Hutchison, 1968, p. 212).

40. Reynolds, 1975, p. 171.

41. For the following discussion of Nathaniel Hone, 'The Pictorial Conjuror, Displaying the Whole Art of Deception', 1775 (Dublin: National Gallery of Ireland) see Hutchison, 1968, 58–9: Martin Butlin, 'Angelika und 'The Conjuror', in *Angelika Kauffmann und ihre Zeitgenossen*, exh. cat., ed. Oscar Sandner (Bregenz, Aus.: Vorarlberger Landesmuseum: and Vienna: Österreichisches Museum für Angewandte Kunst, 1968) pp. 29–36. In the present context, the most important study of Hone's painting is John Newman, 'Reynolds and Hone: "The Conjuror" Unmasked', in Penny, 1986, 344–54.

42. See Reynolds, 1975, p. 27 (as quoted above).

43. For an excellent account of the elaborated syntax of eighteenth-century reproductive engravings see William M. Ivins, Jr, 'The Tyranny of the Rule: The Seventeenth and Eighteenth Centuries', in *Prints and Visual Communication* (London: Routledge & Kegan Paul, 1953) pp. 71–92.

44. Blake, who knew the requisite vocabulary well enough, first suffered such 'standardization' at the hands of Schiavonetti and then attacked it violently in his 'Public Address'. The best exposition of the theoretical implications of Blake's somewhat idiosyncratic position is Eaves, 1977.

45. Landseer, 1807, pp. 176–8.

46. In 1769, however, Reynolds had already employed the concept of 'translating' for the contrary purpose (Reynolds, 1975, p. 28); see also John W. Draper, 'The Theory of Translation in the Eighteenth Century', *Neophilologus* 6 (1921) pp. 241–54.

47. For the belated recognition of engraving as one of the fine arts see Trevor Fawcett, 'Graphic versus Photographic in the Nineteenth-Century Reproduction', *Art History* 9 (1986) pp. 185–212.

48. The fate of the engravers at the London Royal Academy thus resembles that of the female artists: there had at least been two women, Mary Moser and Angelica Kauffmann, among the founding members of 1768; however, just as the Associate Engravers, they were not accepted as equals and were not allowed to take an active part in the administration of the Academy, its schools and exhibitions. It took a full 150 years until, during the 1920s, the male academicians could make up their minds to elect another woman as an R.A. See Hutchison, 1968, pp. 47, 60–1.

49. Hazlitt, 1931 and 1967, p. 267.

50. Paul Oskar Kristeller, 'Das moderne System der Künste', *Humanismus und Renaissance II: Philosophie, Bildung und Kunst*, ed. Eckhard Keßler, trans. Renate Schweyen-Ott, UTB 915 (Munich: Wilhelm Fink, n.d. [1980]), pp. 164–5.

9

The Sins of the Fathers: Patriarchal Criticism and *The Book of Thel*

HELEN BRUDER

Feminist literary criticism, since its very inception, has worked to turn critical orthodoxies upside down and, in Blakean cadence, to reveal the infinite which was hid and the sexism which had been ignored. One of the most valuable ways in which this re-visioning has been achieved is through fiercely direct (as well as subtly oblique) polemical assaults on the truths and truisms of patriarchal criticism. The ground of academic debate has been so radically shifted because feminists have, quite simply, moved it from under the feet of their institutionally ensconced fathers.

Feminist criticism of Blake, however, has largely failed to undertake this enterprise. Faced by an urbanely sexist critical establishment, feminist Blakeans opted for assimilation. Though these writers employed some diversity of methodology they shared the desire to complement rather than violently challenge orthodox readings of Blake's work; with a few honourable exceptions (eg. Langland, 1987; McClenahan 1990, in their keenness to offer (just) another perspective they seem, sadly, to have forgotten the importance of mental fight.

In this essay I hope to show that a historically engaged and combative feminism is intellectually productive and urgently needed. Taking Blake's dictum 'Severity of judgment is a great virtue' (*Ann. Lav.* 36, E585) as my guiding principle, I intend both to demonstrate that patriarchal critics (and their acolytes) have got away with numerous unchastised interpretative transgressions, and to establish the existence of a neglected feminist dimension to Blake's long acknowledged radicalism. I have limited myself to analysing *The Book of Thel* and the criticism ensnaring it, but the validity of my case-study has wider implications.

147

The Book of Thel may seem a rather diminutive example but it is an immensely important poem. Dated 1789, it appears to be the first illuminated narrative Blake produced and one he continued to offer for sale throughout his life (see Bogen, 1971: xiii–xiv). Blake's evident commitment to the work, however, was not shared by those men who worked for his canonization; they found it a deeply embarrassing poem and strove, through critical assessments of extravagant condescension, to marginalize it comprehensively. Northrop Frye blushed even to comment on such a fragile work, merely noting how deft Blake was at avoiding the 'namby-pamby' (Frye, 1947: 233). David Erdman was similarly uninterested in a work written before the ardour of Orc had arisen and he waved the poem aside as 'a sort of mystery play for adolescents' (Erdman [1954] 1977: 130, 132). S. Foster Damon (although chronologically prior to Frye and Erdman), completed the trinity with his patronizing declaration that this was merely an aberration, Thel being 'far too nice a girl to fit in amongst Blake's furious elementals' (Damon [1965] 1988: 401).

Although such stances have left as their legacy the constant assertion that *Thel* is 'completely accessible' (Nurmi, 1975: 69) in its 'delicacy and gentleness' (Fuller, 1988: 33), these three respected patriarchs of Blake studies were, for once, not at all prophetic. Once the metaphysicians had been displaced and the poem's protagonist acknowledged to be an inquisitive and slightly truculent young woman there was an explosion of works impelled by moral imperatives.

The first blast of this particular trumpet was issued by Robert F. Gleckner who, at the end of the 1950s, savaged Thel's behaviour with an almost rabid ferocity.[1] Not only is she a selfish and vain spiritual failure whose 'real self' is 'ugly, cold, mean' and 'dark' but she is also a despot, bearing 'no distant resemblance' to Urizen who presides over the Vales of Har as its Queen, wearing 'the crown of luxury, pride, material comfort' and 'power'. Gleckner ended his orations with the definitive statement 'In Blake's eyes Thel is obviously a sinner' and it would be fascinating to trace in detail the manifold ways in which critics following Gleckner have demanded her repentance. In *Thel* criticism, prescriptiveness and didacticism reign to an extent unprecedented in Blake studies. The corpus of criticism forms a kind of dictatorial conduct book of the sort which abounded at the time *Thel* was written and whose motivations, I would argue, the poem exposes.[2] For *The Book of Thel* is a poem in which the sceptical enquiries of a determined young woman thoroughly unmask patriarchal ideology, an ideology which promised women that conventional romantic and maternal roles equalled heavenly fulfilment but which, Thel discovers, amount to nothing less than death. According to *The Book of Thel*, life under patriarchy is a grave-plot. To elaborate this contention, I'll briefly run through the major events of the narrative.

The first contentious question about Thel's biography is what the realm of the Seraphim is and why Thel chooses to leave it? One popular belief, emanating from Gleckner (1959: 162–3), is that this is a region of deserving higher innocents who, in Michael Ferber's elaboration, live exalted lives circling around God the sun/Son (1980: 49). There is but scanty evidence for such rosy claims, which leave their authors with the problem of explaining why Thel would want to leave such bliss. For a more convincing answer, we need to turn to Mary Wollstonecraft's insight into the motivation behind patriarchal associations of the female with the ethereal. 'Why', Wollstonecraft asked, 'are girls to be told that they resemble angels; but to sink them below women?'[3] This is precisely the fate of Thel's older sisters, confined as they are to the dizzyingly futile task of leading 'round their sunny flocks' (*Thel* 1:1, E3). But Thel, having spent slightly less time amongst the sheep, is not so mesmerized, and sensibly decides to leave such an unimpressive life. She has not, however, got much of an idea of what to do once she reaches the illicit 'secret air' (*Thel* 1:2, E3), and this is why she laments.

Her speeches have received much critical attention, with not a few writers joining David Wagenknecht in his assessment that Thel 'prattles amiably but pointlessly' (1973: 155); even Hilton finds her 'caught in the wilderness of herself' (1983: 3). Nearly all commentators also claim that her main concern is with mortality and the transience of life (e.g. Ferber, 1985: 152). Yet, however strong this critical consensus may be, it fails to account for the almost ludicrous excessiveness of the poem's form. We could, perhaps, believe mortality was worrying Thel if she had simply said 'O life of this our spring! why fades the lotus of the water? / Why fade these children of the spring? born but to smile & fall' (*Thel* 1: 6–7, E3) but once the flow of similes begins we become aware that something rather more subversive is going on.

I think Blake is exploding stereotypical notions of youthful femininity by pushing them to their limits and hence revealing their absurdity. These lines can be read as a kind of satire on Edmund

Burke's highly influential, and roughly contemporaneous, notion of female beauty with its stress on smallness, delicacy and weakness. If we look closely at part of Burke's 'Recapitulation' to the *Philosophical Enquiry*, we find a key intertext:

> On the whole, the qualities of beauty, as they are merely sensible qualities, are the following. First, to be comparatively small. Secondly, to be smooth. Thirdly, to have a variety in the direction of the parts: but, fourthly, to have those parts not angular, but melted into each other. Fifthly, to be of a delicate frame without any remarkable appearance of strength. Sixthly, to have its colours clear and bright, but not very strong and glaring.[4]

As she laments, Thel is not engaged, as Gleckner claims, in 'masterful self-analysis' (1959: 163) but rather mercilessly parodies this flexi-woman construction of femininity. As Lavater puts it, 'The primary matter of which women are constituted appears to be more flexible, irritable, and elastic, than that of man', a sentiment taken up in Wollstonecraft's complaint that 'all women are to be levelled, by meekness and docility, into one character of yielding softness and gentle compliance'.[5]

Having opened her new existence by exploding such notions of female beauty, Thel is ready to 'come out' into a social world where she will defy many other conventional expectations. At this point she is in a parallel situation to William Hayley's appalling paragon, Serena, in *The Triumphs of Temper*: 'For now she enter'd those important years / When the full bosom swells with hopes & fears'. But, as we will see, Thel cherishes a nobler ambition than simply 'To love & be belov'd: she has faculties to unfold and independence to attain.[6]

As we move on to look at Thel's conversations it becomes essential to move away from the virtually undisputed critical assumption of the 'dysfunction' of dialogue within the poem (Linkin, 1987). Although Susan Fox rightly stressed that this is the first poem in which multiple perspective is the governing principle (1976: 7–8), most critics have tended to deny this interactive polyphony by insisting that the Lilly, Cloud and Clod are simply Thel's self-projections; she being, as Marjorie Levinson puts it, basically a ventriloquist (1980: 289: see also Wagenknecht, 1973: 152). In this way Thel's problems are reduced to those of consciousness only and the insights she gains into the functioning of partriarchy and its justificatory ideologies are dismissed as merely examples of her misperception (e.g. Heppner, 1977: 85) As my case unfolds it will become clear how far I diverge from the opinions of the many critics who claim that Thel is ignorant and myopic (e.g. Gleckner, 1960: 573; Read, 1982: 167).

The initial point to make about Thel's dialogue with the Lilly is that it does not provide evidence of the poet's enthusiasm for some harmonious natural cycle to serve as a guide to human action (see Pearce, 1978). Rather, what he is exploring is the naturalizing function of ideology: as the illumination on plate 2 makes clear, the Lilly is a woman much like Thel who has learnt to think of herself as a diminutive weed through patriarchal insinuations. Indeed, through the insinuations of the ultimate patriarch, she knows she is a small, weak, watery plant who loves to dwell in lowly vales (*Thel* 1: 16–18, E3–4) because every morning God the Father spreads His hand over her head and tells her so, daily reminding her that she is a 'humble' 'gentle' 'modest' maid (*Thel* 1: 21–2, E4). This uninspiring message is only slightly sweetened by His promises of life after death in some allegorical abode, and it is the chance of fulfilling this feminine role which is supposed to placate Thel's unease: 'why', asks the Lilly after she has explained her situation, 'should Thel complain, / Why should the mistress of the vales of Har, utter a sigh' (*Thel* 1–2: 25–1, E4)?

Thel continues to object because she has been perceptively observing the situation. The intensity of her gaze is quite marked as she encounters the Lilly on plate 2, and the critics who suggest that she is a victim of her own slipshod perceptions would do well to consider this habit of close and attentive scrutiny which is also evident on the title-page and on plates 4 and 5. She has learnt that the Lilly's lot is a great deal more strenuous and perilous than her words have led us to believe. In particular Thel is distressed by the masochism inherent in giving this kind of nurture. Brenda Webster is right to speak of *Thel* in relation to images of sacrifice and devouring (1983: 31–60) because in minding 'her numerous charge among the verdant grass' (*Thel* 2: 18, E4) the Lilly actually loses her life. She is cropped by infectious lambs and ultimately dismembered to provide a bed for the infant worm. It is this self-annihilation that Thel will not accept, she wants an independent life that leaves a mark and her demand 'who shall find my place' (*Thel* 2: 12, E4) has brought her a great deal of criticism. D.G. Gillham speaks for many when he opines 'Thel has given nothing [. . .] There is no generous

impulse here, only a self-centred and self-pitying wail that contrasts
with the selflessness of the modest Lilly' (1973 1982; see also
Johnson, 1970; and George, 1980: 98). Thel is clearly in trouble for
lacking that 'Propensity to Devotion' which James Fordyce felt to be
such an essential ingredient in any eighteenth-century woman's
character.[7] The painfully credulous Lilly, however, simply takes Thel
at her word: as she has described herself as 'a faint cloud kindled at
the rising sun' (*Thel* 2: 2, E4) the Lilly assumes that a cloud must
obviously be called forth to answer Thel's questions. Having hailed
the next interlocutor, she shuffles off to die in some quiet corner of
the valley.

Thel's encounter with the Lilly has allowed her to unfold her
reasoning faculties and extend her confidence. She is literally buoy-
ant when the Cloud approaches, addressing him as a little figure
and charging him to answer her queries (*Thel* 3: 1, E4). She will need
this self-will, for the Cloud is the only adult male Thel addresses in
the Vales of Har, and her feeling that they share a similar problem of
lack of recognition for their grievances evaporates immediately she
sees his form. Unlike the other creatures Thel encounters, the Cloud
is not self-effacing, pale or earthbound but rather 'shew'd his
golden head & his bright form emerg'd, / Hovering and glittering
on the air' (*Thel* 3: 5–6, E4). Thel had thought he simply shed his
water and vanished but this male youth has a much brighter fate, as
he tells her 'when I pass away, / It is to tenfold life, to love, to peace,
and raptures holy' (*Thel* 3: 10–11, E4–5).

The Cloud, in short, seems to enjoy an eternal life of endless
happy copulation. Although many writers have acknowledged his
sexual significance, what they have not acknowledged is the deeply
suspicious nature of the bliss he enjoys. Annette Levitt roundly condemns Thel for retaining unacted desires in the face of his sexual
appeal, insisting that she finds Comus-like danger in a figure who
has no negative qualities whatever (1978: 72–83; compare Lattin,
1981). But this is an erroneous claim for the Cloud is merely more
honest than Comus about his exploitative masculinist activities, telling us quite openly about his unseen descent upon female flowers
and of the marked lack of enthusiasm displayed by his bride ('the
fair-eyed dew'), who weeps and 'trembling kneels' as a prelude to
their union (*Thel* 3: 12–14, E5). As the title-page's illumination makes
quite clear, aggressive male sexuality is one of the main problems
that Thel has to face: and although Erdman has stressed the
relevance of the botanical machismo of Erasmus Darwin's *Loves of*

the Plants to *Thel*, most critics have preferred to enthuse over the 'whirling vortex of pleasure' (Mitchell, 1978: 105) they find in the sexual encounter depicted on the title-page (despite the posture of upreaching arms repeatedly used by Blake to indicate female distress [see *America*, cancelled plate c]). The now venerable tradition of deploring Thel's 'deep fear of the phallus' (Linkin, 1987: 69) has served only to negate the legitimacy of her complaints: though the majority of *Thel*/Thel critics assume that illogical sexual tentativeness is habitual among young women, why, after all, shouldn't she protest about the prospect of being groped like the woman whose fate she observes on the title-page?

Moreover, such criticism tends to obscure the acute perception Thel now has of the divergent parenting activities of the sexes: having heard the Cloud's account of sexual union and child-rearing Thel declares 'I fear that I am not like thee' (*Thel* 3: 17, E5). One look over the page vividly illuminates why she feels her difference. The headpiece to plate 4 offers an unequivocal message: Thel stands mimicking the outstretched arms of the Cloud, but as he gusts energetically on the breeze she looks down at an infant, lying by her feet. Sex means motherhood, and motherhood in this patriarchal environment means self-sacrifice. All will indeed say 'without a use this shining woman liv'd' (*Thel* 3: 22, E5) if she chooses not to become a mother and yet, as Thel complains, accepting available maternal roles is as good as dying and becoming the food of worms. The speaking of this taboo truth forces the Cloud to reveal his allegiances and he answers her with a piece of exemplary utilitarian sexism.

Pompously reclining upon his airy throne, the Cloud shows himself to be a kind of winged Rousseau: 'Then if thou art the food of worms[...] How great thy use/ how great thy blessing' (*Thel* 3: 25–6, E5).[8] As a woman Thel's greatest blessing is to be useful and that she rejects such logic becomes clear when she gets a chance to exercise this sacrificial feminine prerogative (see Wagenknecht, 1973: 158).

The Worm is a dual symbol, representing both an infant and a penis and Thel reacts to each connotation in a different way. When perceiving the creature as a baby she pities its naked and helpless form but, nevertheless, refuses to answer its cries and nourish it with 'mothers smiles' (*Thel* 4: 6, E5). This is a rejection that has done little to endear Thel to her critics who continue to offer up a near universal cry against her selfishness. Thel's reaction to the Worm's phallic dimensions has done little to ameliorate their displeasure, for her immediate response is to express astonishment at its unimpressiveness.

That Blake entertained no Lawrencian reverence for the penis is well evidenced here. 'The nakedness of woman' may well be 'the work of God' (*MHH* 8: 25, E36) but Thel's smirky 'Is this a Worm?', 'Art thou a Worm? image of weakness. art thou but a Worm?' (*Thel* 4: 2–5, E5) suggests that at least one aspect of the nakedness of man has no such divine associations. This has a good deal of political significance because, although Blake was always able to balance negative images of the vagina (the veil of Vala and so on) with positive ones (the wonderful bursting flower chorus that opens the second book of *Milton*), his feelings about the male genitals became more and more wholeheartedly negative. By the turn of the century erection, for example, is treated not as a pleasure but as a veritable affliction (see the description of the Spectre of Urthona / Los's trials with his 'veiny pipes' *FZ* 50: 11, E333). In *Jerusalem* sexual arousal draws men into ever more intimate contact with their Spectres (see *J* 6: see also Reide, 1981). With the phallus so radically compromised it is but a short step to the act of questioning all phallocratic authority. However suggestive this line of argument, as far as *Thel*'s narrative is concerned it is the Worm's infant needs that are most significant, for they bring forth Thel's final, and most instructive, communicant.

When the Clod of Clay, much critically praised for her 'admirable abjectness', slumps forward to tend the infant worm we see epitomized the version of motherhood which Thel has rejected (Grant, 1969: 342: see also Johnson, 1970: 269; and Hilton, 1983: 30). This decision is made because she is the very antithesis of the rational or republican mother celebrated by Wollstonecraft, and many other contemporary feminists.[9] Unlike Wollstonecraft's reasoning mother who performs her nurturing tasks as a human duty based on a sense of self-worth and adult capability, the Clod has accepted without qualification the Cloud's hypocritical male philosophy: 'we live not for ourselves' (*Thel* 4: 10; cf. 3: 26–7, E5). Hence she has no self-esteem: 'Thou seest me the meanest thing, and so I am indeed', and she has accepted sado-sexual religious rationalizations of her situation: 'But he that loves the lowly, pours his oil upon my head. / And kisses me, and binds his nuptial band around my breast'. Most importantly, the Clod is incapable of questioning her condition: 'But how this is sweet maid, I know not, and I cannot know, / I ponder, and I cannot ponder; yet I live and love' (*Thel* 4: 11–15: 6, E5–6).

Thel, on the other hand, having learnt that she too partakes with man of the gift of reason, soon discovers that the Clod has been seduced into a role if slavery and self-annihilation. Anyone who exhales her life in 'milky fondness' (*Thel* 4: 8–9, E5) has been gulled in the most grotesque way if she believes that this amounts to having 'a crown that none can take away' (*Thel* 5: 4, E5). The Clod, in short, is the living embodiment of Wollstonecraft's claim that 'The being who patiently endures injustice, [. . .] will soon become [. . .] unable to discern right from wrong': 'Man, taking her body, the mind is left to rust'.[10]

We do, however, need to appreciate the totality of the Clod's role because Blake is not only exposing the injustice of her situation, but also wanting us to see the value of her capacity for love, however excessively employed. Hence, although Thel maintains her complaint about fading from a significant role in life (*Thel* 5: 12–13, E6) she is deeply moved by the Clod's suffering example, sufficiently so to make the courageous decision to enter Matron Clay's house.

Plate 6 is where Thel has achieved her general reputation as a cowardly hysterical failure, and I think it is important to note initially how brave a figure she is (see Pearce, 1978, for a general survey of opinion since 1890). Before Thel reaches her grave-plot she passes, without flinching, through a number of utterly agonized wastelands, 'where never smile was seen' (*Thel* 6: 5, E6). That the majority of Blake's expositors find it impossible to imagine a young woman who is courageous must not be allowed to blind us to his capacity to do so. Indeed, the disservice done to the poet's feminism by the existence of sexist critical orthodoxy is nowhere more evident than in commentary on the voice from Thel's grave.

Most critics aim at denying the validity of Thel's vision of her future life, choosing rather to read the voice as yet another example of her perverted understanding (see Lattin, 1981: 21). As Gleckner explained, it is only because Thel is dazzled 'by her own brilliance' that experience looks like 'a chamber of horror' (1959: 169). After all, the voice is speaking of what Thel's life will be like if she grows up in the Clay's house, as part of the community we have seen throughout the poem, and any perception of that as destructive must surely be wrong. 'No reader questions the vast difference [. . .] between the vales Thel inhabits [. . .] and the startling land unknown' (Linkin, 1987: 71). My reading is a questioning of this distinction. What Thel is actually hearing is a bitingly honest account of what her life as a woman will be like in an environment where males, through either charm or violence, invade her senses, and as I've tried to show, when stripped of its obfuscating quasi-religious and pastoral imagery, this invasion is precisely the situation that exists in the Vales of Har.

What makes the poem really valuable is that Thel's voice also manages to hint at a solution: by exclaiming against the patriarchal fetishizing of the hymen as an oppressive curb to an erotics of mutual delight, Thel offers a way beyond the deathly future which had seemed to be her, and indeed every woman's, fate.[11] To hear such a vibrant and sexually challenging message emerge from the lips of a young woman who was so unimpressed by earlier displays of the phallus has thrown the critics into disarray, even leading some to wonder whether Thel actually speaks the final two lines (e.g. Wagenknecht; 1973: 162: see also Levitt, 1978: 81; and George, 1980: 94, 97). Yet it is only because of Thel's cumulative scepticism about phallocentric practices that this particular insight is at all possible.

Her final shriek, as Anne Mellor hints (1971), is one of violent denunciation and Thel flees back to Har to reanimate her dissenting 'sighs' and 'moans' which the patriarchally saturated Clod had momentarily called down (*Thel* 5: 14, 15, E6).[12] Thel could indeed, as Nancy Bogen suggested nearly twenty years ago, become the leader of a protest movement, and the sexual politics displayed on plate 6, which ushers her back into the vales, certainly tend to reinforce this claim: a young girl confidently holds the reins of the phallic serpent whilst a young boy directs his attention to caring for a straggling infant (Bogen, 1973: 30) This is 'innocence organized' in a very new way. At the poem's close, then, Thel is certainly set to shake things up in the Vales of Har. Through her encounters with both the female Moles and the male Eagles, Thel has achieved some of that strength of body and mind which Wollstonecraft thought essential for women's advancement, and there is no saying what kind of 'revolution' in 'Female manners' that might lead to.[13]

Sadly, this is not a standard reading of the text. Apart from K.D. Everest's excellent discussion of Thel's specifically female dilemma (1987), no one has pursued any of the feminist implications of this luminously woman-centred poem (e.g. Simpkins, 1988; Swearingen, 1989–90), and this must now amount to a critical scandal. If my contribution has begun convincingly to address this negligence it will have achieved my primary aim, but if it encourages others to join in this salutary corroding of the critical establishment something much more significant will have been set in motion. Perhaps by the start of the next century the sinning fathers of Blake studies will have been comprehensively exposed, and their tomes left ragged and increasingly dusty. As ever we must wait and see, but one thing is certain: if feminists do not set about liberating a new Blake we can be sure that others will step forward only too happy to 'repeat the same dull round over again' (b: E3), and 'May God us keep' from such stultifying 'Single vision' (E722).

Notes

1. See Gleckner's work over thirty years (1959: 157–74 [esp. p. 168]; 1960: 574–80, [esp. 578–9]; 1985: 28–47, 287–302). The seminal importance of Gleckner's censorious work has been noted by Mary Lynn Johnson: 'Together [. . .] Gleckner and Tolley shifted critical attention from the metaphysical to the moral sphere, where it now rests' (1985: 215).

2. For a discussion of this material see Nancy Armstrong and Leonard Tennenhouse, *The Ideology of Conduct* (New York and London: Methuen, 1987), and William St. Clair, *The Godwins and the Shelleys* (London: Faber & Faber, 1991) pp. 504–11.

3. Mary Wollstonecraft, *Vindication of the Rights of Woman: with strictures on political and moral subjects* (1792), *The Works of Mary Wollstonecraft*, 7 vols, Janet Todd and Marilyn Butler (eds) (London: William Pickering, 1989) vol. 5, p. 164.

4. Edmund Burke, *A Philosophical Enquiry into the Origin of our Ideas of the Sublime and Beautiful* (1757) 6th edn 1770, pp. 222–3.

5. Reverend John Caspar Lavater, quoted in *Britannic Magazine* 4 (1796) p. 109. See also Wollstonecraft (1989) vol. 5, p. 165.

6. William Hayley, *The Triumphs of Temper* (1781) 10th edn 1799, pp. 2, 6. Compare Wollstonecraft (1989) vol. 5, pp. 73, 65–6, 94–5.

7. James Fordyce, *The Character and Conduct of the Female Sex* (1776) p. 45.

8. See the extract from Rousseau quoted, with no little displeasure, by Mary Wollstonecraft (1989) p. 149.

9. One of the best discussions of the rise of the moral mother is provided by Jane Rendall, *The Origins of Modern Feminism* (London: Macmillan, 1985) pp. 33–65.

10. See also Wollstonecraft's question, 'Who made man the exclusive judge, if woman partake with him of the gift of reason?' (1989) vol. 5, p. 67, and Blake's 'A Little Boy Lost' (*Songs* II, 15–16, E29). Blake scholars have not agreed with Wollstonecraft's censure of Cloddish ponderlessness. While Wollstonecraft stressed that 'when forbearance confounds right and wrong, it ceases to be a virtue' (1989) vol. 5, p. 102, Thel's critics have praised the Clod's limitless self-sacrifice. As Gleckner explains, the Clod 'gives to all; she is the great earth mother [. . .] By merely living and loving, acting and being, she has attained the higher innocence and this is all you know and all you need to know' (1959: 169).

11. When Thel's voice exclaims against the 'little curtain of flesh on the bed of our desire' (*Thel* 6: 20 E6) she is not protesting at the physical existence of the hymen (in itself a diminutive membrane of 'little' importance) but rather, as Hilton says, against 'the significance *invested* in it' (1983: 130–2). For an account of some eighteenth-century significances see Paul Gabriel Bouce, 'Some Sexual Beliefs and Myths in Eighteenth Century Britain', *Sexuality in Eighteenth Century Britain*, P.G. Bouce (ed.) (Manchester: Manchester University Press, 1982) pp. 28–46 (see esp. 33–5).

12. But see also Mellor's recent unflinchingly hostile article on *Songs* (1988) which suggests that she has departed from this position.

13. See Wollstonecraft, 1989, vol. 5, p. 114.

10

Blake's Changing View of History: The Impact of the Book of Enoch

JOHN BEER

Previous essays in this collection have discussed and demonstrated Blake's responsiveness to the historical processes that were unfolding about him during his lifetime, particularly in the last decade of the eighteenth century. The events of the French Revolution, the rise of industrialism, the ravages of war, domestic English politics, all find some reflection in his pages. He was equally perceptive concerning the manner in which the poor are overlooked and marginalized in every age.

It is also important to recognize the extent to which Blake sometimes *avoided* documentary presentations of events. Even in the writings that are 'historical' in nature there are occasional distortions: for *The French Revolution* he invented, as the 'ancientest Peer', the Duke of Burgundy, thus enabling himself to introduce the symbolism of blood and wine, while the 'sickening' of the Archbishop of York in *America* seems to have had no counterpart in real life.[1] In *Europe* 'Golden Verulam' is sited on the 'infinite shores of Thames'; and if Erdman is right to identify the 'Guardian of the secret codes' there with Chancellor Thurlow's behaviour in 1792 history is then turned back on itself, for that episode is followed by Newton rising up to blow 'the Trump of the last doom' (Erdman 1977: 216–18, *Eur* 10: 5, 12: 15, 13: 2, E63–5). As one looks at these and other documents it becomes clear that Blake would not concern himself with chronological or geographical accuracy if a change or invention provided a vivid means of suggesting a significance. When he dealt in prophecy, similarly, it was not a matter of trying to foretell future events; as he remarked in his annotations on Watson's *Apology for the Bible*:

159

Prophets in the modern sense of the word have never existed
Jonah was no prophet in the modern sense for his prophecy of
Nineveh failed Every honest man is a Prophet he utters his opinion both of private & public matters / Thus / If you go on So /
the result is So / He never says such a thing shall happen let you
do what you will. a Prophet is a Seer not an Arbitrary Dictator.

(*Ann. Wat.*, E617)

He was not attempting to escape from history; his concern was
rather with the extent to which events in history might themselves
be shaped by the interpretation placed on history by the par-
ticipants. If one particular pattern was imposed the future course of
action likely to be extrapolated differed from the one that might be
authorized by another. Blake believed the history of his time to be
shaped by an interpretation of the Bible that made central the rule of
law. On the other hand, if instead of adhering to the priestly record
in the Old Testament which constantly emphasized the importance
of observing God's commandments one attended to the moments of
prophetic vision contained in it, one's view of history would be
correspondingly transformed. Maintaining that Isaiah and Ezekiel
had been among his earliest guides, Blake wanted to deter his
readers from reading the Bible as the record of God's dealings with
a wayward and fickle nation and encourage them to see instead a
book of visions, in which 'seers' from time to time emerged to pro-
claim their view of events. In his own epic narrative, *The Four Zoas*,
similarly, characters would from time to time emerge to speak of
dreams or visions that had impressed them and which, once put
together by the reader, could be seen to reveal interlocking segments
of the great story that underlay all history – the story of the sleep of
true humanity.

During the 1790s this was a growing feature of Blake's work. As he
became pessimistic concerning the outcome of current events the
segments of mythology presented in the interpretative 'Preludia' that
stood at the beginning of *America* and *Europe* were drawn into the
full-blown myth-making venture that formed the basis of *The Four
Zoas*. But the seeds of such writing lay further back. When in *Tiriel* he
rewrote the story of Adam and Eve as a narrative in which not they
but the serpent, the principle of energy, had been expelled from the
garden, leaving them still in paradise as the ineffective Har and
Heva, growing old in a state of impotent innocence, it was a fore-

shadowing of the rewriting of the Bible in which he engaged during the 1790s, working toward the construction of what in *The Marriage of Heaven and Hell* he called 'The Bible of Hell' (*MHH* 24, E44).

He had been much helped in that enterprise by the rising interest in Swedenborgianism, with its attempt to read both the Bible and nature in a symbolic fashion. About Swedenborg himself he became disillusioned, concluding that he had used such methods to arrive at interpretations differing little from those regarded as orthodox (*MHH* 21–2, E42–3). This did not mean that the methods themselves were invalid, simply that Swedenborg had not been willing to allow his own imaginative vision free play. There were in any case other received methods of interpretation that suggested different or additional meanings for the biblical record, notably the cabbalistic. Philosophic traditions such as Neoplatonism, which suggested further interpretations of history and religion, had been applied to Christianity by older theologians long before. In England, equally, the idea that Western civilization had been dominated by priests and kings who wished to impose on society an uncritical respect for the law was not confined to the revolutionaries in France; it could be found in the writings of earlier Englishmen.[2] Blake was particularly interested in the further possibility that one effect of a reading of history dominated by the forces of law had been the active suppression of the true, visionary tradition – a possibility inviting those who were attracted by it to look into all the records that might be thought to embody its remains. He would be likely to investigate eagerly any hint of secret traditions or apocryphal writings for signs of such a lost wisdom.

One of the most absorbing of these alternative traditions – not least because it appeared fleetingly in the Bible itself, in the Book of Genesis – was the story of how the sons of God had visited the daughters of men:

> And it came to pass, when men began to multiply on the face of the earth, and daughters were born unto them,
> That the sons of God saw the daughters of men that they were fair; and they took them wives of all which they chose.

The rest of the story contains the well-known phrase 'There were giants in the land in those days' (Genesis 6: 1–4). The importance of the tradition was that it offered a possible version of the fall in which the problems of the human condition were created not by original sin but by the existence of a commixture of the divine with the human. This differs from the received account, whereby evil came into the world through man's disobedience, presupposing rather the presence in human beings of a portion of the divine creative powers, capable of being turned to either good or evil ends. It would then follow, at least on one reading, that the way to a better state of things lay not in a search for forgiveness from an impossibly distant and withdrawn God but through illumination and under-standing of the true human condition and a reawakening of the creative powers. In terms of the philosophy that lay behind the French Revolution, with its stress on the original good in human beings, this was bound to be attractive, offering a means of satisfy-ing human aspirations without betraying religious ideals.

For the same reason, it must have been fascinating for those who were drawn by this idea to learn that the same tradition appeared in one of the most intriguing of 'lost' ancient writings, the Ethiopic Book of Enoch.

This was a text of some resonance during the period for another reason. It had been known about and mentioned for centuries, having even – or so it seemed – been quoted in the Bible: in the general epistle of Jude there was a passage which began 'And Enoch also, the seventh from Adam, prophesied of these, saying, Behold, the Lord cometh with ten thousands of his saints, To execute judg-ment upon all . . .' (Jude: 14–15). The work itself, however, had fallen from view. There had been other references in the early fathers, even some quotation from it, but in Europe it disappeared so completely that its very existence was doubted. In the Church of Ethiopia, on the other hand, it was said to be regarded as a canonical book, and there were various attempts to discover whether copies might still exist in that country. Colbert, minister of Louis XIV, tried to obtain one for the king but his emissary was refused permission to enter the country and a volume that was brought away was found to be another work altogether. It was left to James Bruce, the explorer who set out in search of the sources of the Nile, to discover a copy and bring it back, giving a brief account of it in his famous *Travels*.[3] The work had a glamorous appeal, enhanced at that time of cultural enquiry into origins just after the French Revolution by the fact that Bruce's exploration could be regarded as a quest for the source not just of a great river but possibly of civilization itself. Abyssinia, it will be recalled, was the site of Milton's Mount Amara, 'By some suppos'd / True Paradise under the *Ethiop* Line / By Nilus head,

enclos'd with shining Rock, / A whole days journey high . . .'
(*Paradise Lost* IV: 281–4). Bruce's account was read with delight by
the young Romantics; his natural descriptions were among those
that entered Coleridge's imagination, to re-emerge in some of his
most magical poetic descriptions.[4]

Bruce gave an account of the copy he brought back, but did not
reproduce more than a little of its contents. What he had to say,
however, was tantalizingly suggestive:

> . . . the book of Enoch . . . is a Gnostic book, containing the age of
> the Emims, Anakims and Egregores, supposed descendants of the
> sons of God, when they fell in love with the daughters of men,
> and had sons that were giants.[5]

He brought three copies back to Europe: one was left in Paris for the
library of Louis XV, one was given to the Bodleian Library in Oxford
and one he kept for himself. Despite some interest, however, little
happened. Silvestre de Sacy published a Latin translation of some
chapters in the *Magasin Encyclopédique* in 1800 but it was not until
1821 that a complete translation into English appeared.[6]

At the time when Bruce's account appeared the story of the
seduction of the daughters of men had already been well known
from the account in Genesis quoted above. The full text of the Book
of Enoch as it emerged extended the story in various ways, particularly in making it clear that the seduction of the daughters of men
was carried out by those among the angels who were known as the
Watchers. In the Bible the wickedness of the proceedings is said to
have been the occasion of the Deluge and the building of Noah's
Ark. Enoch amplifies this by saying that the Watchers co-habited
with their wives, 'teaching them sorcery, incantations, and the
dividing of roots and trees' as well as 'the making of swords, knives,
shields, breastplates, the fabrication of mirrors, and the workmanship of bracelets and ornaments, the use of paint, the beautifying of
the eyebrows, the use of stones of every valuable and select kind,
and of all sorts of dyes, so that the world became altered.'[7] The
women also bore giants five hundred feet tall who devoured all the
fruits of their labour and then became carnivores. Enoch found himself called upon to plead for the Watchers, whereupon he was told
to go and teach them repentance.

Another element in the book which was of great interest to
those who read it for the first time was a visionary episode which

culminated in the midst of a vibrating flame, with a throne on which sat 'one great in glory', 'Whose robe was brighter than the sun, and whiter than snow'.[8]

This was one of the most sublime accounts of God yet recorded, which could immediately take its place in a long tradition. And if the Book of Enoch appealed to those who lived in the Romantic period by offering an account of evil as brought about not by disobedience to the law but through an intermingling of the divine with the human in a daemonic form, it was not the only document of its kind: a story had been related in Milton's *History of Britain*, according to which the daughters of Dioclesian, king of Syria, had murdered their husbands and been cast away on the island of Britain, where they met with devils and bore them a giant race who tyrannized over the island until the arrival of Brutus.[9] Coleridge made notes in an early notebook from this account which may well have provided one source for his woman wailing for her daemon lover in *Kubla Khan*.[10]

Blake's interest in the Book of Enoch is demonstrated most strongly by a short series of pencil drawings, some of which are of unusually fine quality, yet which are still comparatively little known. In 1863 they were in the collection of John Linnell, where they were traced by W.M. Rossetti. Later they were acquired first by Allan R. Brown and then by Lessing J. Rosenwald, who gave them to the National Gallery of Art in the United States. One was included by Sir Geoffrey Keynes in the first series of *Pencil Drawings* in 1927; this and four others were reproduced in the *Burlington Magazine*, with a discussion by their then owner, Allan Brown, and again in Keynes's second series of the *Pencil Drawings* (Brown 1940; Keynes 1927 and 1956). In 1974, Peter Alan Taylor contended that many of Allan Brown's more plausible-looking interpretations were vitiated by the fact that he was using a modern translation of the Book of Enoch instead of the one published in Blake's time.[11] Taylor also reproduced an additional item discovered by John E. Grant on the back of another drawing entitled the 'Circle of Carnal Sinners' which was associated with Blake's Dante illustrations. The most comprehensive account is by G.E. Bentley Jr in an article entitled 'A Jewel in an Ethiop's Ear' (Bentley 1978). Martin Butlin also reproduces the illustrations but, because descriptive titles and numberings are conjectural, they appear in a different order (Butlin 1981 cat. no. 827). For the purposes of the present discussion I normally refer directly to Bentley, since his article summarizes the available material. While I draw heavily on his account, particularly for factual points, I also wish to raise a few questions, including one of crucial importance.

One of Bentley's major contributions to the discussion has been to point out that the publication of the full English translation of the Book of Enoch in 1821 stimulated more than one writer to produce works on the theme of the angels descending to the daughters of men. Tom Moore, who was then writing his only novel, *The Epicurean*, included in it an episode entitled *The Loves of the Angels* and published that separately, with illustrations by Westall. At about the same time Byron wrote a drama, *Heaven and Earth*, on the same subject. Drawings on the same theme by Flaxman are also dated by Bentley to this period, shortly before his death in 1826.

The most interesting response to the Book of Enoch, however, is undoubtedly to be found in Blake's pencil drawings. There are, as mentioned earlier, six: all are inscribed 'Book of Enoch' and four are numbered, though it is not clear whether the numbering is Blake's.

The first numbered drawing (Figure 1) is described by Bentley as 'A Watcher surrounded by four Daughters of Men': he goes on to say, 'A bearded hero, with an heroic penis, is surrounded by four women whose breasts are emphasized'. The reproduction, at least, does not reveal the heroism of the penis, but according to Bentley it is enormous, and across the figure's hip. The description of him as one of the Watchers differs from that by Keynes, who, drawing no doubt on his memory of other illustrations by Blake showing Jesus in human form, describes him as 'The Son of Man, or Messiah, surrounded by four attendant spirits'; it might equally well be intended as an opening depiction of Enoch himself (Butlin sees these figures as related to the Book of Enoch xl, 1–9, Michael, Raphael, Gabriel and Phanuel; repro. 1981 cat. no.: 827. 5).

The second drawing (Figure 2) is described by Bentley as 'A Watcher seducing a Daughter of Men, with two offspring'. The central incident is fairly obvious, but the burning figures on either side might be allegorical of what the woman is losing in the moment of seduction, as full bodily desire shrivels into a more petty lust concentrated in the genitals (repro. Butlin 1981 cat. no.: 827. 2).

The third drawing (Figure 3), described as 'Two Watchers descending to a Daughter of Men', is particularly splendid (repro. Butlin 1981 cat. no. 827. 1). Bentley comments, 'The orgiastic implications are made plain by the carefully emphasized vulva of the woman and the giant, light-giving phalli of the men.' His further comment that 'the woman appears to be tantalized by the difficulty of deciding which phallus to choose first' is more open to question: her expression might rather seem anxious and bewildered.

The fourth drawing (Figure 4) is described as 'Two Daughters of Men with a prone figure' (repro. Butlin 1981 cat. no. 827. 3). This can be taken a little further. There appears to be the outline of a tree in the centre of the design and the figures can be pursued into Blake's allegory, as I shall try to show.

The next drawing (Figure 5), which is unnumbered, is described as 'Enoch before the throne of One great in glory' (repro. Butlin 1981 cat. no. 827. 4). Although plausible as describing an important incident in the book itself, this does not explain why there should be two figures before the throne. Keynes describes them as 'Enoch with his guiding angel'.

According to Bentley's description of the final drawing (Figure 6), also unnumbered, 'A figure tethered by the ankles soars upward between the stars' (repro. Butlin 1981 cat. no. 812. 11). His title for the drawing is 'A Watcher punished'. This also is plausible, though the appearance of the name Enoch in block capitals might equally justify an interpretation of the figure as that of Enoch himself. It could also be argued that he is only *trying* to soar upward, and that the stars appear to be falling to one side of him.

The most important question that remains to be addressed concerns the dating of the drawings. When Sir Geoffrey Keynes printed his first, single example of the illustrations (the third) he wrote '. . . they unquestionably belong to the last period of Blake's life, the first English translation of the Ethiopic original of *The Book of Enoch* having appeared only in 1821' (caption to Keynes 1927 pl. 80) and since then those who have examined them have agreed with that dating, following Keynes's persuasive argument. The discovery of another in the series on the other side of a drawing for the Dante illustrations, which also of course date from the very end of his life, has offered further evidence in support of Keynes's dating. Blake, it would seem, was joining in the fashionable interest which he shared with Moore and Byron.

There is at least one consideration that might give us pause before finally accepting Keynes's dating, however. Three of the drawings are on paper bearing the watermark 'WELGAR 1796' and the other three are watermarked with a crown that is almost certainly a part of the same design. This is not such a strong pointer as it might at first seem, since such watermarks as are to be found on the paper of the Dante illustrations are of the same kind; these drawings therefore were almost certainly made on paper from the same stock. But although paper can lie around for many years before it is used, twenty-five years seems a long time, particularly since Blake, who was a poor man, would have been likely to use up his stocks rather than keep them. Was there somewhere a stock of unused paper upon which he could call?

Leaving aside this matter it is worth putting a more radical question. If it had not been for the fact that the first full English translation of the Book of Enoch appeared only in 1821 would we have been quite so ready to assign them to so late a stage in his career? If we had been simply trying to fit them sequentially among the work that appeared during his lifetime might we not have found ourselves proposing a different place?

The question is not, as it turns out, a hypothetical one. As mentioned earlier, some parts of the fuller translation were published in a French journal in 1800: they were in Latin, however, and to suppose that Blake even knew of their existence might seem to stretch credulity, for that would seem to presuppose the existence of some hitherto unknown Parisian connection. The fact that in 1800 England was apprehensive concerning a possible invasion by the French makes this even more unlikely.

There is, however, one further place of publishing which has apparently been overlooked by everyone who has looked at the problem – including even the 1821 translator, Richard Laurence, who printed in an appendix the Latin translation that had been published in Paris. In *The Monthly Magazine* for 1 February 1801 there appeared an unsigned article entitled 'Concerning the Writings and Readings of Jude'. This article not only discussed Jude, who as mentioned above was one of the early sources for knowledge that the Book of Enoch existed, but went on to present some extracts from the book itself, translated into English. These are characterized by a language still more powerful than Laurence's, further enhanced by condensation into dramatic passages such as the following:

And behold another house greater than the former was builded before me, and the gates were open: it was built of flame, and paved with stars, its pillars were of lightning, and its roof of beams; and it abounded in all glory and all pomp; and I saw sitting within on a throne one whose countenance was as snow, and whose garment as a shining sun, that he could not be looked on even by an angel. His voice was as the voice of cherubs, and from under his throne went forth rivers of fire.[12]

The author of this piece had evidently gained access to the French article and its Latin translation (which he acknowledged) for he extracted precisely the same passages as had been printed there in Latin. Its existence changes the picture so far as Blake's possible knowledge of the book is concerned. In 1801 he was living in Felpham, but *The Monthly Magazine* had a good circulation and it is by no means unlikely that he saw it. He was closely in touch at the time with Flaxman, for example, who could have provided the necessary channel of communication; indeed, by the same token it is possible that Flaxman's drawings too were earlier than we think, though this requires further investigation. The important point for present purposes is that the extracts published in *The Monthly Magazine* contained the most crucial of the events on which Blake drew for his main illustrations.

The question of chronology may be pursued a little further by turning to some of the drawings that appear in the text of the poem *The Four Zoas*. These are on paper watermarked 1794; and although they are not in exactly the same visual style as the Enoch illustrations some of them have strikingly similar features, making them plausible precedents for Blake's designs.

Further features in the Enoch illustrations would support a date of execution shortly before Blake worked on his prophetic book *Milton*, which according to its title-page was completed in 1804. If we look for anything like the giant stars in the last drawing, for instance, we find three examples, all in *Milton* (see for example, *Milton* pls. 2, 29[32], 33[37]); there are further interesting parallels in designs of the subsequent period, as we shall see, notably in the illustrations to Milton's poems.

So far we have been looking at visual motifs, but it is also the case that elements in the text of the book *Milton*, also, bear an interesting resemblance to themes in the Enoch drawings. One of the points that has been mentioned as emerging from the fuller translations was that the sons of God who had seduced the daughters of men were the heavenly beings known as the Watchers appear in the Bible on only one occasion, in the Book of Daniel (IV. 13, 17, 23).

When Blake uses the concept of watching in his writings it has primarily to do with guardianship – particularly, as in the Bible, that of the watchmen who protect cities.[13] In at least one early place, however, he made a connection between watching and the stars. Some apocalyptic lines in his poem *The French Revolution* (1791) contain a reference to a time:

> When the heavens were seal'd with a stone, and the
> terrible sun clos'd in an orb, and the moon
> Rent from the nations, and each star appointed for
> watchers of night . . . (p. 11, lines 211–12, E295)

This appointment of the stars as watchers is a result of the fall. Under the dominion of Urizen watching becomes a more locked and sinister matter: the hero of the *The Book of Los* is 'compell'd to watch Urizens shadow' and in *The Four Zoas* he sits 'in showers of Urizen watching cold Enitharmon'; one of the finest of the drawings for that book shows a figure, bound apparently in the bonds of his own analytic power, watching a female figure who smiles back at him in all her polymorphous perversity.[14] In the poem *Milton*, and to a lesser extent, *Jerusalem*, the Watchers take on a more precise significance. There they belong to the world of Urizen in which seeing has become confined into locked analysis. They are described in fact as 'Satans watch-fiends' and the effect of their work is to fix the perceiving powers of human beings into such rigid modes that the expansiveness of true vision can never take place.

This is particularly so in the plate of *Milton* where Blake writes of the fall of the seven starry ones. He first asserts that mortals should not seek their heavenly father beyond the skies:

> There Chaos dwells & ancient Night & Og & Anak old:
> For every human heart has gates of brass & bars of
> adamant,
> Which few dare unbar because dread Og & Anak guard the
> gates
> Terrific! and each mortal brain is walld and moated round
> Within: and Og & Anak watch here; here is the Seat
> Of Satan in its Webs . . .

This is followed within a few lines by the anger of the Eternals when they see what is going on:

wrathful, fill'd with rage!
They rend the heavens round the Watchers in a fiery circle:
And round the Shadowy Eighth: the Eight close up the Couch
Into a tabernacle, and flee with cries down to the Deeps:
Where Los opens his three wide gates, surrounded by raging
     fires!
They soon find their own place & join the Watchers of the
     Ulro.[15]

It may be a coincidence that two of the most fearsome watchers
are called Og and Anak (the Anakim being the giants mentioned
in the Book of Enoch), but it is noticeable that the power of
watching, which in *The Four Zoas* tended to be a process associated with the lovers, has here become a hallmark of the Urizenic,
to be summed up, perhaps, in the evolution of the Watch-fiends
who are the agents of Blake's Satan and who can only be escaped
in the moment of true vision. These Watch-fiends are seen as con-
taminating the true experience of love and indeed of all full
human feeling. Yet this is not the whole story. In one of the finest
passages of the book – and indeed of all his prophetic books –
Blake affirms that:

There is a Moment in each Day that Satan cannot find
Nor can his Watch Fiends find it, but the Industrious find
This Moment & it multiply. & when it once is found
It renovates every Moment of the Day if rightly placed[.]

(*Milton* 35[39]: 42–5, E136)

This moment is then identified by Blake with the sensuous moment
when the lark soars and the wild thyme expands into scent (*Milton*
35[39]: 48–36[40]: 12, E136).
     If we suspend our belief in the assumption that Blake could not
have known the Book of Enoch before 1821, his encounter with it
falls into a very natural development: his meditations on the fate of
the Watcher suggesting a contamination of sexual and mental
experience by the intervention of analytic vision that stands somewhere between the half-farcical, half-nightmare experiences of *The
Four Zoas* and the themes of the new poem, *Milton*, where he is still
more concerned with the effect of a narrow analytic watching upon

the development of humane vision. The drawings can be seen to relate to the pencil drawings for *The Four Zoas* and the etched plates for *Milton*, while the book itself produces a version of the fall which could stand equally between the two.

The existence of a link between early knowledge of Enoch by way of *The Monthly Magazine* and the text of *Milton* can be argued for more easily than one with the pencil drawings: indeed those who wish to keep to the received belief that Blake produced the designs after the publication of Laurence's full translation have some points in their favour. That translation speaks of Enoch being assisted by an angel when he was approaching the glory of God and there is also mention of the son of man, both of which might be thought to be reflected in certain details of Blake's drawings. The evidence of the watermarks, meanwhile, is inconclusive. The fact that the 1796 paper was used also for the Dante drawings negates conclusions that might otherwise be drawn; it also raises questions concerning the date at which those drawings themselves might have been begun.[16] If the Enoch drawings are indeed late, on the other hand, the use of explicit genital detail in the nude figures is surprising, since it corresponds more to features of *The Four Zoas* drawings than to the later work. This is not easy to explain – unless, perhaps, one looks to the story that some of Blake's drawings were destroyed after his death and supposes that further late examples of such work might have been among those that perished.[17]

Blake commonly developed a new style for a new series of prints, whether it was an illuminated book or a set of designs to illustrate another author. The Enoch designs do not relate in a straightforward way to any existing series and the resemblances which are traceable cover a wide range of works; it is also difficult to determine which way the influence might be running. Since there are variations of style within the series itself, moreover, the possibility that Blake executed some of the designs later than others cannot be excluded.

Some of the more striking resemblances may be mentioned. The central figure in the first plate has features in common with the figure of Milton rising to offer himself in plate 16 of Blake's prophetic book of that name and to that of the Archangel Michael leading Adam and Eve from Eden in the *Paradise Lost* designs (1807, 1808) (Dunbar 1980 pls. 50–1; Butlin 1981 cat. no.: 529. 12; 536. 12). He might also be related to the figure of the Spirit in the Arlington Court

picture illustrating Revelation, 'The Spirit and the bride say "Come!"'
(1821; see Beer 1969 pp. 288–94; Butlin 1981 cat. no.: 803). The
manner of the female figure at the centre of the second of the Enoch
drawings (Figure 2) is not unlike that of the pencil design for the
plate 'The Queen of Heaven in Glory' of the Dante illustrations,
while the seducer who is descending to her looks rather like one of
the devils from 'Baffled Devils Fighting' in the same series; yet the
figures to either side, which look rather like burning sunflowers, are
more reminiscent of certain elements in the designs for Gray's poems
and of the design known as 'The Bowman' (c. 1797–8; Figure 2).[18] The
bold drawing of the woman in the third Enoch picture (Figure 3),
with her genitals clearly visible, is reminiscent of some female
figures in *The Four Zoas* (Bentley 1963 ms page 86). The fourth Enoch
drawing (Figure 4), on the other hand, bears resemblances to some of
the illustrations to Milton's *Paradise Lost*, where a central tree provides the main feature (Figure 7). The female figure rising up to the
left is like the figure of Mirth in the illustration to 'L'Allegro' (c. 1816–
20; Figure 8) while the scales on her body can be matched by those
(in a similar but more sophisticated version) on female figures in the
feast temptation scene from the *Paradise Regained* illustrations
(c. 1816–20; Butlin 1981 cat. no.: 544.6). The figure of Christ on the
right, raising his hands in horror, is not unlike that of Adam seeing
the effects of Eve's Fall, which is taking place behind him (Figure 7).
The figure on the throne and the two figures before him in the fifth
drawing of the Enoch sequence (Figure 5) form a grouping like that
of 'The Angel of the Divine Presence clothing Adam and Eve' (1803;
Butlin 1981 cat. no.: 436), while that in the sixth Enoch drawing
(Figure 6), tethered yet trying to fly, takes one back to *The Four Zoas*
illustrations, where there is at the end a similar figure (apparently
untethered) rising aloft (Bentley 1963 ms. page 139).

These resemblances are in each case general ones and their
cumulative effect does not furnish a convincing date for the composition of the series. While the explicit sexual detail on its own would
suggest a time near to the composition of *The Four Zoas*, parts of the
seduction scene are closer to the late Dante illustrations; other
features suggest his various engagements with Milton over the
years. But if one supposes that the hitherto accepted dating in the
1820s is correct, it is still possible to trace a possible continuing effect
from the 1801 article; in that case it might be suggested that the
immediate impact was on the body of ideas and images that went to
make up 'Milton', and that when Blake's fascination with the lost

Book of Enoch was revived by the publication of the full translation, ideas, images and visual motifs that had been lying dormant for many years were reawakened into life.

Whatever the dating, is it possible to find a convincing interpretation of the drawings as a whole? If the numbering on them is accepted as Blake's the first four form a series, supplemented in some way by the other two, unnumbered, ones (although the authenticity of the numbering is disputed in Butlin 1981 cat. no.: 827). In that case it might be thought that the first represents Enoch embarking on his career and surrounded by guiding and admonitory figures. The second would then portray a woman falling under the dominion of lust, with two of the Watchers burning in their vegetative form, innocent but enslaved. In the next, on this reading, the Watchers are seen presenting themselves to one of the daughters of men who is unable to cope with their divine energy and feels herself in danger of destruction, while in the fourth a spectrous version of herself is seen splitting off from her, leaving her half-horrified. The next shows Enoch attended by an angel before the throne of a great being (who may be the God depicted in the Book of Enoch but seems less awful than the description there would suggest) and we are left in the final one with a picture of the prophet subsisting in a state of aspiration and bondage, visionary and aspiring, yet ineffective.

Such reasoning remains inconclusive so far as a likely date for the drawings is concerned. If they were indeed executed in the 1820s we are led again to the complex hypothesis set forth above: that the late efflorescence of his art to be seen in the illustrations to Bunyan and Dante (1824–7) and in his later sets for *The Book of Job* (c. 1805–6; c. 1821–7) included in this instance a more decisive return by him to motifs evolved much earlier, especially in *The Four Zoas* and *Milton*, an early excitement when he first read the vivid paragraphs extracted from the Book of Enoch in *The Monthly Magazine* being renewed by the publication of Laurence's fuller translation. In the absence of more compelling evidence it is difficult to proceed much further.

Whatever hypothesis is proposed concerning the drawings and their dating, however, the evidence that Blake read the extracts in *The Monthly Magazine* and that they affected his writing of *Milton* remains strangely persuasive. And here a further point may be made. One passage among them that could be expected to strike Blake with particular force was the description of Enoch's supreme visionary moment as he approached the figure that showed itself 'in great glory'. That begins:

> This was the vision that appeared. Clouds embraced me, and a little cloud wrapped round me, and the paths of stars and lightnings were beside me, and storm-winds lifted me on high, and bore me to the walls of heaven: and the walls are built of hailstone and tongues of fire sit upon them. Then I was afraid, and I entered into a tongue of fire, and was moved toward a great house, also of hail-stone. And the walls of the house and the floor of the house were tables of blocks of ice; and on the roof ran to and fro lightnings and stars and cherubs of fire. And I entered into the house, and it was as hot as fire, and cold as frost; but there is no solace neither life within. Fear covered me, and trembling came upon me; I was sore moved and fell on my face.[20]

The movement of that passage, particulary at the end, is surprisingly close to that of the climactic incident in *Milton* when Blake describes his own moment of inspiration:

> Terror struck in the Vale I stood at that immortal sound
> My bones trembled. I fell outstretchd upon the path
> A moment, & my Soul returnd into its mortal state
> To Resurrection & Judgment in the Vegetable Body
> And my sweet Shadow of Delight stood trembling by my side
>
> (*Milton* 42[49]: 24–8, E143)

This suggests that the extracts from the Book of Enoch might have prompted not just the conception of Satan's Watch-fiends in *Milton* but a touch of inspiration for the apocalyptic climax in that poem as well. That, it will be recalled, was seen to have implications for contemporary history and for mankind in general:

> Los listens to the Cry of the Poor Man: his Cloud
> Over London in volume terrific, low bended in anger.
>
> Rintrah & Palamabron view the Human Harvest beneath
> Their Wine-presses & Barns stand open; the Ovens are
>   prepar'd
> The Waggons ready: terrific Lions and Tygers sport & play

> All Animals upon the Earth, are prepared in all their
>   strength
>
> To go forth to the Great Harvest & Vintage of the Nations
>
> (*Milton* 42[49]: 34–9, 43[50]: 1, E144)

It was the climactic version of an apocalyptic vision that had been haunting his prophetic books during the previous decade. Throughout that time he had been repeatedly visited by a sense of the ambiguity of the current political situation, which seemed to be about to erupt into a fearfully destructive war yet which might still, just conceivably, produce an absolute revolution in human behaviour, restoring human beings to awareness of their full humanity. It was a vision that, so far from removing him from contemporary history, found him situated in its very depths as its most essential prophet.

With the return of political stability in Europe and a hardening of the existing political forms, however, the prospect of such an imminent and general apocalypse had faded. Faced with the rise of Napoleon and the threat to England's independence, Blake was even willing to create great icons of Pitt and Nelson as necessary rallying spirits for the cause of British freedom.[21]

In his 'Public Address' (c. 1809–10), correspondingly, he had come to take a detached and sardonic view of political institutions:

> I am really sorry to see my Countrymen trouble themselves about Politics. If men were wise <the Most arbitrary> Princes could not hurt them If they are not Wise the Freest Government is compelld to be a Tyranny[.] Princes appear to me to be Fools Houses of Commons & Houses of Lords appear to me to be fools they seem to me to be something Else besides Human Life (p. 18, E580)

He had by no means lost interest in politics, though his trial for sedition had no doubt prompted caution in expressing his own views too openly. Even the numbers of *The Monthly Magazine* surrounding that in which the Enoch extracts had appeared provided a reminder that this could be visited upon anyone, for they contained successive articles by Gilbert Wakefield addressed from Dorchester Gaol, where he was serving a sentence for publishing a book condemned as seditious – a sentence considered by many to be an outrageous abuse of the right to freedom of speech.

Meanwhile, his aspirations for humanity had turned in another direction. On 19 October 1801, just over six months after *The Monthly Magazine* article appeared, he wrote to John Flaxman: 'The Kingdoms of this World are now become the Kingdoms of God & his Christ, & we shall reign with him for ever & ever. The Reign of Literature & the Arts Commences. Blessed are those who are found studious of Literature & Humane & polite accomplishments. Such have their lamps burning & such shall shine as the stars' (E717–18). As Kathleen Raine has pointed out, this new initiative found an Old Testament patron in the very figure who has become familiar in this essay. Although little is known from the Bible about Enoch except that he 'walked with God' and in the end did not die but was translated into heaven (Genesis V: 18–24; Hebrews XI: 5), Jewish tradition had represented him as the inventor of letters, arithmetic, and astronomy, and as the first author. A book containing his visions and prophecies was said to have been preserved by Noah in the ark – a tradition which Blake, who saw in the story of the ark on the waters a symbol of the survival of vision would have found congenial. In 1807 he produced in his only surviving lithograph a representation of Enoch in a posture remarkably like that of the Job of the later plates, surrounded by figures representing literature, art and music (repro. Essick 1983: cat. no. XV). It seems, therefore, that just as he found in Elijah an image of the immortality of the prophet in his fiery chariot, Enoch represented for him the heroic survival of artistic vision.

This shift corresponds to an internalization of apocalypse that was another effect of his changing view of history. In this new conception the Last Judgement was not a cataclysm at the end of time but an event that could happen to anyone at any time: as he put it in his long manuscript note on the Last Judgement, '. . . whenever any Individual Rejects Error & Embraces Truth a Last Judgment passes upon that Individual' (p. 84, E562). The nature of that rejecting and embracing had been expressed in more positive images a little before in the same manuscript:

If the Spectator could Enter into these Images in his Imagination approaching them on the Fiery Chariot of his Contemplative Thought if he could Enter into Noahs Rainbow or into his bosom or could make a Friend & Companion of one of these Images of wonder which always intreats him to leave mortal things as he must know then would he arise from his Grave then would he meet the Lord in the Air & then would he be happy (p. 82, E560)

Instead of a cataclysmic climax to world events Blake was now pro-
jecting a Last Judgement that existed within the capabilities of
everyone and was infinitely repeatable yet no less potentially wide-
spread in its effects: for 'The Last Judgment is an Overwhelming of
Bad Art & Science' (p. 94, E565).

He would continue to survey current events with a detached and
amused eye but his central vision was now firmly expressed as that
of someone who looked through his eye and not with it.[22] Consequently his perspective on history had also changed. Society, he
now grasped, was not going to be either destroyed or redeemed
through a single apocalyptic event; it would be renewed, but only
to the extent that artists remained true to their vision and prophetic
powers. And if I am correct in believing that Enoch's warnings
against the corrupters of art and sexual desire in his own time and
his experience of fear and prostration before the revelation of the
divine glory had been a potent force in sparking the attacks in
Milton on the geometric art of his time and the account of Blake's
own moment of prostration and personal apocalypse, we can see
why he should have chosen to represent him so favourably in his
lithograph. Enoch, seer and prophet, who had known what it was
to keep faith with both aspects of his vision 'in fear and trembling'
had become a central emblem of the true art which represented for
him the only true means by which human history could be
redeemed.

Notes

1. The line of Burgundy had died out in 1717, see Erdman 1977 pp. 166–8.
   For details of York, see Erdman 1977, p. 61. See also Thompson (1963)
   p. 192.
2. See, for example, Matthew Tindal's *Christianity as Old as the Creation:
   or Christianity a Republication of the Religion of Nature* (1730).
3. James Bruce, *Travels to Discover the Source of the Nile. In the Years 1768,
   1769, 1770, 1771, 1772, and 1773* (1790), 5 vols.
4. See J.L. Lowes, *The Road to Xanadu* (1927) on, for example, the star-
   dogged moon in *The Ancient Mariner* and the fountain, the Mount
   Abora and the floating hair of *Kubla Khan* (pp. 183, 370–9).
5. Bruce, *Travels*, vol. I, p. 499.
6. Bruce, *Travels*, vol. I, p. 382; *The Book of Enoch The Prophet: An Apocryphal Production. Supposed to Have Been Lost for Ages; But Discovered at
   the Close of the Last Century in Abyssinia; now First Translated from An
   Ethiopic MS. in the Bodleian Library*, trans. Richard Laurence (1821).
7. *Enoch*, chaps vii. 10; viii. 1, pp. 6–7.
8. *Enoch*, chap. xiv. 14–24, pp. 17–18.

9. John Milton, *The History of Britain, That part especially call'd England* (1670) in *Works*, ed. J. Toland (1694–8), vol. I, p. 4.

10. *The Notebooks of Samuel Taylor Coleridge*, ed. Kathleen Coburn, 5 vols in progress, (Princeton, NJ: Princeton University Press, 1957–73) vol. I, p. 39 and n., citing Lowes, *The Road to Xanadu* (1927) pp. 14–15, 457.

11. Taylor (1974) pointed out that Brown and Keynes had both used a translation of 1912 instead of that of 1821, and that some suggestions in their interpretations could not be supported from the 1821 text.

12. Anon., 'Concerning the Readings and Writings of Jude', *Monthly Magazine*, 1 February 1801, XI, p. 22.

13. This is particularly the role of Los, 'dividing / The horrible night into watches' as he binds Urizen (*The First Book of Urizen* 10: 10, E75) and named as the guardian of Enitharmon's Watchman in Night the Seventh, p. 98 {VIIb 92–122}: 5–7, E362 of *The Four Zoas*, as 'the Watchman of Eternity' in *Milton* 24 [26]: 9, E119 and as 'Albions Watchman' in *Jerusalem* in 56: 32, E206.

14. *The Book of Los* 3: 32, E91; *The Four Zoas* p. 81 {VII 160–94}: 7, E356. See the illustration on page 27 in the original MS of Vala, reproduced in Bentley 1963.

15. *Milton* 20[22]: 33–8, 45–50, E114–15. Enoch himself receives a passing mention in *Milton* 37 [41]: 36, E138.

16. The fact that one of the Enoch drawings appeared on the 'back' of one for Dante does not of course mean that it must have been produced later. It may also be noted that the evidence concerning the date of the Dante illustrations presented by A.S. Roe in his edition (1953) shows him to have been hard at work on them in the 1820s, but does not preclude his having started work on them some (even many) years earlier.

17. The story is told and discussed in various places, notably in Samuel Calvert's *A Memoir of Edward Calvert, Artist* (1893) p. 59, Garnett (1895) p. 71, and Symons 1907 pp. 240–1; these sources are brought together and judiciously appraised in Bentley 1969 pp. 417–18n.

18. For Dante, see Roe 1953 plates 99, 42E; Butlin 1981 cat. no.: 812. 99; 812. 42. For Gray, see the illustration (c. 1800) to page 86 ('Hyperion's march they spy . . .') of *Gray's Poems* (1790) in Keynes 1971; Keynes 1956 pl. 22; Butlin 1981 cat. no.: 336.

19. See Dunbar 1980 pls. 39 and 40; Butlin 1981 cat. nos.: 529.9; 536.9. Later, as Michael foretells the Crucifixion, the Cross replaces the tree (Dunbar 1980 pls. 47–9; Butlin 1981 cat. nos.: 536, 11; 537.3).

20. 'Concerning the Writings and Readings of Jude', *The Monthly Magazine* 1, Feb. 1801, XI, 22.

21. See the accounts of his pictures 'The spiritual form of Nelson guiding Leviathan' and 'The spiritual form of Pitt, guiding Behemoth' in his *A Descriptive Catalogue* (1809) pp. 1–2, E530–1.

22. See Blake's testing of Samuel Palmer on this point in 1824, Bentley 1969 p. 291.

Blake Bibliography

Aers, David, 'Representations of Revolution: from the French Revolution to "The Four Zoas"', D. Ault et al. (eds) *Critical Paths: Blake and the Question of Method* (Durham, NC: Duke University Press, 1987) pp. 244–70.

Ault, Donald D., *Visionary Physics: Blake's Response to Newton* (Chicago: University of Chicago Press, 1974).

Barrell, John, *The Political Theory of Painting from Reynolds to Hazlitt: the Body of the Public* (New Haven, Conn.: Yale University Press, 1986).

Beer, John, *Blake's Visionary Universe* (Manchester: Manchester University Press, 1969).

Bentley, G.E., Jr. *Vala or The Four Zoas, A Facsimile of the Manuscript* (Oxford: Clarendon Press, 1963).

Bentley G.E. Jr, *Blake Records* (Oxford: Clarendon Press, 1969).

—— *Blake Books* (Oxford: Clarendon Press, 1977).

—— 'A Jewel in an Ethiop's Ear', *Blake in His Time*, eds Robert N. Essick and Donald Pearce (Bloomington: University of Indiana Press, 1978) pp. 213–40.

—— 'The Great Illustrated-Book Publishers of the 1790's and William Blake', *Editing Illustrated Books: Papers Given at the Fifteenth Annual Conference on Editorial Problems*, ed. William Blisset (New York: Garland, 1980) pp. 57–96.

Bindman, David, 'Blake's "Gothicised Imagination" and the History of England', *William Blake: Essays in Honour of Sir Geoffrey Keynes*, (eds) Morton D. Paley and Michael Phillips (Oxford: Clarendon Press, 1973) pp. 29–49.

—— 'William Blake and Popular Religious Imagery', *Burlington Magazine* 128 (October 1986) pp. 712–18.

Bogen, Nancy (ed.), *The Book of Thel: A Facsimile and Critical Text*, (Providence, RI: Brown University Press, 1971).

Bronowski, Jacob, *William Blake and the Age of Revolution* (London: Routledge & Kegan Paul, 1972).

Brown, Allan R., 'Blake's Drawings for *The Book of Enoch'*, *The Burlington Magazine* 77 (Sept. 1940) pp. 80–5.

Butlin, Martin, *The Paintings and Drawings of William Blake*, 2 vols (New Haven, Conn. and London: Yale University Press, 1981).

Carretta, Vincent, *George III and the Satirists from Hogarth to Byron* (Athens, Ga: University of Georgia Press, 1990).

Christiansen, Bryce J., 'The Apple in the Vortex: Newton, Blake, and Descartes', *Philosophy and Literature* 6 (1982) pp. 141–61.

Curtis, F.B., 'Blake and the "Moment of Time": An Eighteenth Century Controversy in Mathematics', *Philological Quarterly* 51 (1972) pp. 460–70.

Damon, S. Foster, *A Blake Dictionary*, ed. Morris Eaves (Providence, RI: Brown University Press, 1965, revised edn. 1988).

Damrosch, Leopold, Jr, *Symbol and Truth in Blake's Myth* (Princeton, NJ: Princeton University Press, 1980).

Dunbar, Pamela *William Blake's Illustrations to the Poetry of Milton* (Oxford: Clarendon Press, 1980).

Eaves, Morris, 'Blake and the Artistic Machine: An Essay in Decorum and Technology', *Publications of the Modern Language Association of America* 92 (1977) pp. 903–27.

Erdman, David V., *Blake, Prophet Against Empire* (Princeton, NJ: Princeton University Press, 1954; 3rd edn revised, 1977).

—— *The Illuminated Blake* (New York: Anchor/Doubleday, 1974).

—— with Donald K. Moore, (eds) *The Notebook of William Blake: A Photographic and Typographic Facsimile* (1973: rev. edn, New York: Readex Books, 1977).

Essick, Robert N., *The Separate Plates of William Blake* (Princeton: Princeton University Press, 1983).

—— 'William Blake, William Hamilton, and the Materials of Graphic Meaning', *English Literary History* 52 (1985) pp. 833–72.

—— 'Dating Blake's "Enoch" Lithograph Once Again', *Blake/An Illustrated Quarterly* 22 (1988) pp. 71–3.

—— *William Blake and the Language of Adam* (Oxford: Clarendon Press, 1989).

Everest, Kelvin D., 'Thel's Dilemma', *Essays in Criticism* 37 (1987) pp. 193–208.

Ferber, Michael, 'Blake's *Thel* and the Bride of Christ', *Blake Studies* 9 (1980) pp. 45–56.

—— *The Social Vision of William Blake* (Princeton, NJ: Princeton University Press, 1985).

Fox, Susan, *Poetic Form in Blake's "Milton"* (Princeton, NJ: Princeton University Press, 1976).

Frye, Northrop, *Fearful Symmetry. A Study of William Blake* (Princeton, NJ: Princeton University Press, 1947; 4th paperback edn. 1974).

Fuller, David, *Blake's heroic argument* (London: Croom Helm, 1988).

Garnett, Richard, *William Blake: Painter and Poet* (London: Seeley, 1895).

George, Diana Hume, *Blake and Freud* (London and Ithaca: Cornell University Press, 1980).

Gillham, D.G., *William Blake* (Cambridge: Cambridge University Press, 1973).

Glausser, Wayne, 'Atomistic Simulacra in the Enlightenment and in Blake's Post-Enlightenment', *The Eighteenth-Century: Theory and Interpretation* 32 (1991) pp. 73–88.

Gleckner, Robert F., *The Piper and the Bard* (Detroit: Wayne University Press, 1959).

—— 'Blake's Thel and the Bible', *Bulletin of the New York Public Library* 64 (1960) pp. 574–80.

—— *Blake and Spenser* (Baltimore and London: Johns Hopkins University Press, 1985).

Grant, John E., 'Two Flowers in the Garden of Experience', in *William Blake: Essays for S. Foster Damon*, ed. Alvin H. Rosenfeld (Providence, RI: Brown University Press, 1969) pp. 333–67.

Grant, J.E., E.J. Rose, and M.J. Tolley, with D.V. Erdman, (eds) *William Blake's Designs for Edward Young's "Night Thoughts": A Complete Edition*, 2 vols, (Oxford: Clarendon Press, 1980).

Heppner, Christopher, '"A Desire of Being": Identity and *The Book of Thel'*, *Colby Library Quarterly* 13 (1977) pp. 79–98.

Hilton, Nelson, *Literal Imagination: Blake's Vision of Words* (Berkeley: University of California Press, 1983).

—— and Thomas A. Vogler (eds), *Unnam'd Forms: Blake and Textuality* (Berkeley: University of California Press, 1986).

Hirst, Désirée, *Hidden Riches: Traditional Symbolism from the Renaissance to Blake* (London: Eyre & Spottiswood, 1964).

Johnson, Mary Lynn, 'Beulah, "Mme Seraphim", and Blake's Thel', *Journal of English and Germanic Philology* 69 (1970) pp. 258–77.

—— *The English Romantic Poets, A Review of Research and Criticism*, ed. Frank Jordan, 4th edn (New York: MLA, 1985), p. 215.

—— and Brian Wilkie, *Blake's "The Four Zoas": The Design of a Dream* (Cambridge, Mass.: Harvard University Press, 1978).

Keynes, Sir Geoffrey, ed., *The Pencil Drawings by William Blake* (n.p. [London]: Nonesuch Press, 1927).

Keynes, Sir Geoffrey, ed., *Blake's Pencil Drawings, Second Series*, (n.p. [London]: Nonesuch Press,1956).

—— *William Blake's Water Colour Designs for the Poems of Thomas Gray* (London: Eyre Methuen, 1972).

Langland, Elizabeth, 'Blake's Feminist Revision of Literary Tradition in "The SICK ROSE"', *Critical Paths: Blake and the Argument of Method*, eds Donald Ault, Mark Bracher and Dan Miller (Durham, NC and London: Duke University Press, 1987) pp. 225–43.

Larrissy, Edward, *William Blake* (Oxford: Basil Blackwell, 1985).

—— 'Blake and the Hutchinsonians', *Blake/An Illustrated Quarterly* 20 (1986) pp. 44–7.

Lattin, Vernon E., 'Blake's Thel and Oothoon: Sexual Awakening in the Eighteenth Century', *Literary Criterion*, 16 (1981) pp. 11–24.

Leader, Zachary, *Reading Blake's Songs* (Boston, London and Henley: Routledge & Kegan Paul, 1981).

Levinson, Marjorie, '*The Book of Thel* By William Blake: A Critical Reading', *English Literary History* 47 (1980) pp. 287–303.

Levitt, Annette, 'Comus, Cloud and Thel's "Unacted Desires"', *Colby Library Quarterly*, 14 (1978) pp. 72–83.

Linkin, Harriet Kramer, 'The Function of Dialogue in *The Book of Thel'*, *Colby Library Quarterly*, 23 (1987) pp. 66–76.

Lucas, John, *England and Englishness: Ideas of Nationhood in English Poetry 1688–1900* (London: Hogarth, 1990).

McCalman, Iain, *Radical Underworld: Prophets, Revolutionaries and Pornographers in London, 1795–1840* (Cambridge: Cambridge University Press, 1988).

McClenahan, Catherine L., 'No Face Like the Human Divine?: Women and Gender in Blake's Pickering Manuscript', *Spirits of Fire: English Romantic Writers and Contemporary Historical Methods*, (eds) G.A. Rosso and B.P. Watkins (Rutherford: Fairleigh Dickinson University Press, 1990) pp. 189–207.

McGann, Jerome J., *The Romantic Ideology* (Chicago: University of Chicago Press, 1983).

—— *A Critique of Modern Textual Criticism* (Chicago: University of Chicago Press, 1983).

—— *Textual Criticism and Literary Interpretation* (Chicago: University of Chicago Press, 1985).

—— *The Beauty of Inflections: Literary Investigations In Historical Method and Theory* (Oxford: Oxford University Press, 1985).

—— *Social Values and Poetic Acts: the Historical Judgement of Literary Work* (Cambridge, Mass.: Harvard University Press, 1988).

—— *Towards a Literature of Knowledge* (Oxford: Oxford University Press, 1989).

—— *The Textual Condition* (Princeton, NJ: Princeton University Press, and London: Routledge, 1991).

Matthews, Susan, '*Jerusalem* and Nationalism', in Stephen Copley and John Whale, *Beyond Romanticism: New Approaches to Text and Context, 1780–1832* (London: Routledge, 1992) pp. 79–100.

Mellor, Anne K., 'Blake's Designs for *The Book of Thel*: An Affirmation of Innocence', *Philological Quarterly* 50 (1971) pp. 193–207.

—— 'Blake's *Songs of Innocence and Experience*: A Feminist Perspective', *Nineteenth Century Studies* 2 (1988) pp. 1–17.

Miller, Dan, Mark Bracher, and Donald Ault (eds), *Critical Paths: Blake and the Argument of Method* (Durham, NC: Duke University Press, 1987).

Mitchell, W.J.T., *Blake's Composite Art* (Princeton NJ: Princeton University Press, 1978).

Morton, A.L., *The Everlasting Gospel: A Study of the Sources of William Blake*, (London: Lawrence & Wishart 1958).

Murray, E.B., 'Thel, *Thelyphthora*, and the Daughters of Albion', *Studies in Romanticism* 20 (1981) pp. 275–97.

Nicolson, Marjorie Hope, *Newton Demands The Muse: Newton's "Opticks" And The Eighteenth Century Poets* (Princeton, NJ: Princeton University Press, 1946).

Nurmi, Martin K., 'Blake's "Ancient of Days" and Motte's Frontispiece to Newton's *Principia*', *The Divine Vision*, ed. V. de S. Pinto (London: Victor Gollancz, 1957) pp. 207–16.

Nurmi, Martin K., *William Blake* (London: Hutchinson, 1975).

Ostriker, Alicia (ed.), *William Blake: The Complete Poems* (Harmondsworth: Penguin, 1977).

Paley, Morton, 'William Blake, the Prince of the Hebrews, and the Woman Clothed with the Sun', *William Blake: Essays in Honour of Sir Geoffrey Keynes*, eds Morton D. Paley and Michael Phillips (Oxford: Clarendon Press, 1973) pp. 260–93.

Pearce, Donald R., 'Natural Religion and the Plight of Thel', *Blake Studies* 8 (1978) pp. 23–35.

Percival, Milton O. *William Blake's Circle of Destiny* (New York: Columbia University Press, 1938).

Peterfreund, Stuart, 'Blake on Charters, Weights, and Measures as Forms of Social Control', *Studies in the Literary Imagination* 22 (1989) pp. 37–59.

—— (1990a), 'Blake and Anti-Newtonian Thought', Judith Yaross Lee and Joseph W. Slade (eds), *Beyond the Two Cultures: Essays on Science, Technology, and Literature* (Ames: Iowa State University Press, 1990) pp. 141–60.

—— (1990b), 'Blake, Priestley, and the "Gnostic Moment"', Stuart Peter-freund (ed.), *Literature and Society: Theory & Practice* (Boston: North-eastern University Press, 1990) pp. 139–66.

Pinto, Vivian de Sola (ed.), *The Divine Vision: Studies in the Poetry and Art of William Blake* (London: Victor Gollancz, 1957).

Raine, Kathleen, *Blake and Tradition*, 2 vols (Princeton, NJ: Princeton University Press, 1969).

Read Dennis M., 'The Context of Blake's "Public Address": Cromek and The Chalcographic Society', *Philological Quarterly* 60 (1981) pp. 69–86.

—— 'Blake's "Tender Stranger": Thel and Hervey's Meditations', *Colby Library Quarterly* 18 (1982) pp. 160–7

Reide, David G., 'The Symbolism of the Loins in Blake's *Jerusalem*', *Studies in English Literature*, 21 (1981) pp. 547–61.

Roe, Albert S., *Blake's Illustrations to the Divine Comedy*, (Princeton, NJ: Princeton University Press, 1953).

SCBSG (Santa Cruz Blake Study Group), review of David V. Erdman (ed.), *The Complete Poetry and Prose of William Blake*, New York: Anchor Books, Doubleday, 1982, in *Blake/An Illustrated Quarterly*, 18 (1984) pp. 4–31.

Simpkins, Scott, 'The Book of Thel and the Romantic Lament', *South Central Review* 5 (1988) pp. 25–39.

Swearingen, James E., 'Will and Desire in Blake's *Thel*', *Eighteenth-Century Studies* 23 (1989–90) pp. 123–39.

—— 'William Blake's Figural Politics', *English Literary History* 59 (1992) pp. 125–44.

Symons, Arthur, *William Blake* (London: Constable, 1907).

Taylor, Peter Alan, 'Blake's Text for the *Enoch* Drawings', *Blake Newsletter* VIII (1974), pp. 82–6.

Thompson, E.P., *The Making of the English Working Class* (London: Victor Gollancz, 1963).

—— 'London', in *Interpreting Blake*, ed. Michael Phillips, (Cambridge: Cambridge University Press, 1978).

Wagenknecht, David, *Blake's Night: William Blake and the Idea of Pastoral* (Cambridge, Mass.: Belknap Press of Harvard University Press, 1973).

Walker, C.R. (ed.), *William Blake in the Art of His Time* (Santa Barbara, Calif.: University Art Galleries, 1976).

Webster, Brenda, *Blake's Prophetic Psychology* (London: Macmillan, 1983).

Wilkie, Brian and Johnson, Mary Lynn, *Blake's "Four Zoas": the Design of a Dream* (Cambridge, Mass.: Harvard University Press, 1978).

Worrall, David, 'Blake and the Night Sky, I: "The Immortal Tent"', *Bulletin of Research in the Humanities* 84 (1981) pp. 273–93.

—— *Radical Culture: Discourse, Resistance and Surveillance, 1790–1820* (Hemel Hempstead: Harvester Wheatsheaf, 1992).

Index

The index entries do not include endnote citations.